GOVERNING INDEPENDENCE AND EXPERTISE

Governing, Independence and Expertise tells the story of the 'not-for-profit' housing sector in England, focusing on its representative body, the National Housing Federation. The story tells of how the Federation and associations influenced their own space of governing through deploying discourses of independence and expertise; how being governed, and governing, become at times one and the same.

The National Federation of Housing Societies was born in 1935 out of the apparent failure of housing societies, associations and charitable trusts to tackle the 'problem of the slums'. Its story was a familiar one—organisations have often set up collective structures to facilitate intervention in government. Viewed historically, the success of the project is, nevertheless, remarkable, given that the housing association sector is now a major force in social housing provision. Moreover, housing associations have pioneered many programmes which are central to our 'modernised' welfare state—such as private finance, independence and entrepreneurialism. Through the story of the Federation, the book examines the role of non-governmental sectors in mechanisms of governing, engaging contemporary debates about public services and the nature of the 'social'—the limits of the role of the 'not-for-profit sector'; the impact of private funders; and the disappearance of the notion of 'public'.

Governing Independence and Expertise

The Business of Housing Associations

Morag McDermont

·HART·
PUBLISHING

OXFORD AND PORTLAND, OREGON
2010

Published in North America (US and Canada) by
Hart Publishing
c/o International Specialized Book Services
920 NE 58th Avenue, Suite 300
Portland, OR 97213–3786
USA
Tel: +1 503 287 3093 or toll-free: (1) 800 944 6190
Fax: +1 503 280 8832
E-mail: orders@isbs.com
Website: http://www.isbs.com

Hart Publishing Ltd, 16C Worcester Place, Oxford, OX1 2JW
Telephone: +44 (0)1865 517530 Fax: +44 (0)1865 510710
E-mail: mail@hartpub.co.uk
Website: http://www.hartpub.co.uk

British Library Cataloguing in Publication Data
Data Available

ISBN: 978-1-84113-0-989-0

Typeset by Columns Design Ltd, Reading
Printed and bound in Great Britain by
CPI Antony Rowe Ltd, Chippenham

Preface

The title of this book reflects an intersection of my personal, economic and organisational interests. Fifteen years of working in the social housing sector, a life-long involvement in politics, and several years studying and teaching public law all provided the personal motivation to understand how *governing* operated in the social housing sector. As luck would have it, when in search for funding for a PhD, I discovered that both the National Housing Federation (NHF, the representative body for housing associations, set up in 1935) and Professor Peter Malpass also had an interest in the historical role the Federation had played in governing social housing in England. With a studentship funded by the Economic and Social Research Council (award number S42200134042) and the NHF I was provided with the time and resources to conduct an academic study. I had great fun delving into archives, uncovering old journals and interviewing anyone I could get hold of in an attempt to understand how the housing association sector, as we see it now, had come about. Part of the fascination was that here was a group of organisations that had seemed insignificant for much of their existence, but are now at centre-stage of the delivery of housing for those in housing need. The work of Michel Foucault and the 'histories of the present' scholars has provided an important foundation for analysing governing and power relations. Nevertheless, I have been keen to speak to an audience much broader than social theorists. So, in using, developing and adding to the empirical work carried out for the PhD for this book I have made every attempt to avoid technical and theoretical language.

I began to see *independence* as a driving motivation for the housing association sector as the result of an article by James Tickell, written in 2002 when he was Deputy Chief Executive of the NHF. In 'Independent Spirit'[1] he argued that housing associations would only survive and flourish if they broke away from a dependence on the state. This concern that associations must be seen as independent, private organisations had arisen in a case I had written about, *Poplar HARCA v Donoghue.*[2] Here the question was whether a housing association, Poplar HARCA, was a public authority in law. The Housing Corporation (regulator and funder for the housing association sector) argued that the billions of

[1] J Tickell, (2002) 'Independent Spirit' *Inside Housing* 13 September, 22–3

[2] (2001) 33 HLR 823–46; see M McDermont, 'The Elusive Nature of the 'Public Function': *Poplar Housing and Regeneration Community Association Ltd v Donoghue*' Year 66(1) *Modern Law Review* 113–23

pounds of private funding raised by the sector would be at risk if the courts decided that associations were public bodies. My research into the Federation's history suggested, however, that the relationship between the state and associations was not so straight-forward. At various points in its history the Federation had argued *for* an understanding of associations as some form of public organisation. As the project neared its completion in 2009, the sector's anxieties about its independence from the state increased. The NHF saw the Housing and Regeneration Bill (now Act) as a threat because it (apparently) increased the powers of the state regulator. In the courts a High Court judge decided that London and Quadrant Housing Trust was exercising public functions for the purposes of the Human Rights Act 1998 when allocating and managing its housing stock.[3]

Claims that housing associations had particular forms of *expertise* were important in positioning associations in the centre-stage of social housing. The Housing Act 1974 had enabled them to promote their expertise in buying-up and improving inner-city terraced housing as a popular way forward for a government housing policy. This was at a time when many questioned local government's high-rise developments on the edges of towns and cities. However, such a focus on expertise was not new. From the formation of the National Federation of Housing Societies (as it was then called), the organisation put a great deal of energy and resources into turning associations into experts.

All of these factors go towards making up *the business of housing associations.* So too has the ascendancy of financial values and financial thinking. Decision-making in the sector – whether it be the regulatory code of the Housing Corporation which informed its regulatory decisions, or the daily operational decisions of housing officers about whether to pursue rent arrears or provide tenancy support – have become dominated by this financial thinking. Such a focus on financial values has produced a type-change in the sector; it has become commercialised to the extent that we are often unable to distinguish a housing association from a private commercial housing developer. In this book I question whether associations' pursuit of the business model and their increasing dependence on the world of private finance has left by the wayside the ideal of the 'social' in social housing.

As work on this book drew to a close, the financial world went into crisis. Given the dependence on private finance and private business modes of operation, the crisis had a significant (and continuing) impact on the sector. Associations' increasing involvement in home-ownership – whether shared-ownership or outright sales meant to subsidise social housing – led some associations to

[3] *R (on the application of Weaver) v London & Quadrant Housing Trust* [2008] EWHC 1377 (Admin); [2009] 1 All ER 17. The Court of Appeal dismissed LQHT's appeal ([2009] EWCA Civ 587, [2009] HRLR 29, 18 June 2009). The UK Supreme Court refused permission to appeal on 19 November 2009. However, that will not be the end of the story, as the Supreme Court invited a 'leap-frog' appeal in another case that raised the same issues.

show very large accounting deficits in Autumn 2008. Associations who, like private developers, had gone in for 'land-banking' on a large scale, suffered as land values plummeted.[4] On top of this, the increasingly complex and intricate financial arrangements set up by some associations created more difficulties. As interest rates fell, those associations who had entered into 'stand-alone swaps' were threatened as banks called on them to raise £398 million in collateral.[5] How associations change and adapt to these and other challenges of the twenty-first century is not a story that this book can tell. However, I hope that in writing a book which shows the importance of historical struggles for ideals as well as practical advances, I have provided some food for reflection on how associations might approach this threatening future.

****

A book is seldom a solitary effort; a book like this is a collaborative project, reliant on the ideas, support, expertise and resources of many. However, for this book in particular one person has been key all the way through. Professor Peter Malpass not only managed to obtain funding through the highly competitive process of the ESRC CASE studentship programme, but was then open and generous in appointing me to the studentship, even though it would have been clear that my approach was not his own. All the way through Peter shared my enthusiasm for the project, shared his own vast knowledge of the social housing world, and provided support and constructive criticism. Then, as I developed my ideas after completing the PhD, Peter has continued to be there to provide inspiration and to challenge. Thank you Peter; without you, this book would never have been written.

Others have also been inspirational in the writing of this book. Professor Dave Cowan introduced me to and fired my enthusiasm for the work of Foucault. Dave engaged thoroughly with my project, arguing and advising as I became more and more fascinated by the theoretical analysis. Dave and I have continued to work together on social housing research, and aspects of those collaborative projects have also found there way into this book.

James Tickell, both when at the National Housing Federation and after he left, was invaluable in providing links and insights into the world of the Federation and associations that have enriched this book. James was also instrumental in obtaining the initial funding from the ESRC and NHF, and his enthusiasm for the project helped provide some of its depth.

Many people gave generously of their time to be interviewed for this book. Their contribution has brought the subject matter alive in many places, as well as providing insights that would otherwise have been missed. Many thanks to them all (listed in the Appendix). John Coward not only agreed to be interviewed, but then provided lengthy and thought-provoking comments on a subsequent paper

[4] C Dowler 'Battered accounts reveal extent of downturn damage' (2008) 10 Oct *Inside Housing* 4.

[5] C Dowler 'Cash calls hit landlord' (2008) 12 Dec *Inside Housing* 1.

that developed from part of the research.[6] The chapter about Shelter (chapter seven) benefited enormously from the leads to publications provided by Les Burrows recently retired after over thirty years of working for Shelter. Les also provided detailed comments on several drafts of that chapter.

In a project like this, the support of friends and colleagues is always a vital ingredient. Professors Davina Cooper and Rob Atkinson, as thesis examiners, provided stimulating ideas that helped to develop the thesis into a book. Peter and Dave continued to read and comment on subsequent papers and draft chapters, as did Ann Baines, Tom Bermingham, Lois Bibbings, Jim Coulter, Sharon Gilad, Alex Marsh and Bronwen Morgan. Sarah Webber proof-read several chapters.

Chapter 5 draws upon 'Territorializing Regulation: A Case study of "Social Housing" in England', which was published in (2007) 32(2) *Law & Social Inquiry 373–98*. Davina Cooper, Mariana Valverde, Richard Young and three anonymous referees all provided many insightful comments and observations on drafts of that paper which also enriched the chapter.

My children, Rosie and Brendan, warmly supported their idiosyncratic mother throughout the PhD and the writing of the book, as did my own mother. Tom too provided much support, challenged many of my ideas, and provided me with a refuge in the West of Ireland where I could complete the writing project.

This book is dedicated to my Dad, Andrew – I wish that he too had been able to be part of the journey I have travelled to produce it. As an engineer he spent much of his life building bridges. This book is my own attempt at building a bridge between the professional world of housing, where I once worked, and the academic world of research and theory I now inhabit.

****

The photograph on page 22 was reproduced from the very first edition of the NFHS *Official Bulletin*, and the reproduction of the Shelter poster on page 139 was reproduced from Shelter's 1970 publication, *The Shelter Story: A Brief History of the First Three Years of SHELTER's National Campaign for the Homeless.* In each case every effort has been made to trace the copyright owner, and anyone claiming copyright should get in touch with the author.

[6] M McDermont, 'Housing associations, the creation of communities and power relations' (2004) 19 (6) Housing Studies 855–74.

Contents

Abbreviations

CIoH	Chartered Institute of Housing (previously IoH, Institute of Housing)
COS	Charity Organisation Society
DoE	Department of the Environment
DETR	Department of the Environment, Transport and the Regions
GCTPA	Garden Cities and Town Planning Association
GLC	Greater London Council
HAG	Housing Association Grant
I&P society	Industrial and Provident Society registered under the Industrial and Provident Societies Act 1965
LCC	London County Council
MHLG	Ministry of Housing and Local Government
NFHA	National Federation of Housing Associations
NFHS	National Federation of Housing Societies
NHF	National Housing Federation
ODPM	Office of the Deputy Prime Minister
PSBR	Public Sector Borrowing Requirement
PUS	Public Utility Society
RFS	Registrar of Friendly Societies
RSL	Register Social Landlord
SORP	Statements of Recommended Practice (as agreed by the Accounting Standard Board)
TNA	The National Archives

Note on referencing in footnotes:
The Federation's *Official Bulletin* has been abbreviated to *OB*; it then became the *Quarterly Bulletin*, abbreviated to *QB*. All files accessed at the National Archives begin with 'TNA'.

1

Housing, Governing and History

Introduction

NOT SO MANY years ago, a book on housing associations would have been about small, not-for-profit organisations, run on a voluntary basis by well-meaning philanthropists; organisations providing housing for people with insufficient resources to be owner-occupiers or to rent from private landlords, or those ineligible for local authority housing. They were considered as under-funded, insignificant and marginal.[1] Today, the story is very different. Housing associations in England[2] will soon be the second largest form of housing tenure[3] next to owner-occupation; their use of private finance to provide social housing has been hailed as the most successful private finance initiative of the (once) welfare state and they are now a central part of housing policy. It is this transformation that has been the motivation for this book. The story concerns the role played by housing associations and their national representative body, the National Housing Federation in this transformation.[4] It concerns the power relations that govern what we now call 'social housing'.[5] One central thesis is that the expansion of the housing association sector into *the* principal provider of social housing can be located in a narrative that has been created by the sector

[1] P Malpass, *Housing and the Welfare State: The Development of Housing Policy in Britain* (London, Palgrave, 2005) 115.

[2] For the most part, I have confined the geographical scope of this book to England in an attempt not to over-complicate. At the time the Federation was formed, it covered the whole of the UK; now there are different systems of funding and regulating housing association activity in England, Wales, Scotland and Northern Ireland and the Federation only represents associations in England.

[3] The term 'tenure' is used here in the sense frequently employed by housing academics and policy makers, not property lawyers who may see it as a *mis*-appropriation of a legal term: see D Cowan, *Housing Law and Policy* (Basingstoke, Macmillan, 1999) 5–9.

[4] The National Housing Federation (NHF) was established as the National Federation of Housing Societies (NFHS) in 1935. It became the National Federation of Housing Associations (NFHA) in 1973 and the National Housing Federation in 1996. The reasons for the change in name are discussed in ch 2. Throughout this book I have referred to the organisation simply as the 'Federation', or, where this might cause confusion, the 'National Federation'. It was colloquially known as the 'Nat Fed' and this terminology appears in some interviews.

[5] See D Cowan and M McDermont, *Regulating Social Housing: Governing Decline* (London, Routledge, 2006) ch 1 for a discussion of the term 'social housing'.

itself. The Federation's story is one of the promotion of expertise and the defence of independence by organisations that have variously portrayed themselves as voluntary, public interest and private businesses. In telling and re-telling this history, housing associations have created a set of 'truths' that has enabled a once 'voluntary housing movement' to transform itself into a sector of entrepreneurial private businesses, now seen as the (principal) solution to present-day problems in social housing provision.

Whilst the focus of this study is on an organisation that operates now in England alone, the issues that it raises, of the role of the private sector and the blurring of the public and private domains, are certainly not confined to this single nation-state. The complex roles played by non-state bodies in systems of governing, including the diverse ways in which such organisations work with, beyond and resist the State, should resonate beyond this small, highly-populated country. For many Western countries have also chosen the route of using the private and not-for-profit sectors to deliver public services, a move that raises new questions about accountability and control. This book is intended as a detailed study of some particular pragmatic responses, at the same time prompting new thinking about the rationalities that both lie behind and are created by the importation of different practices and value systems into services that we once thought of as a 'welfare state'.

Every writing project has its own story of what motivated the author to embark on the journey. This story itself can inform the perspective of the book, explaining where the author is taking the reader. The main body of this chapter introduces the concepts I explore in the rest of the book, using the personal journey that I have travelled in arriving at the point of writing this book to explain the ideas. The final section sets out a brief description of the arguments in each of the subsequent chapters; in part as a means of explaining the whole, in part to enable those readers who wish to dip in and out to find what they are looking for. The study approaches the question of what makes up the housing association sector through two broad 'organising modes'. The first is the idea that housing associations inhabit a number of 'spaces' in which they are 'regulated': chapters three to six follow this schema. The second organising mode, for chapters seven and eight, is that 'ideas' too have motivated housing association actors and that whilst 'ideas' may also motivate regulatory spaces, these ideas in themselves are worth investigating for the ways in which they might have shaped past practices and present-day modes.

Housing, Governing and History as Inspiration

Inspiration for this book has come from three separate, but interlocking interests developed over many years: an interest in housing, and in particular, the role of housing in addressing poverty, what is often termed addressing *housing need*;[6] an interest in *governing*, in how we are governed and how we are participants in our own governing; and an interest in the role of history, or more specifically, in the way *historical narratives* shape how we perceive our present condition. Each of these has shaped the way I have approached this project.

On Housing

For many currently working in or just 'retiring' from housing, the homelessness charity Shelter has been influential in shaping concerns for housing as a social issue. Shelter's launch in 1966 coincided with the BBC showing of the seminal film *Cathy Come Home*,[7] which led to donations pouring in at a rate undreamed of by the charity's initiators. Shelter itself plays a significant part in the Federation's story, its influence referred to in several of the chapters. My own entry into housing issues began nearly a decade later, with memories of shaking Shelter collecting tins on a wet, windy street in the centre of a predominantly middle-class Scottish town. Such were the mixed public reactions to issues of homelessness that, despite Shelter's success, my memory here is of a grey-haired, well-dressed lady shouting at my friend 'You students' (he was not a student, but the father of teenage sons), 'you're just a load of lazy layabouts'.

Whilst her anger was misdirected, it is certainly the case that student demand for housing has been a contributory factor in creating housing shortages. It was the 'students' angle that began my life-long engagement with the dynamics of housing supply and demand in the UK, when several years later, as a student union officer, I took over responsibility for housing issues. Then, as now, in towns and cities with significant student populations, the need for student housing and the ability of a middle-class student population to pay, strained local supplies of private rented housing. The thrust of the student union housing campaign was to pressurise the universities and colleges to provide more housing for students. We attempted (largely unsuccessfully, I suspect) to align the interests of students with others in housing need. However, our demands were not that local government (dominant suppliers of rented housing at the time) should meet that need; rather we focused our attention on the institutions of education. This story demonstrates one of the strands of this book—the complexity of what we call the 'housing system', with its multiple and often conflicting sources of need and the multiple identities of the institutional actors that we demand should meet housing need. This book is concerned with one sector of that system—the

[6] For a detailed discussion on the various meanings of 'housing need' over time, see Cowan and McDermont, *ibid*, ch 3.

[7] According to a biography of the film's director, Ken Loach, '*Cathy Come Home's* exposure of homelessness as a social problem, at a time when the media was preoccupied with the hedonistic fantasy of the "swinging sixties" aroused national concern' (Ken Loach, BFI Online, www.screenonline.org.ukl/people/id/458945/).

housing association sector, or what has at times been called the voluntary housing sector and even the Voluntary Housing Movement (*with* the capital letters and discussed in chapter seven). These multiple identities can be the cause of problems of definition, even identity crises. For example, taking the housing needs of students, it might be questioned why they should be housed by institutions whose role is the provision of education, not housing. Some would certainly argue that universities should concentrate on their primary objective of education and leave the provision of housing to organisations whose expertise lies there. Indeed, this is the strategy many universities now adopt, establishing partnerships with housing associations and private companies to build and manage new blocks of accommodation for an expanding student population. For the housing association sector, their entrepreneurialism and a specific *expertise* (to which I return in the next section), brought them new possibilities.

The term 'housing association' can be seen as an umbrella term, under which can be grouped a wide range of organisations—almshouses, charitable housing trusts, housing societies (a term used in the early and mid-twentieth century) and organisations registered as Industrial and Provident Societies. They can be loosely identified as not-for-profit organisations, but *identity* is a much contested aspect of the sector, in particular whether they are located in the public, private, voluntary or 'third sector'. Over time, housing associations have sought and been able to adopt various identities. When I began working within the housing system, in a housing department in local government, housing associations were seen as something entirely other. Indeed, to many in local government they were highly suspect bodies, seen particularly by Labour Party politicians as an extension of the Tory Party.[8] This was despite attempts by housing associations in the 1970s to align themselves with the public sector and their predominant mode of funding, grants and loans from central or local government. Indeed, since the Housing Act 1974 when the Housing Corporation was established as the state regulator for the sector, the identity 'housing association' has been intertwined with state regulation to the extent that the term commonly used now for housing association is 'registered social landlord' or RSL. This terminology arose out of the Housing Act 1996 which defined an RSL as an organisation registered with the Housing Corporation and therefore eligible to receive state subsidy for its activities in the form of social housing grant.[9] More recently, it has been their self-identification as *private* social businesses that has become the current mode, but not without considerable controversy. It is this question of identity, and how identity has been used as a tactic for positioning the housing association sector, that motivates much of the inquiry in this book.

Returning to *housing need* and the campaigning work of Shelter on homelessness. Since beginning this project, a remarkable change has taken place in the

[8] Glenn Back discusses the way that support for housing associations has been kicked between political parties in 'Association Football'. *ROOF* (May/June 1983) 26–27.

[9] Housing Act 1996, s 1.

political perception of *housing*. Throughout the 1980s and 1990s, the low priority of housing in the political system was a source of continual frustration to practitioners and activists in the housing system. However, all that seems to have changed. By 2007, it seemed that Tony Blair's 1997 slogan of 'education, education, education' had been replaced by 'housing, housing, housing'. Since 2004, when the majority of the fieldwork for this book was completed, the following research reports have been published, all with major implications for social housing, all initiated by central government: the Barker review of housing supply;[10] the Hills review of the future of social housing;[11] the Lyons Inquiry into local government;[12] the Cave review of the future of social housing regulation,[13] which led to a Communities and Local Government consultation paper.[14] There has also been Gordon Brown's announcement, made within days of becoming Prime Minister, that local councils would once again be allowed to build their own housing; a pledge to build three million new homes by 2020;[15] and another new Housing Green Paper.[16] Then in November 2007, the Housing and Regeneration Bill was introduced into Parliament in the Queen's Speech. The Bill became an Act in July 2008 and introduced a new system for regulating and funding social housing. As Shelter's August 2007 letter to supporters expressed it, housing 'went from nowhere to the top of the political agenda'.[17]

Shelter, quite rightly, takes some of the credit for moving housing up the political agenda. However, the inexorable shift towards home ownership that has taken place in Britain, particularly since Margaret Thatcher's political promotion of the 'right-to-buy' for Council tenants in the Housing Act 1980, means that its demand that 750,000 of these new homes should be social rented is a demand that is unlikely to be met.[18]

[10] K Barker, *Delivering Stability: Securing Our Future Housing Needs* (2004) (www.barkerreview.org.uk).

[11] J Hills, *Ends and Means: The Future Roles of Social Housing in England* (ESRC Research Centre for Analysis of Social Exclusion, CASEreport 34, 2007).

[12] M Lyons, *Lyons Inquiry into Local Government, Place-shaping: A Shared Ambition for the Future of Local Government* (London, TSO, March 2007) and www.lyonsinquiry.org.uk.

[13] M Cave, *Every Tenant Matters: A Review of Social Housing Regulation* (Communities and Local Government Publications, Wetherby, Yorks, 2007) and www.communities.gov.uk/index.asp?id=1511391.

[14] *Delivering Housing and Regeneration: Communities England and the Future of Social Housing Regulation* (www.communities.gov.uk/index.asp?id=1511392); another interesting change in this period has been in departmental responsibility and indeed the naming of the responsible department. No longer does housing come under the Office of the Deputy Prime Minster (ODPM), the department seemingly concocted to keep John Prescott happy. In May 2006, a new department was formed, but in a move seemed designed to distance it from being identified as a government department, it was snappily named 'Communites and Local Government'.

[15] P Wintour, 'Brown promises 3m new homes' *Guardian* (London, 12 July 2007).

[16] Communities and Local Government, *Homes for the Future: More Affordable, More Sustainable* (Cm 7191, 2007) at http://www.communities.gov.uk/index.asp?id=1511890.

[17] Letter from Adam Sampson, chief executive, Shelter, to Shelter supporters, August 2007 (copy with author).

[18] *Ibid.*

On Governing

A concern for the ways in which power is exercised arose from two arenas which have shaped the responses of many of my generation: first, a political involvement with Labour Party politics during the period of 'Thatcherism' in England; and secondly, a pragmatic involvement as practitioner in public service delivery during the same period, the 1980s and 1990s. From both arose a perspective on the politics of resistance and what might be termed 'the art of the possible'. Labour councillors, party members and Labour local authorities were involved in this period in high profile acts of resistance to the politics of Thatcherism—the miners' strike, the campaign against the poll tax and rate-capping[19] and the campaign against section 28.[20] For housing practitioners and activists it was a period when council housing was privatised through the right-to-buy, the resources and power of local government diminished and interest rates and levels of homelessness soared. 'The art of the possible', for housing practitioners, was how to utilise the resources that could be accessed for meeting increasing levels of housing need. It was a period when practitioners turned to alternative funding and provision mechanisms to house increasing numbers of homeless families whose only 'home' was in bed and breakfast. So local authorities set up schemes to lease houses from private landlords to house homeless families, and when the rules of the game were changed by central government, turned to housing associations as vehicles for tackling homelessness. For associations, too, the 1980s was a period when a change in the funding regime began to produce a significant shift in how they functioned, and ultimately, in their identity. The regime of 100 per cent state funding (through a mix of grants and local government loans) went out, to be replaced by 'mixed funding', state grants and loans from banks, building societies and later, even through stock flotation. The inevitable increase in the control that private funders could exercise over the shaping of the sector has meant not only a dropping of the 'voluntary' label and image, but a new identification with the private sector.

The exercise of power, or governing, seen in this practical way, can no longer be thought of an activity remote from each of us. Banks, building societies and funding intermediaries exercise significant control over the decisions of housing association officers and their management boards, and large financially strong housing associations exercise influence over the decisions of local government. Governing is no longer confined to the State, but occurs in many varied and

[19] Rate capping: an attempt by central government to control both the aggregate expenditure of local government and the individual expenditure of local authorities by 'capping' the amount by which a local authority was allowed to raise its rates in any one year: see, eg, M McVicar and R Atkinson, 'Rate Capping and Local Government' (1985) 19 *Social Policy & Administration* 121–33.

[20] S 28 of the Local Government Act 1988 prevented local authorities from, among other things, promoting homosexuality and purportedly prohibited teachers from discussions of homosexuality in schools.

dispersed sites—it is, in fact, an activity that each and every one of us attempts to engage in. Governing here encompasses 'all endeavours to shape, guide, direct the conduct of others, whether these be the crew of a ship, the members of a household, the employees of a boss, the children of a family or the inhabitants of a territory'.[21] It is not about domination, or simply commanding and directing, but is concerned with the shaping and altering of the ways in which we see and think about ourselves and others and the norms by which we operate. It is about how we create a sense of what is 'common sense'.[22] We are each of us subjects of, and to, governing.[23] Governing seen in this way recognises our capacity as subjects of governing to think and act. It takes this capacity into account and uses it to construct new ways of governing, what might be termed 'programmes of government';[24] for example, the introduction of 'choice' into education, health and housing. This, then, is a second central thesis of this book: that housing associations, as subjects *of* governing, are themselves involved in that construction of governmental strategies and programmes.

Governance: A Note on Terminology

Throughout this book I have chosen to use 'governing' or 'government' when many would have used 'governance'. This has been a deliberate choice. 'Governance' is one of those tricky words with a number of interconnected but nevertheless distinct meanings. It has become one of those 'buzz' words in academic, policy and practitioner communities. At one level, it is used to convey the idea of moving beyond a centralised model of governing towards a 'differentiated polity'.[25] When talking of systems of governance, tackling social and economic issues is a task for actors drawn from a wide range of institutions, including those in the role of private and voluntary institutions.[26] Consequently, boundaries become blurred. In the political speak of New Labour, 'governance' has become an essential part of the rhetoric, to denote a movement away from a unitary

[21] N Rose, *Powers of Freedom: Reframing Political Thought* (Cambridge, Cambridge University Press, 1999).
[22] C Geertz, *Local Knowledge: Further Essays in Interpretive Anthropology* 3rd edn (New York, Basic Books, 2000).
[23] M Foucault, 'Afterword: the subject and power' in H Dreyfus and P Rabinow (eds), *Michel Foucault: Beyond Structuralism and Hermeneutics* 2nd edn (Chicago, The University of Chicago Press, 1983).
[24] Eg, M Dean, *Governmentality: Power and Rule in Modern Society* (London, Sage, 1999); P Miller and N Rose, 'Governing Economic Life' (1990) 19 *Economy & Society* 1–31.
[25] R Rhodes, *Understanding Governance: Policy Networks, Governance, Reflexivity and Accountability* (Buckingham, Open University Press, 1997).
[26] G Stoker, 'Governance as theory: five propositions' (1998) 50(1) *International Journal of Social Sciences* 17–28.

system of government; from the 'Westminster model' to a more open one based on concepts of the 'active citizen', participation and partnership, particularly at the community level.[27]

However, governance has also found a more particular meaning in the world of corporations and business, which has, by and large, been imported into housing association terminology. Here, governance means 'corporate governance', 'the system by which companies are run' by company boards.[28] As discussed in chapter eight, the control of associations by their voluntary committee members has been an essential element in their claims to independence. Particularly since the 1990s, the housing association sector has embraced what has been described as 'a whole new science' of corporate governance.[29] The Federation has developed training programmes, conferences and manuals which describe the many ways in which associations, through their boards, are given strategic direction and are held accountable externally and internally.[30] Because of this very specific meaning found in much of the housing literature, I have used 'governing' throughout the book to convey a broad understanding, confining the use of 'governance' to the context of the role of housing association boards.

Knowledge, Expertise and Professionalisation

The book is an analysis of systems and modes of governing within a particular sector, the housing association sector. It is an examination of relationships of power, and in power relations, *knowledge* is never very far away. In the Federation's attempts at providing leadership, guidance and support for the sector, knowledge in the form of *expertise* has played a leading role: it has been through claims to possessing expert knowledge and expertise that the Federation and housing associations have sought to influence the governing of social housing. Because of the centrality of expertise in this book, it is worth looking at some elements of this expertise and the ways in which it led to the *professionalisation* of the housing association sector.

When, in the 1930s, housing associations decided to form the National Federation of Housing Societies, they viewed the inculcation of expert and professional practices in the voluntary housing societies as vital for the sector's

[27] C Durose and K Rummery, 'Governance and Collaboration: Review Article' (2006) 5(2) *Social Policy & Society* 315–21 at 315.

[28] The Cadbury Report (1992), *Committee on the Financial Aspects of Corporate Governance, Draft Report* London, Financial Reporting Council: see below, ch 8.

[29] M Arden, 'The Challenge of Corporate Governance' (2003) 3(1) *Journal of Corporate Law Studies* 1.

[30] Eg, J Ashby, *In Control: The Board Members' Handbook* (London, NHF, 2005); C Tickell, *Governance…The Small Print: A Range of Model Documents Covering Key Policy Areas* 2nd edn (London, NHF, 2008). For a discussion of the impact of 'governance' on other organisations providing 'public' services, see A Greer and P Hoggett, 'Patterns of governance in local public spending bodies' (1997) 10(3) *International Journal of Public Sector Management* 214–27.

progress. In 1935, housing societies were viewed by some in central government as 'bodies neither efficient nor easy to deal with … they had only a very small contribution to offer at the price of much inconvenience',[31] and as 'totally inadequate organisation[s] with which to replace [local authorities]'.[32] It was not the Federation's strategy to consider *replacing* local authorities, and indeed it would not have been possible to compete with local authorities as housing providers in terms of *quantity* of provision. What the sector did claim was an expertise in *managing* housing. Indeed, many housing societies expected their managers to go through a period of training in the 'Octavia Hill system'. This consisted of methods of managing housing and, more particularly, tenants, which had been developed by the Victorian philanthropist Octavia Hill.[33] Thus, in the first decades of the twentieth century, the her followers established their expertise as housing managers, setting up the Institute of Women Housing Managers and advising ministers through the Central Housing Advisory Council.[34]

The Federation also laid claim to another form of expertise for housing associations: the improvement and repair of existing housing, rather than large-scale programmes of demolishing slums and building new that was the territory of local government. This, the Federation claimed, was the historical role of the sector, and indeed for some of the older housing societies such as the St Pancras Housing Society, Rowe Housing Trust (based in Kensington, London)[35] and the Oxford Cottage Improvement Society[36] this was their primary contribution to housing provision. For years the Federation campaigned (somewhat in vain) for more funding for this type of work. However, by the 1970s the strategies of local councils of demolishing large swathes of 'slum' housing and re-providing in tower-blocks and periphery council estates were being called into question from a range of directions. It was at this time that housing associations' claim to expertise in 'urban renewal' became a critical factor in enabling the sector to begin significant expansion. For, by calling into question the housing expertise of local government and at the same time claiming expertise of their own, the Federation helped to bring about a shift in common understandings of housing policy. This shift was very much in the interests of the sector: the primary function of the Housing Act 1974 was to make housing renewal a central plank of

[31] Sir Arthur Robinson, Permanent Secretary to the Minister for Health in 1933 (in TNA HLG 29/213).

[32] A briefing note to the Chancellor of the Exchequer found in TNA, *ibid* (note dated 6 December 1933).

[33] See, eg, M Brion and A Tinker, *Women in Housing: Access and Influence* (London, Housing Centre Trust, 1980); P Malpass, *The Work of the Century: The Origins and Growth of the Octavia Hill Housing Trust in Notting Hill* (London, Octavia Hill Housing Trust, 1999).

[34] The Central Housing Advisory Committee (CHAC) had been set up by the Housing Act 1935 as a committee of experts to advise ministers on housing matters.

[35] Previously the Improved Tenements Association; an article about Rowe HT appeared in the *QB* 76, January 1956, 11–12.

[36] See R Mole, *Cottage Improvement to Sheltered Housing: Oxford Citizens Housing Association—The First 120 years* (Oxford, Oxford Citizens Housing Association, 1987).

housing policy, bringing associations' experience of housing improvement and renewal to the fore. The Act also established a funding and regulation system that significantly strengthened the sector and made housing associations a key partner. This was the beginning of housing associations moving to 'centre stage',[37] and had been achieved in part by the valorising of a specific expertise held by associations.

In using expertise as a conduit for entering the territory of government, housing associations had followed in the footsteps of many other professions. The development of the welfare state had enabled the authority of experts to become inextricably linked to political institutions and mechanisms of governing.[38] The professionalisation of local and central government enabled engineers, architects, planners, teachers and social workers to become invaluable in systems of government, providing solutions to the problems of governing. Independent accreditation by professional bodies such as the British Medical Association, the Royal Institute of British Architects and the Royal Town Planning Institute,[39] provided professionals with apparent authority and an image of neutrality which separated them from the messiness of politics. Moreover, under the guise of 'neutrality', it was experts rather than politicians who established norms and standards.

However, latterly there has been a significant shift in modes of expertise. Since the 1970s, the political rhetoric that has gained ascendancy has been for a diminished role for the State, both in managing the economy and providing welfare services. More recently, strident voices inside and outside politics have proclaimed the superiority of the market place and the rules of business. This 'new welfare'[40] has brought to the fore *managerialism*, displacing and pushing out professionalism. Managerialism—'behaving in a businesslike way'[41]—brings with it a shift in expertise: business managers, accountants and auditors, with their budgets, targets and performance indicators, now increasingly set the agenda. Where once politicians listened to those who worked in the 'social' space—social services, social security, social housing—now it is the rhetoric of the market, consumerism and 'choice', that determines what, and how, services are delivered. New forms of knowledge and ways of thinking inform policy making. Auditors and accountants inspect and check, ensuring 'value for money'. This is Michael Power's 'audit society'.[42] Here accountants and economists

[37] M Langstaff, 'Housing Associations: A Move to Centre Stage' in J Birchall (ed), *Housing Policy in the 1990s* (London, Routledge, 1992).

[38] N Rose, 'Government, authority and expertise in advanced liberalism' (1993) 22 *Economy & Society* 283–99.

[39] Previously the Garden Cities and Town Planning Association, which supported housing associations and was instrumental in the formation of the Federation in the 1930s: see below, ch 2.

[40] J Clarke, S Gewirtz and E McLaughlin, *New Managerisialism, New Welfare?* (London, Sage/Open University, 2000).

[41] See, eg, J Clarke and J Newman, *The Managerial State* (London, Sage Publications, 1997).

[42] M Power, *The Audit Society: Rituals of Verification* (Oxford, Oxford University Press, 1997).

provide the research for policy makers to bring in new targets for house building, a new planning system and new institutional forms for regulating social as well as private providers of housing (Kate Barker, John Hills and Martin Cave, the authors of three of the key government reports referred to above, are all trained economists). Within organisations, it is finance directors, financial advisers and providers of private finance who become critical in setting the agenda, whether it be in devising spreadsheets to determine whether a proposed housing development is sustainable, or deciding rent policies and maintenance programmes. Here again, the Federation used the sector's financial experts—their accountants and finance directors—to place themselves in such a way as to fit snugly with the new priorities of a managerial, privately financed welfare state. Forms of housing association accounts (the public face of associations) were changed to conform with 'plc accounting',[43] to make associations intelligible to funders.

Regulation, Regulatory Space and being 'Placed'

Regulation is a term that frequently occurs in the pages of this book. Indeed, *regulation* seems of late to have become all pervasive. It has become the subject of new government departments, the Better Regulation Unit;[44] a range of academic research centres;[45] and a whole new literature with its own language, programmes, tools and tool-kits to make it seem like a new science.[46] This makes it necessary to clarify terms once again: *regulation* as used in this book and in much of the regulation literature, refers not simply to the acts of regulatory agencies such as OFWAT, OFCOM and the Housing Corporation;[47] it has a much wider meaning used to denote any attempt to alter the behaviour of others according to a defined set of values with the intention of achieving a set of identified outcomes.[48] As such, a wide range of actors become *regulators*, from regulatory agencies to audit and inspection agencies (such as the National Audit Office and the Audit Commission) and trade bodies such as the Federation. In this perspective on regulation, regulatory controls are no longer always hierarchical: in 1989

[43] 'Plc accounting' is the form of accounts used by Public Limited Companies: see below, ch 6.

[44] Placed within the Cabinet Office to demonstrate its centrality to government.

[45] Eg, Centre for Risk and Regulation (CARR) at the London School of Economics, Centre for Competition Policy, at the University of East Anglia.

[46] The literature on regulation is vast. See, eg: www.lse.ac.uk/publications/CARR/documents/Default.htn.

[47] The Housing and Regeneration Act 2008 brought about major changes to the system for regulation and funding housing associations. The Housing Corporation was replaced by the Tenant Services Agency for the regulatory role and the funding role has been taken over by the Homes and Communities Agency.

[48] See, eg, R Baldwin and M Cave, *Understanding Regulation* (Oxford, Oxford University Press, 1999) 2; J Black, 'Enrolling Actors in Regulatory Systems: Examples from UK Financial Services Regulation' (2003) *Public Law* 63–91 at 65.

Hancher and Moran[49] coined the term 'regulatory space' as a way of conceptualising the complex forms of control, relationships and the deployment of resources that occur in these decentred regulatory environments. Since then, it has become for some a useful interpretive lens. The main idea of regulatory space as a metaphor is that resources of regulatory power are dispersed and fragmented. Resources are not restricted to formal, state authority that arise from, for example, legislation or contracts; they also include information, wealth and organisational capacities. Relationships in regulatory space are characterised as complex, dynamic and horizontal, involving negotiated interdependence.[50]

In studying governing it is easy to become narrowly focused on programmes of government; for example, the Thatcher Government's New Public Management (NPM) reforms,[51] and New Labour's modernisation programme.[52] Sometimes we can lose sight of the ways in which *actors*, in their everyday mundane practices, produce the space they occupy.[53] Through the relations and associations they create, actors in regulatory spaces come to form collective understandings of norms, creating new forms of common sense. The regulatory practices that develop become powerful modes of governing, which can exclude others through lack of knowledge of jargon, appropriate forms of acting and the prevailing common sense.

Through conceptualising the exercise of power in *spacial terms*, the processes of *placing* oneself, and *being placed*, become useful ways of seeing. Placing oneself in certain spaces, in certain relations to others, becomes a way of signifying difference (or sameness); placing oneself in certain relation to others can signify skills, create alliances and associations that can further one's interest.[54] The space that one occupies, not alone but with others, becomes important for creating networks, associations and altered forms of common sense.[55] Returning to that

[49] L Hancher and M Moran, 'Organizing Regulatory Space' in L Hancher and M Moran (eds), *Capitalism, Culture and Economic Regulation* (Oxford, Clarendon Press, 1989).

[50] C Scott, 'Analysing Regulatory Space: Fragmented Resources and Institutional Design' [2001] *Public Law* 329–53 at 330.

[51] For some of the academic literature on NPM see: C Hood, 'A Public Management for All Seasons' (1991) 69 *Public Administration* 3–19; E Ferlie, L Ashburner, I Fitzgerald and A Pettigrew, *The New Public Management in Action* (Oxford, Oxford University Press, 1995); J Newman, 'Beyond the New Public Management: Modernising Public Services' in Clarke, Gewirtz and McLaughlin (eds), *New Managerialism, New Welfare*, above n 40. On the effect of NPM on housing, see D Mullins and A Murie, *Housing Policy in the UK* (Basingstoke, Palgrave Macmillan, 2006) ch 7.

[52] Eg, J Newman, *Modernising Governance: New Labour, Policy and Society* (London, Sage Publications, 2001).

[53] See H Lefebvre, *The Production of Space* (trans D Nicholson-Smith) (Oxford, Blackwell, 1991).

[54] Henry James' novel *The Golden Bowl* (Harmondsworth, Penguin Books, 1966). The prince and Charlotte find themselves 'placed' in such a position by the continuing close relationship between Maggie (the prince's wife) and her father after Maggie's marriage to the prince that almost the only option available to them is to enter into a very close relationship that we assume (but is never stated) is an affair.

[55] On networks, see, eg, RAW Rhodes, *Beyond Whitehall and Westminster* (London, Allen and Unwin, 1988) and RAW Rhodes, *The National World of Local Government* (London, Allen and Unwin, 1986); on associations see, eg, M Callon and B Latour, 'Unscrewing the Big Leviathan: How Actors

pivotal moment in the recent history of the Federation, the making of the Housing Act 1974, it was the placing of a specific expertise (agents of inner-city development) alongside anxieties within central government that current modes of provision and governing were no longer working (local government's housing role), which enabled a shift in ways of thinking about the place of housing associations in housing policy. It was the placing of the flexibility and the relative smallness of housing associations alongside the desire of local communities to remain as communities, their placing in *contrast to* the largeness of local government housing solutions (their programmes of demolition and removal to the periphery of towns and cities), which made associations attractive as agents for a revitalisation of housing policy. These placings created relations and alliances that enabled a new way of providing and governing, which became inscribed into the (Conservative) Government's Housing and Planning Bill. The strength of this placing was such that the Bill survived a change of government in February 1974; the Bill, piloted through Parliament by a Conservative housing minister, became the Housing Act 1974 under the Labour Government in July 1974.

Similarly, in the spacial analysis of power 'proximity' provides further insight. Being in close proximity, or 'neighbourhood', implies a responsibility to those who are one's neighbours.[56] Those in close proximity are more likely to share similar understandings or outlooks on the world.[57] Proximity can be a positive and a negative property. So, on the one hand Federation actors have frequently achieved change through their proximity to civil servants and ministers; on the other hand, members of the Joint Charities Group,[58] campaigning in the 1970s for legislation to make local government have a duty towards homeless households, became worried about the close relationship of their de facto leader to civil servants.[59]

It is the concept of a number of regulatory spaces that is one of the ordering ideas for the material in this book. The multiple identities of housing associations may, at times, cause confusion, but nevertheless enables them to take advantage of different understandings of *form*, or modes of arrangement. So the *charitable*

Macro-Structure Reality and How Sociologists Help Them to Do So' in K Knorr-Cetina and A Cicourel (eds), *Advances in Social Theory* (London, Routledge & Kegan Paul, 1981); B Latour, 'The Powers of Association' in J Law (ed), *Power, Action and Belief A New Sociology of Knowledge?* Sociological Review Monograph 32 (London, Routledge & Kegan Paul, 1986); on common sense see, eg, B Latour, 'Visualisation and Cognition: Thinking with Eyes and Hands' (1986b) 6 *Knowledge and Society: Studies in the Sociology of Culture, Past and Present* 1–40.

56 Lord Atkins in *Donoghue v Stevenson* [1932] AC 562, at 580; on proximity see, D Manderson, *Proximity, Levinas and the Soul of Law* (Montreal & Kingston, McGill-Queen's University Press, 2006).

57 P Bourdieu, 'What Makes a Social Class? On The Theoretical and Practical Existence of Groups' (1987) 32(1) *Berkeley Journal of Sociology* 1–17, 5: 'Those who occupy the same positions have every chance of having the same habitus'.

58 A group comprising Shelter, SHAC, Child Poverty Action Group, Catholic Housing Aid Society and the Campaign for Homeless and Rootless.

59 B Widdowson, 'Making the Law' *ROOF* (November/December 2007) 32–33; see below, ch 7.

form, and the understandings that go along with being charitable, have been useful to some associations at various points in their history (for example, by giving access to tax benefits, to charitable funding, or a label of respectability).[60] At times, the *local* has been important; being seen as local organisations operating in a locality has meant intervening in the regulatory space of local government and all the negotiations that go along with such a position. In different times, it has been the national sphere of state regulation that has been the space in which intervention has proved most fruitful. This view of multiple, overlapping spaces or spheres in which governing happens and can be influenced becomes a lens for understanding the role of the National Federation and housing associations in governing social housing.

On History

This project was initially conceived as a joint collaboration between the University of the West of England and the National Housing Federation to research the organisation's history. The focus was on the role of the Federation in the governance of social housing. This need for a historical perspective brought a new dimension to the analysis of how power is exercised, or processes of governing. Central to the thinking behind this book has been the works of the French social theorist and philosopher Michel Foucault, and the scholars who developed his project of creating 'histories of the present'—understandings of the conditions that have made possible the particular present we occupy.[61]

The coincidence of the Federation's desire to have a record of its own history and my own concern to explore the regulation of the social housing sector produced an interesting set of possibilities. It also raised new questions; what work are we expecting history to do? What questions are we asking our historical sources? Taking a historical perspective is not a search for one linear 'true' story of the Federation. Rather, the historical perspective is intended to ask the questions: what made it possible for present-day 'truths' to be accepted as such? What was it that made our particular view of 'common sense', common? History is not a search for one clear line that leads us to the present; in fact, a historical perspective should disrupt that conception. Rather, 'history' appears as many tangled, interconnected stories that create possibilities for our present. Such histories do not work with a hierarchy of what counts as relevant sources, for in effect *everything* becomes relevant. All documents have their own story to tell;

[60] See below, ch 3.

[61] M Foucault, *Discipline and Punish* (trans AM Sheridan) (London, Penguin Books, 1977) 31; on scholars who have used this 'method' see, eg, M Dean, *Critical and Effective Histories: Foucault's Methods and Historical Sociology* (London, Routledge, 1994); D Garland, *The Culture of Control: Crime and Social Order in Contemporary Society* (Oxford, Oxford University Press, 2001) ch 1.

however, the importance is not simply in the document, but in the context—the question becomes, what were the conditions that made this particular text possible?[62]

There are, of course, many choices made for us, many avenues cut off before we begin the historical exploration. Bureaucracies are seldom concerned with their own (or other's) history, and frequently destroy information in the quest for more space, or in organisational expansions, contractions and relocations. Many organisations, including the Federation itself, have little documentary evidence that does not relate to immediate concerns. In trying to track down sources, chance plays no small part in history's processes of source discrimination. For this research, finding in an association's dusty basement an almost complete set of the quarterly *Bulletin*, the Federation's official mouthpiece from 1936, opened up avenues that may otherwise have been closed. Chance, as well as civil servants and archivists' decisions, also led to the retention of some government files held at the National Archives; these files opened windows onto the relationship between government and the Federation that were not available through annual reports or interviews. Chance also lost data: files discarded by civil servants or archivists, or lost in the system.

However, stories of a researcher's frustrations can hide the far more important point that archives are *always* intimately tied up with power relations. This is not simply a product of the resources that governments can put into maintaining archives, and make choices about what is retained and discarded, who can have access and who is excluded. There is a more subtle point here about the voices that are not just silenced, but never come to the surface. We may think this can be solved by looking at other, non-archival sources, and indeed in this research I relied heavily on interviews with 'key actors' in the history of the Federation. This, however, raises other questions of versions of truth.

The first question relates to whose voices are to be privileged through the choice of interviewees. It was the Federation's institutional memory of those people who had been involved in the organisation's history *and* who were still alive that became a critical determining factor. My interviewees were past and present staff and members of the Federation Council; generally these were the people who had won battles for control of the organisation. They provided, in the main, an official view of the Federation.

The second question relates to the relationship between interviewer and interviewee. The interview interaction is not simply a one-way 'confession' of the interviewee, but an active co-production of the 'facts' between researcher and

[62] See, eg, K Jenkins, 'A Postmodern Reply to Perez Zagorin' (2000) 39(2) *History and Theory* 181–200; N Royle, *After Derrida* (Manchester, Manchester University Press, 1995); and see M Foucault: 'One ought to read everything, study everything [..] have at one's disposal the general archive of a period at a given moment' in *The History of Sexuality: Part 1 The Will to Knowledge* (trans R Hurley) (London, Penguin Books, 1998) 263.

interviewer.[63] The interviewer's understanding of the past formulates questions and interprets the answers; the interviewee's version of past events is filtered through their present-day understandings and social position. There is no objective 'truth'; the journey becomes a pilgrimage to understand how certain versions of history become *accepted as truth*, to investigate the emergence and transformation of systems of truth. The interview becomes like any other text, to be read for what it says, not a search for hidden meaning.[64] That there will be more than one version of historical events is inevitable, for each text is itself attempting to create the past as a justification for its own historical present. What becomes of concern is to trace the emergence of the present version of history, the battles won that have authorised the speaker to exercise power for a particular end and the lost battles that have silenced speakers and the discourses for which they were speaking.

The Rest of the Book

Just as this book is attempting to tell a number of overlapping, interconnected stories at once, it has also been written with several different readers in mind. One reader I hope will be like many of my interviewees; those who have spent years working in social housing, who care passionately about it but are also curious about why it is the way it is. Perhaps this reader, like the author, is worried about the encroaching privatisation of the sector, both in legal form and in changes of culture. I also hope that those who are not housing professionals but have a connection through, for example, sitting on the governing body of a housing association, may find the inquiry interesting, perhaps stimulating. My other audience would be made up of those who are interested in modes of governing and control, either as academics or practitioners. My audiences may be overlapping. I have tried to write the different stories in the chapters in such a way that they can be critical and questioning, without allowing the theory to intrude. I have used footnotes to develop some of the theoretical ideas that might have hindered the flow of the text.

The book has been written so that the chapters can be read individually, or not in the order they appear in the book. This leads to a certain amount of repetition, but this is the price you pay for approaching history in a thematic rather than chronological way. To conclude this introduction, I provide a brief overview of the remaining chapters. As previously explained, two 'organising modes' have

[63] See, eg, J Mason, 'Qualitative Interviewing: Asking, listening and interpreting' in T May (ed), *Qualitative Research in Action* (London, Sage, 2002).

[64] Having said that, research ethics and data protection rules do not allow me to treat interviews as texts like articles or books. Interviewees agreed to be interviewed for this research I made it a condition that they would be able to see any of their quotes being used for this book and, if desired, correct my transcript of what they said. Therefore, I am unable to make interviews available to others and interview transcripts do not appear in the bibliography.

been employed to arrange the material within these pages. The first, followed in chapters three to six, is the idea that housing associations inhabit a variety of 'regulatory spaces'. The second, that alongside governmental programmes and strategies it has been 'ideas' that have motivated housing association actors, forms the framework for chapters seven and eight. However, following this introduction and before these modes are explored there is an overview chapter which provides a guide to the time period covered in the book. What follows expands on the content of each of these chapters.

The difficulty with telling a historical story thematically is that the sense of a *whole* story can become obscured. To help remedy this, chapter two—**The Story of the National Housing Federation: An Overview**—looks at the role of the Federation since its formation in 1935 as the National Federation of Housing Societies to its present incarnation as the National Housing Federation. From the failure of associations in 1935 to become an important plank of housing policy dealing with the slums, the Federation was born. Despite the recommendations of a government committee that a central funding body for voluntary housing bodies should be established, the social relations of associations could not compete with the strength and allies of local government. When the Federation emerged, its most pressing task was to address the perceived failure of an amateur, voluntary housing association sector, by providing and promoting expertise.

In this is demonstrated the themes for the Federation's story: using social relations, creating expertise. The Federation began to become an organisation with an eye to governing: forming alliances to remove war-time rent restrictions; working to turn associations into experts; and working *on* associations to remind them of responsibilities arising from success. The public–private divide is frequently contested, as associations seek 'public' status to gain access to resources. Transformation begins in the 1960s, as social relations between the House of Lords, civil servants, ministers and members of the Federation enable the restructuring of the Federation; this time so that central government can promote its programme of market-based housing solutions to counteract local government's monopoly of rented housing. With the launch of Shelter in 1966, homelessness and poor housing became political. Associations created highly productive relations, and in the 1970s the Federation achieved where it had failed in the 1930s: the Housing Corporation is established as a central funder and regulator for the whole housing association sector and housing associations become recognised as an essential 'third arm' of housing policy.

In the remainder of the chapter tensions within the sector become dominant. Expansion becomes the norm: some thrive in it, others struggle. The regional agenda becomes more important as public resources become scarce. And most critically, concern for private lenders' support becomes focused on the necessity for independence from state control. For some, this move raises significant questions of values systems, moving away from a 'movement' of community-based philanthropic organisations towards organisations dominated by the values of the market.

Chapter three—**Unacceptable Boundaries of Charity Regulation**—explores the space delineated by charitable status, the oldest form of regulation of voluntary intervention into housing need. At the heart of this chapter is the highly problematic nature of charity, at least in its regulatory forms. Events that took place in the 1960s provide a pivotal point for housing associations' relationships with charity. The identification of homelessness as a central social issue and the formation of the homelessness charity Shelter in 1966, motivated the search for a *transformation* of the housing association sector. The principal aim of this chapter is to examine the space in which state regulators of the charitable sphere, the Charity Commission and the Inland Revenue, have sought to produce hierarchical regulatory practices. An attempt to impose a particular normative view led not to domination and control, but to a rejection of those norms and the sector turning away from charity as an organising mode. Chapter three concludes by considering whether the housing association form provides a model for the development of a 'third sector' as provider of welfare services in many fields beyond housing.

Chapter four—**Governing Locally: Housing Associations and Local Government**—aims to reflect on the importance of local regulatory space, as a particular dimension *distinct* from national regulatory spaces. Local government has long been important to housing associations as a site of resources and expertise, but governing locally has always also taken place within the context of local government's powers determined at the national level. The first part of this chapter explores the broad context of the relations between local government and housing associations in the context of these resources. The second part focuses on a particular set of relations based around the *nomination* of tenants by local authorities to associations. Nomination agreements, as quasi-legal agreements between associations and local authorities, have been a battleground throughout the history of the Federation, used by both parties to structure and re-structure power relations. In the late 1980s, with spiralling homelessness and diminishing public subsidy to housing associations, associations and local government entered into partnerships to tackle housing need. *Partners in Meeting Housing Need*,[65] a joint publication of the Federation and London local authorities associations, attempted to standardise nomination procedures, tying associations into local authority assessments of need. This was soon followed, however, by the Page report[66] which criticised the approach of *Partners*, urging associations to assert control over who they housed and the types of developments they took on.

[65] D Levison and I Robertson, *Partners in Meeting Housing Need—Local Authority Nominations to Housing Associations in London: Good Practice Guide* (London, NFHA, 1989).

[66] D Page, *Building for Communities: A Study of New Housing Association Estates* (York, Joseph Rowntree Foundation, 1993).

Chapter four closes with recent research about nomination agreements which shows that nomination arrangments continue to be problematic.

Chapter five—**Territorialising Regulation: Creating a National Regulatory Community**—looks at the creation of a regulatory community at a national level. With the rejection of charitable regulation came the Housing Act 1974, which enabled a new regulatory community to come into being with the housing associations as important actors alongside the state regulator, the Housing Corporation. Government officials and housing association actors jointly carved out a new territory of governance and developed regulatory practices, enabling this community to exercise a large element of control over the regulatory territory. The analysis challenges an understanding of the making of law as top-down, substituting a more nuanced, three-dimensional understanding of the production of norms and common sense. Regulatees become not only subjects of regulation, but exercise power within the regulatory space through their expertise and social relations.

In chapter six—**Money**—the housing association actors successfully defend and expand their borders, redefining social housing so that it becomes seen almost exclusively through a financial projection. This chapter focuses on the regulatory space created by money and the power of *financial expertise*. Money governs 'at a distance', imposing the norms of the financial sphere onto fields of social policy. In social housing, the gap between the costs of provision and what poor households could afford has always created a need for subsidy; it is this subsidy that has created direct governing relationships between housing associations and their funders. Funding relationships create multiple tensions when, for example, responsibilities to shareholders clash with responsibilities towards tenants and local government funders. More recently, reliance on private lenders has shaped both associations and the state regulator and has brought into the regulatory sphere a new set of regulators, the ratings agencies and financial institutions.

Financial affairs also foreground the critical role played by those who are able to inscribe financial knowledge, to interpret the activities and functions of organisations in forms that can be understood by external funders. In the 1990s, the Federation co-ordinated the expertise of housing association accountants and finance managers, putting their knowledge to work in re-shaping the sector through reformatting accounting systems. When the sector began to have access to financial resources that made significant expansion possible, these experts first sought to 'rationalise' the financial affairs of associations through a standard form of accounts, and then to mould these accounting forms to those of the private sector. This latter move enabled the sector to successfully engage with the private finance industry. By altering housing association accounts to a more commercial format, accountants have helped to create a new image for housing associations, shaping their operations and translating them into the normative values of the private, commercial sphere.

In chapter seven—**Shelter, the Federation and Social Movements**—I consider the ways in which the idea of being a *housing movement* has shaped the housing association sector. To explore this concept I return to the 1960s, often seen as the decade of the emergence of social movements, and to the formation of the charity Shelter—'a national campaign for the homeless'.[67] As noted above, partly as a result of the screening of the BBC documentary *Cathy Come Home* in 1966, Shelter's fundraising activities were phenomenally successful from the start. Initially Shelter and the Federation worked closely together with, for example, the Federation being involved in the distribution of Shelter's charitable funds to housing associations. However, by the 1970s Shelter was becoming critical of the housing association sector; some considered that associations were adopting the 'conservative mantle' once associated with local authorities. Through an examination of the coming together and then moving apart of Shelter and housing associations, this chapter examines the importance of a social movement campaigning for better housing and an end to homelessness in the shaping of the housing association sector.

Finally, in chapter eight—**'Independent Spirit'**—it is the idea of the *independence* of that is examined as a force for shaping the sector. Independence has become something of a mantra for the housing association sector, particularly strident in the Federation's campaigning against the Housing and Regeneration Bill 2007.[68] The chapter examines how the idea of independence has been put to work as a tool of governing, and how in recent times it has come to mean just one thing; independence from the State. The chapter aims to unpick this idea and demonstrate that a narrow focus on imagining associations as private businesses misses their complexity. The first part of chapter eight draws together material from previous chapters to explore the different meanings independence has held at different times. It looks at how the Federation sought to prepare associations for meeting the demands of the Housing Act 1974 and to set associations free of a dependency on charity and of their image as well-meaning but amateur voluntary organisations. It moves on to examine the Federation's response to what has been particularly important in making claims of independence—the governance of housing associations by their voluntary committees, or boards of management. The second part of chapter eight looks at the 'iN Business' campaign, which in fact, despite its focus on independence, brings into focus associations in their hybrid form; in being not simply housing providers, but community builders, with the desire to develop health, education and employment resources as alongside housing, deploying state-like powers such as Anti-social Behaviour Orders and Parenting Orders. Chapter eight concludes by arguing that the recent Court of Appeal decision that the London and Quadrant

[67] The organisation was originally named 'Shelter—a national campaign for the homeless'.

[68] Introduced in the 2007–08 parliamentary session. The Bill received Royal Assent on 22 July 2008.

Housing Trust is a *hybrid* public authority[69] acknowledges the complex nature of associations, in-between the public and the private.

In organising the book in this way, I have tried to show the myriad of relationships, spaces, regimes and ideas that have created the conditions that made possible the present-day housing association sector. I have very deliberately set out to write the story from the perspective of the Federation and housing associations, and my sources have primarily arisen from this context. This will mean that at times readers may feel that other external political and economic factors are missing. That, however, is inevitable, for despite Foucault's exhortation to read everything, it is never possible to have more than a partial view of history. The point of this story, however, is that the particular, partial story that the Federation and associations have been able to tell about themselves has been a critical aspect in creating their own *particular* present.

[69] *London and Quadrant Housing Trust v Weaver* [2009] EWCA Civ 587.

2

The Story of the National Housing Federation: An Overview

H.M. King Edward VIII at Broadcasting House, March 1st, 1936

This nation cannot afford, from an economic point of view, the perpetuation of the slums. No one can calculate what their cost really is. It is an incalculable factor which adds to the expenditure on social and health services. Slums are radiating centres of disease, ill health and discontent. How much loss of working time is due to slums! What extra burden is placed on the shoulders of approved societies, what extra burden on local authorities in the provision of hospital services!

. . .

Let public opinion awaken. Great tasks require great energy, vision and determination. Let us put forward a great national effort, irrespective of party or politics. Every generation has a dominating social task, and so let our age, our generation, be remembered as the one in which we swept away this blot that disgraces our national life. This is an age of planning and building. Let us build a new Britain and provide houses worthy of the dignity and greatness of our race.[1]

[1] *Official Bulletin* No 1, April 1936, 1. This was the journal established by the Federation to communicate with its members. Hereafter, *Official Bulletin* abbreviated to *OB*. The *OB* became the *Quarterly Bulletin*, hereafter abbreviated to *QB*.

Beginnings: The Problem of the Slums

SO SPOKE KING EDWARD VIII in May 1933. His speech was printed in the first *Official Bulletin*, published by the National Federation of Housing Societies in April 1936. By the 1930s the 'problem' of the slums had become a 'great crusade'[2], calling into question housing policies of central and local government. The formation of the Federation in 1935 came from such an environment, for many a mere by-product no doubt; but for those voluntary housing organisations that saw themselves as part of the solution, a new representative body was a critical event.

Responding to the slum problem had motivated the formation of voluntary housing organisations since at least the middle of the nineteenth century. Industrialisation, impelling many to move from rural communities to urban areas, created crises in housing provision. The upper classes, fearing the 'moral evils directly traceable to the wretched dwellings of the poor',[3] had set up model dwelling companies and charitable housing trusts to provide a better standard of housing. Nevertheless, in the 1930s, slums remained despite several Housing Acts in the early decades of the twentieth century which enabled local authorities to build their own council housing.[4] The Housing and Town Planning Act 1909 was significant for voluntary housing; under the Act 'public utility societies' (limited profit organisations registered as Industrial and Provident Societies) were allowed much greater access to loans from the Public Works Loans Board.[5] The Act also gave local authorities powers to define land use in town extension schemes, by promoting the principle of low-density suburbs, the 'garden cities', so linking the public utility societies and the garden city movement.[6] The Garden Cities and Town Planning Association (GCTPA), a professional association for architects and town planners, provided advice and assistance for new public utility societies and those developing housing schemes.[7] Later, through conferences organised by the GCTPA, the idea of a centralised co-ordinating body for the 'voluntary housing movement' emerged. A national GCPTA conference in

[2] National Housing and Town Planning Council, *Memorandum upon the progress of the anti-slum campaign and the main features of the Housing Act 1930* (revised April 1935) (London, NHTPA, 1935).

[3] From the first report to the directors of the Metropolitan Association for Improving the Dwellings of the Industrial Working Classes, quoted in S Morris, 'Private Profit and Public Interest: Model Dwelling Companies and the Housing of the Working Classes in London 1840–1914' (unpublished PhD thesis, University of Oxford, 1998) 38.

[4] In particular, the Housing and Town Planning Act 1919 introduced central government subsidy for local authority house building: see, eg, D Mullins and A Murie, *Housing Policy in the UK* (Basingstoke, Palgrave Macmillan, 2006) ch 2.

[5] The Public Works Loan Board is a statutory body whose function is to lend money from the National Loans Fund to local authorities and other prescribed bodies, and to collect the repayments. See: www.dmo.gov.uk/index.aspx?page=PWLB/Introduction.

[6] P Malpass, *Housing Associations and Housing Policy: A Historical Perspective* (Basingstoke, Macmillan, 2000) 52.

[7] D Hardy, *From Garden Cities to New Towns: Campaigning for Town and Country Planning 1899–1946* (London, E & FN Spon, 1991) 204.

September 1934 unanimously approved proposals for a National Federation for Housing Societies.[8] A drafting committee prepared a constitution, which was approved by four regional conferences in London, Birmingham, Manchester and Newcastle. The National Federation of Housing Societies was incorporated on 24 June 1935, supported by a central government grant under the Housing Act 1935.

Such government support for the Federation was, however, not the triumph the housing societies had campaigned for; their goal had been for a more central role in dealing with the problem of the slums. In 1933, in a move typical of governments in a policy crisis, a departmental committee was set up. The Committee was chaired by Lord Moyne; its remit was to consider how to secure a proper fitness standard in houses not subject to clearance, and to determine

> [w]hat, if any, further steps are necessary or desirable to promote the supply of houses for the working classes, without public charge, through the agency of public utility societies or other bodies subject to similar limitations in particular areas or otherwise.[9]

The Committee, 'conscious that it must not encroach on local authority territory', steered clear of slum clearance policy.[10] In its recommendations it sought to address 'a gap in the Government's housing policy' relating to those who have to live in 'poorly managed, inadequately repaired and grossly overcrowded privately owned property managed by landlords'.[11] Lord Moyne proposed the 'extension on a large scale' of the activities of public utility societies in acquiring poor quality, badly maintained properties owned by private landlords, which they should manage along the lines of the Octavia Hill system.[12] It recommended setting up a central public utility council, to 'promote and supervise the societies and to give help and guidance to Societies', alongside a central financing authority which would have powers to make advances to housing societies to cover up to 100 per cent of the costs of acquiring and improving properties.[13]

The public utility societies may have had allies within the committee but, outside, stronger alliances were in formation. Lord Moyne's recommendations could not withstand vigorous opposition from local government who, allied with private landlords and house builders, had considerable lobbying power within the Ministry of Health.[14] The subsequent Housing Act 1935 contained no provisions for a central funding body or a public utility council; voluntary housing organisations were left dependent on discretionary support from local

8 Garden Cities and Town Planning Association *Town and County Planning* (1935) Vol 1(2), 45
9 Moyne, *Report of the Departmental Committee on Housing* (Cmd 4397, 1933) 1.
10 *Ibid*, 51
11 *Ibid.*
12 *Ibid*, para 126.
13 *Ibid*, paras 69, 70 and 80.
14 PL Garside, 'Central Government, Local Authorities and the Voluntary Housing Sector' in A O'Day, (ed), *Government and Institutions in the Post 1832 UK* (Lampeter, Mellon Press, 1995).

authorities.[15] A government grant for a new central co-ordinating body must have seemed a minor advance. From our present vantage point, the formation of the Federation with state support was nevertheless significant; nearly forty years later, in the Housing Act 1974, the Federation was to become a key actor in delivering centralised state funding for voluntary housing

For the moment, however, the voluntary housing organisations had failed to alter ways of thinking about housing policy. From failure, the National Federation had to secure a role for itself and the organisations it represented. The aims of the new organisation were not ideological; indeed its frequent claim in subsequent years was of its *non-political* nature. Its aims appear as a practical list of functions, attempts to alter external perceptions of competence through directing, in some respects governing, its members. It intended to:

(1) Act as a clearing-house for all information.
(2) Supply model forms for accounts, rent collecting, management, etc.
(3) Circulate, in the form of bulletins, reports on the rehousing of tenants, or on various aspects of the Societies' work.
(4) Provide experienced technical advice, available both before and during the preparation of schemes.[16]

In announcing its formation, the Federation's promoters remained silent about those sections of the voluntary housing sector that remained outside. Whilst the regional conferences demonstrated a geographical spread of support, diversity in *types* of members was not apparent. None of the large pre-1914 charitable housing trusts (Guinness, Peabody, Sutton and Samuel Lewis) were among the founding members, nor any of the Victorian model dwelling companies. A sign, perhaps, of unspoken divisions, for garden cities had been established partly in opposition to the dense urban developments of the model dwelling companies.[17]

In 1936, the Federation set up the *Official Bulletin,* a quarterly magazine for members, which it was also hoped would be passed on to potential allies in local government. This *Bulletin* remains the main source of information we have about the Federation's activities over the next 25 years. Tensions did not surface in its drily-written pages, but nevertheless seemed to underlie the reorganisation of the Federation that took place eleven years later.

[15] See Malpass, *Housing Associations and Housing Policy,* above n 6 at 104; P Malpass, 'The Uneven Development of "Social Rented Housing": Explaining the Historically Marginal Position of Housing Associations in Britain' (2001) 16 *Housing Studies* 225–42.

[16] Garden Cities and Town Planning Association (1935) 3(10) *Town and Country Planning* 45.

[17] Malpass, *above* n 6, 106–07.

'A New Start':[18] The Federation after the Second World War

New starts, new beginnings; organisations silently acknowledge failure in their need to break with the past. 'A new start' was the message from the Federation's chairman in March 1946. Reginald Rowe, president and chairman from the Federation's formation, had died in January 1945; Reginald Browne, its secretary had resigned and Meg Merrylees had taken over. The pre-war concerns of the Federation with the 'slum problem' had disappeared from the pages of the *Bulletin*, to be replaced with a focus on economic issues: the need for full employment (and the contribution that house building could make), subsidies, rents and keeping interest rates down.

The 'new start' was primarily about organisational changes in the Federation:

> With the return of many of its members to active work after the war, the Council of the Federation realised the enormous amount of work necessary to ensure that housing associations take their proper place in the present housing drive … started to set up an entirely new organisation … seven regional branches will co-ordinate the work in their area … new standing committees of the Council … Finance and Development, Legal and Parliamentary, Bulletin and Publications, and Executive.[19]

In this period, the Federation begins to be an organisation with an eye to governing: it forms successful alliances in its campaign to lift rent restrictions; it gains a certain proximity to government; it claims successes for its members and uses these successes to remind them that proximity means *responsibility* too; and it works to replace *amateurism* with *expertise*. In particular, it attempts to stake out a territory for associations where housing societies can claim expertise, marking them out as distinct from local government: expertise as innovators and an entrepreneurialism that is to become a key theme for the sector's development.

A 'Proper Place' for Housing Associations: Rents, Subsidies and the Public–Private Divide

A concern for housing associations to have a 'proper place' in the post-war Government's housing policy was a continuing theme in the *Bulletin*.[20] The Government's planning of a post-war housing policy had begun as early as 1941 with a 'detailed and ambitious programme' in place well before the end of the

[18] The title of the leading article in the March 1946 edition of the *Official Bulletin*, by the chairman of the Federation Council, RSF Simson.

[19] Article by RSF Simson, *OB* 37, March 1946, 1.

[20] Unfortunately, I have been unable to locate copies of the *Bulletin* between January 1938 and October 1943, except January 1942.

war.[21] Here was an ideal opportunity for the Federation to shape a role for housing associations. It was asked to submit proposals to the Ministry of Health and to the Department of Health for Scotland; the Conservative Party's Post-War Problems Committee also sought its views.[22] Nevertheless, in December 1945, Alderman Pike[23] writes with concern about 'uncertainty' as to whether housing societies will be included in post-war housing plans.[24] Housing societies, always able to mobilise political actors, were supported in their cause by members of the Lords and the House of Commons. In 1946, Ronald Chamberlain, previously secretary of the Federation and now an MP, writes in the *Bulletin* of 'secur[ing] from the Minster of Health assurances which form the charter for the future activities of the movement'.[25]

One key issue about 'proper place' revolved around the positioning of housing associations on the public–private divide. The pragmatic response of the Federation was that they must not be considered as *private* developers, for this would prejudice their access to subsidy, as well as building materials. The attitude of the post-war Labour Government to the sector initially caused concern. The Federation's president commented on a new 'note of hesitation' in its dealings with associations; Aneurin Bevan, newly elected and appointed as Minister of Health, referred to the role of housing associations as 'supplementary' to local authorities.[26] By March 1946, however, the new chairman of the Federation, reported

> an entirely new attitude on the part of the Government, which proposes to give first place to housing to be provided by local authorities, but has also made provision for a large increase in the work of housing associations.[27]

The Federation's lobbying for the non-private status of associations had achieved a significant success: the Housing (Financial and Miscellaneous Provisions) Act 1946 put housing associations' eligibility for subsidy on the same terms as local authorities.[28]

Lobbying for access to public subsidy was a central activity for the Federation. With Reginald Rowe as president, civil servants complained about being 'bombarded', their files becoming bulky with long and detailed submissions from Rowe.[29] Ministers had resisted claims for special subsidy for associations, questioning whether the difficulties experienced by associations were caused by

[21] P Malpass, 'Wartime planning for post-war housing in Britain: the Whitehall debate, 1941–5' (2003) 18 *Planning Perspectives* 177–96, 177.

[22] *OB* 30, October 1943, 2.

[23] The first secretary of the National Federation of Housing Societies (NFHS) and then honorary consultant.

[24] *OB* 35, September 1945, 2.

[25] *OB* 38, June 1946, 1.

[26] *OB* 37, March 1946, 11.

[27] *Ibid*, 1.

[28] Malpass, *Housing Associations and Housing Policy*, above n 6 at 121.

[29] TNA HLG 52/810 and HLG 37/16. 'TNA' denotes a file held at The National Archives.

mismanagement rather than difficulties in the type of work.[30] Eventually, lobbying paid off. The Housing Act 1949 gave local authorities the power to provide improvement grants to associations and to 'make arrangements' with housing associations and development corporations for new dwellings to be provided through conversion and the improvement of existing houses or other buildings.[31]

Identity as public or private affected not only state subsidies. Statutory rent restrictions, imposed at the beginning of the war on private landlords, had included housing associations and were not removed at the end of the war. Rising costs of building work and materials after the war were coupled with an inability to raise rents; landlords complained of deteriorating property as they were unable to fund repairs. The Federation campaigned for the lifting of the statutory restrictions, joined by others, including *The Times* newspaper. The Housing Repairs and Rents Act 1954 finally removed the restrictions, with the Federation claiming, among its members, full credit for this success. This was one example, among many, of the Federation putting its 'social connectedness' to work as their president, Lord Gage, was able to speak for the sector in the House of Lords.

This story is told in chapter six. It is one where the Federation, through its proximity to political actors, claims success in shaping government policy. With success, the Federation sought to shape associations themselves, reminding associations that these new powers to raise rents brought new *responsibilities,* both to *act responsibly* in increasing rents and to become more involved in the acquisition and improvement works that the government aimed to promote in the 1949 Act. We tend to think that the agenda of responsibilisation is a very modern one, frequently heard in speeches from ministers in a new Labour Government. In the Federation's use of its social connections, we see it as a much older technique of governing.

From Amateurs to Experts: Innovation and Entrepreneurialism

Establishing housing associations as experts in their field, so combating images of amateurism, was a goal set out in the Federation's founding aims. These first aims were *technical,* ordering and structuring the processes of associations so that their modes of working would give the appearance of efficient and trustworthy organisations, for example, by providing standard formats for accounting, rent collecting and other management functions and providing technical advice for scheme development. Attempts to model associations in the image of bureaucratic local government (though considered essential in the 1970s)[32] were not likely to succeed as a strategy for expanding the sector at this stage, once the central funding council idea had been abandoned. Associations had to find their

[30] TNA HLG 52/810.

[31] Housing Act 1949, ss 20 and 31.

[32] See below, chs 5 and 8.

own *niche*, using the small-scale nature of their operations as an asset. It was their lack of bureaucratic form, their flexibility of purpose and practice, which could be exploited. The Federation sought to support and develop the more innovative forms of housing that the large, politically-controlled local authorities could not. The Moyne committee had recognised this by supporting funding for a system of improvement grants to enable associations to buy up and renovate existing housing, whilst local authorities got on with slum clearance and new build. This support for flexibility also took the form of promoting the *innovative* aspects of the work of housing associations.

Self-build associations were one development that Harold Macmillan, as Minister of Housing and Local Government, was 'specially pleased' to see the Federation supporting.[33] The *Bulletin* described self-builders as generally ex-servicemen, 'unwilling to wait five or six years on a council waiting list', who decided to build their own.[34] Developing housing for *elderly people* was another area in which the post-war Labour Government 'showed great interest in and appreciation' of associations' work.[35] For this work associations received financial support from a range of sources: from the State, under the National Assistance Act 1948; and through a relationship with the charitable National Corporation for the Care of Old People, which provided grants to homes for old people 'in which the more infirm old people will be cared for'.[36] By 1947, nearly one-fifth of the Federation's membership was made up of housing societies for older people.[37]

A further specialist role taken up by a few associations towards the end of the 1950s was housing for immigrant workers. Workers, particularly from the Caribbean, had been invited into Britain by the Government to fill low-paid service jobs. In housing they were disadvantaged and discriminated against by landlords, and local government gave these new applicants low priority. The housing association sector responded in some areas: specialist associations were set up in Birmingham, Nottingham, Leeds and London.[38] Some associations claimed that when they housed 'immigrants' their other tenants complained, which led the founder of two associations in Leeds to set up a separate association for black immigrant workers.[39]

Here we can see the use of quasi-autonomous bodies, such as housing associations, as political tools in 'governing at a distance'.[40] The issue became political and the subject of debate in the House of Commons. The Ministry of

[33] In his 1952 message to the Federation, reported in *QB* 62, July 1952, 2.

[34] *QB* 82, July 1957, 21.

[35] *OB* 40, December 1946, 1, reporting on new Minister of Health.

[36] *QB* 52, January 1950, 21.

[37] *OB* 43, October 1947, 14.

[38] TNA HLG 117/121.

[39] Letter from the Ministry of Housing and Local Government (MHLG) Leeds office to minister office, 3 December 1957, providing information about Aggrey Housing Ltd, as association set up by Charlesworth, secretary of two other housing associations in Leeds; in TNA, *ibid.*

[40] See above, ch 1.

Housing and Local Government turned to the Federation to 'stimulate' the efforts of associations, at the same time stressing that 'the Minister must always be careful not to identify himself too closely with projects of this kind'.[41] Associations offered a distinct advantage in the implementation of such contested programmes. Nevertheless, despite apparent enthusiasm for entrepreneurial strategies, by the end of the 1950s the Federation was dominated by housing for older people and self-build, and found it difficult to comprehend the issues of discrimination facing the new ethnic minority households in the inner city. Later, this area of housing need was in part addressed by Shelter and the new inner city associations. However, addressing discrimination through targeted funding did not become a priority of government until the 1980s, when the Housing Corporation introduced a black and minority ethnic (BME) programme.

Assessing the First Twenty-five Years: Finding a Role, Issues of Control

In these first years, a reckoning of the contribution of the housing association sector to the 'housing crisis' would not have been measured in the number of homes, as Table 1 below demonstrates. Rather, the image of housing associations that the Federation sought to promote was of flexible, independent organisations that could respond to specific needs. Their supporters in the political system proclaimed their advantages over local authorities: they were 'in a more favourable position to experiment and take the lead in the continued effort for improvement in standards and new and better management'; local authorities had to be more conservative, as mistakes meant loss of political prestige.[42]

[41] Notes of meeting between civil servants and the NFHS, 14 April 1958 in TNA HLG 117/121.

[42] Lewis Silkin MP, who became Minister for Town and Country Planning in the Attlee Government in 1945, had previously been a trustee of the Sutton Dwellings. He gave an address to the 1946 AGM of the NFHS reported in *OB* 38, June 1946, supplement.

Table 1. Completions of permanent dwellings 1945–61

England and Wales	Local Authorities	Private Builders	Housing Assocs.
1945–46	741	2,570	n.a.
1946–47	27,159	31,899	145
1947–48	112,183	29,111	1,185
1948–49	117,406	15,958	1,836
1949–50	134,552	22,299	1,229
1950	139,158	24,108	1,540
1951	141,554	20,056	1,658
1952	165,506	31,364	1,868
1953	202,835	59,747	7,707
1954	199,604	87,755	14,761
1955	162,525	109,934	4,444
1956	139,977	119,585	2,518
1957	137,584	122,942	1,913
1958	113,146	124,087	1,133
1959	99,456	146,476	1,113
1960	103,235	162,100	1,650
1961	92,880	170,366	1,585

Source: 1945–46 to 1949–50: MoH Annual Reports; 1950–61: MoHLG Annual Reports. MoH Reports based on years 31 March, MoHLG Reports based on calendar years.

Competing with local authorities in volume was not the aim. This was a sector of *voluntary* organisations, controlled by committees of volunteers. This voluntary base was critical, having potential both in educative terms and for making (political) trouble. A significant number of voluntary committee members were titled; the Federation always had at least one member of the House of Lords as vice-president, and these connections were put to work in attempts to achieve political change. The widespread voluntary base of associations meant the sector had the potential for resisting unpopular programmes and policies of ministers. As one civil servant noted to the Minister, 'they [housing associations] serve as a focus of housing interest in a number of localities and they attract the support of a considerable number of people of interest and influence'.[43]

Nevertheless, criticism of their lack of expertise was evident from the outset; according to one minister's permanent secretary in 1933, they were 'bodies neither efficient nor easy to deal with'.[44] The founding aims of the Federation recognised the importance of providing associations with expertise. In the intervening twenty-five years, it had addressed this through negotiating standard

[43] TNA HLG 101/279: Private Secretary note to new Minister of Health, 1938.
[44] TNA HLG 29/213: this was Sir Arthur Robinson, Permanent Secretary to the Minister of Health

agreements with local authorities, producing model tenancies and instituting the sharing of good practice through the *Bulletin*.

Success meant accepting levels of control: the Federation's attempts at standardising systems and the control that came with a reliance on government subsidies. Principally this was imposed by local government; the Housing Acts of 1935 and 1936[45] required that an association should enter into an agreement with the local authority in order to be eligible for subsidy. Agreements were effectively contractual obligations to provide housing of specified types, in specified locations and for a proportion of tenants to be chosen by the local authority.

Despite twenty-five years of the benefits of a centralised representative body, the housing association sector remained small in scale. The need to develop *expertise*, whilst at the same time preserving *voluntarism*, produced tensions. There was also tension in the diverse range of organisations that made up the sector. All the Federation's attempts at inculcating expertise were also attempts to *govern*, to put in place normative practices. However, the normative values that motivated the different sections within the sector were also diverse: the church-based organisations practising 'practical Christianity';[46] the societies sponsored by supporters of the Garden City movement motivated by the ideals of recreating village life and the self-help motivations of the co-operative and self-build associations. There is silence in the *Bulletin* concerning any tensions these differences may have caused. There is also a virtual silence concerning the practices and procedures of the industrial housing societies, employer-sponsored associations that became very significant providers of housing. These organisations must have been run on a day to day basis by professional housing managers, and yet there is little reference to their practices or policies, which might have informed the work of the voluntary housing associations.

Conservative ministers, and their civil servants, nevertheless continued their support for the Federation through grant aid, though they had to argue with the Treasury to keep it. Their reasons were political, as this memo from the Ministry of Housing to the Treasury shows. The Federation, it was argued

> . . . is the only body which has any general interest in fostering the building of housing to let which is doing anything, in however small a way, to prevent LAs from becoming by gradual steps the universal landlords [. . . we are] considerably impressed by the initiative they are showing.[47]

By the end of the 1950s, the Federation's vision of the role for housing associations was still uncertain. It looked backwards, seeing the 'golden years' as the 1920s and 1930s when societies were the only housing organisations providing

[45] Housing Act 1935, s 27; Housing Act 1936, s 93.

[46] *QB* 47, October 1948, 7.

[47] TNA HLG 101/794: 1957, one of many memos from civil servants in the Ministry of Housing and Local Government to the Treasury defending the continuing of grant aid to the Federation.

housing for labourers and unskilled workers.[48] Its outward image also seemed to look into the past; its *Bulletin* had hardly changed in form, content and tone since its first issues, compiled by the same secretary, Meg Merrylees.

In the following years, this role as a counter-balance to local authorities became part of the story of the sector's expansion; the sector was to become a 'third arm' of housing policy, eventually to become 'first choice' as social housing providers, as the second part of this chapter demonstrates.

Transformations 1: The 1960s, 1970s and 1980s

Reading the Federation's annual reports and bulletins from the 1960s does not bring to mind the 'swinging '60s'. The format and typeface had changed little since 1936 and the tone was still one of self-important pomp. So, for example, of the Federation's work in registering new associations:

> To assist and advise 232 bodies in their legal registration is quite a task, but it is an even more important one that they should have the right background so that they appreciate the work ahead of them...[49]

Awareness of social issues was stated in muted tone; two years before the launch of Shelter as a national campaign against homelessness, the Federation's comment is: 'Most big cities and towns have some "homeless" families'.[50]

Nevertheless, the 1960s was the beginning of a transformation of the Federation and of the housing association sector itself. This transformation was produced from a variety of challenges to existing housing policies: challenges to the domination of rented housing by local government; to the private rented sector through illegality and corruption; and from growing support for owner-occupation. These came from both the Left and Right of the political spectrum. Transformation appears as another new beginning for the Federation; when my interviewees talked about 'the beginning of the Federation', they meant 1973, *not* 1935. But this was not *one* transformation, but a weaving of identities in and out of the public and private spheres. As the Conservative Government in the 1960s attempted a revival of non-municipal renting, the Federation itself was pulled closer to government. Then, as older forms of funding activity through charity appeared unable to meet the acuteness of housing need, housing association provision became *public* housing, 100 per cent publicly funded through state grants and loans. However, as we shall see in the next section, by the end of the 1980s, associations were moving back to a more 'private' form.

48 Address to 1957 AGM by Mrs IT Barclay of St Pancras Housing Society, *QB* 82, July 1957, 20–23.

49 National Federation of Housing Societies (NFHS), *1964 Annual Report*, 3.

50 *Ibid*, 6.

Creating a 'New' Federation

By the beginning of the 1960s, government policy interventions had failed to reverse the decline of the private rented sector. The Conservative Government, intent on attacking the local authority domination of rented housing, looked to Scandinavia for new modes: they imported models of 'co-ownership housing', a form of co-operative housing, providing homes to let or buy on a co-operative basis; and housing at cost, or economic, rents.[51] To help establish new housing societies to run such schemes, the Ministry of Housing and Local Government proposed a £25 million 'pump-priming' fund, but Treasury resistance to government interference in the market meant looking for another vehicle to administer the fund.[52] The Building Society Association and the National House Builders Federation were the ministry's preferred partners but their lack of enthusiasm left the National Federation of Housing Societies as the only option.[53]

These new modes ran counter to some of the deeply-held values of the 'voluntary housing movement'. Committee members of these new societies were professionals gaining fees, or builders getting contracts for the work they produced, motivated by 'enlightened self-interest' not philanthropy.[54] They aimed to house middle-income households who could afford economic rents, not those in poverty. This broke with the charitable purposes of many existing associations and trusts: 'ordinary houses for ordinary people' was *not* the purpose of the older charitable organisations, thundered Viscount Gage, president of the Federation.[55] Nevertheless, the Federation agreed to administer the scheme, as it brought (for the first time) funding from the Ministry for a director.

This may seem to be 'governing beyond the state' but the ministry wanted control. The Federation's Council was exhorted to show 'leadership' by the minister's permanent secretary; the post of director was filled by a candidate effectively chosen by Ministry officials. The Ministry of Housing also worked with the Board of Trade to change the Federation's constitution. The Federation's council had to be 'strengthened by the inclusion of three or more public figures who would take an active part in the £25 million plan'.[56] At the instigation of the civil servants, a consultative committee was formed to act in 'an advisory and consultative capacity' for the Federation's council on the implementation of the Government's plan. The committee comprised the five Ministry nominees plus

[51] TNA HLG 29/511; there are problems of terminology here, as is discussed below in ch 6. When referring to 'cost-rent' ministers meant rents that did not require (state) subsidy. However, the scheme required subsidy in terms of 'pump-priming' funding and the unpaid resource of committee members' time in expectation of future contracts.

[52] TNA T224/403.

[53] Malpass, *Housing Associations and Housing Policy*, above n 6 at 135.

[54] This was the term used by Ministry officials.

[55] TNA HLG 118/179.

[56] *Ibid.*

three other council members. It was the committee, and civil servants, who dealt with all matters connected with the scheme.[57]

In the Housing Act 1964 the Government established a 'quango':[58] the Housing Corporation, which took over the funding of cost rent and co-ownership societies. However, the fact that the Federation was no longer the Government's agent was beside the point; the beginning of change had been set in motion. The Federation's membership expanded dramatically, from 651 societies in 1960 to 1141 in 1964, and the principle of central funding of (some) housing associations through a centralised funding body had been accepted. This was what the associations had failed to achieve in 1935.

Another 'new wave' of associations also emerged in the 1960s. It was not just the Conservative Government which questioned municipal domination of rented housing; residents in run-down inner cities resisted the abandonment of their communities in slum-clearance programmes which relocated them to high-rise estates on the periphery. As earlier, it was often church groups that formed new associations with the aim of buying and rehabilitating older properties, which councils in London (in particular, the Greater London Council)[59] were willing to fund. In 1966 Shelter—the National Campaign for the Homeless—was formed. Shelter's highly successful fundraising raised hundreds of thousands of pounds which were channelled into new and existing housing associations working in the 'stress areas' in London, Birmingham, Liverpool and Glasgow.[60] These were the 'new philanthropists'.

This was a time of considerable change in the housing association sector; the emergence of new forms co-existing alongside the old. In 1969, Federation Council members included: Lord Gage and Lord Strathcona; representatives of the Victorian charitable trusts; the old peoples' housing societies; industrial housing societies; and other associations there at the beginning. The Federation's director, Geoffrey Hall, who had been put in place by the Ministry, was a supporter of the cost-rent and co-ownership housing societies, labelled the 'fee-grabbers' by the new philanthropists (because their committees were made up of architects and other professionals who benefited by getting fees for working on housing schemes for these new associations).[61] Operating more or less outside the Federation, these 'new philanthropists', the inner-city associations supported by Shelter, were out there with a mission to tackle homelessness and poverty. Unsurprising then that this clash of motives led to the taking of sides and a battle for domination of the Federation, and so the housing association sector; a story worth telling for it became a formative event for many of those I interviewed.

[57] *Ibid.*

[58] Quasi Autonomous Non-Governmental Organsiation.

[59] London County Council was replaced by the ILEA and the Greater London Council in 1965.

[60] The story of Shelter and its relationship with the Federation and the housing association sector is told in ch 7, below.

[61] This next section draws from interviews with Richard Best, John Coward, Ken Bartlett, David Bebb and Barry Natton, all of whom came from them 'new philanthropists' camp.

The 'new philanthropists' formed themselves into the Improvement Action Committee to share knowledge about their rehabilitation work. Their priority of urban renewal was now also becoming a priority in shifting government policy, when the Housing Act 1969 introduced the targeting of improvement grants to urban stress areas. With a growing confidence these new associations, the new social entrepreneurs, began to look beyond their own informal organisation. They debated whether they should attempt to work within the Federation, which they saw as dominated by the 'fee-grabbers', or should set up their own organisation:

> … [W]e had a major discussion, the whole evening, about whether we were going to set up an alternative to the Nat Fed, or take it over … we went to a pub, and we said to John Coward [Director of Notting Hill HT and the senior member], you have got to go and see Lewis Waddilove, and you have got to tell Lewis Waddilove that he has got to get rid of Geoffrey Hall.[62]

Lewis Waddilove was the chairman of the Federation. He was also director of the Joseph Rowntree Foundation and a person with a network of political connections. He arranged for the retirement of Geoffrey Hall. Richard Best, who had been secretary to the Improvement Action Committee, became the new director in 1973. The focus for the contest between the 'old' and the 'new' moved to the election of a new chairman: both 'camps' had their own candidates. Whilst a 'compromise' candidate was found that both sides found acceptable, for the 'new philanthropists', who had taken control of the Federation, the outcome signalled support for the 'high-minded, principled' stand that board members should not make personal gain from involvement in associations.[63]

And so another new beginning for the Federation. The Housing Act 1974 brought in a grant system that was to aid housing association transformation and fund their expansion. These elements of the Act were, in part, a result of a new understanding between the Federation and civil servants and ministers. For associations, support from local government was considered haphazard and inadequate, and they were hitting against the boundaries of charitable regulation which could not support attempts at dealing with new understandings of poverty.[64] For central government, there was a need to address the continuing decline of the private rented sector and cross-party criticism of local authorities' monopoly of affordable rented housing.[65] A new funding system for housing associations was needed. The Housing Act 1974, primarily an Act concerned with promoting urban renewal, contained new forms of centralised funding and mechanisms for state control of the assets of the expanding housing association sector. The Housing Corporation became state funder and regulator for the *whole*

62 Interview with David Bebb and Barry Natton (11 August 2003).
63 Interview with Richard Best (12 August 2003).
64 Discussed below in ch 3.
65 Malpass, *Housing Associations and Housing Policy*, above n 6 at 160–61.

housing association sector. Housing associations' claims to expertise in tackling the problems of older housing had brought into being a shared 'regulatory community' in which the Corporation and the associations worked towards the principal priority of spending the grant allocation and expanding the sector. This new, formalised system of regulation came into being as a joint transformation of the field by housing association and government actors with a similar aim: to develop a 'third arm' of housing policy. Personal contacts of ministers and civil servants had been instrumental in shaping the Federation in the 1960s and now personal relationships of Federation members enabled it to influence the outcome of the 1974 Act and the revamped Corporation.

The 1974 Act introduced a generous grant system for associations that were registered with the Housing Corporation and gave housing associations a principal role in inner city renewal, heralding a period of very rapid expansion for the housing association sector. The impact of the Act on the development of the housing association sector cannot be underestimated. Without what was in effect 100 per cent public subsidy, the sector would not have been able to build up a substantial asset base, relatively free from encumbrances. It was this asset base which, in the 1980s, enabled the reintroduction of private finance.

Specialist Housing: Promoting Flexibility and Innovation

In thinking of the governing of organisations or fields of activity, the usual focus is on the legislative changes brought about, the financial deals made, cuts in grants and threats of cuts resisted. This is the story that organisations often wish to tell of themselves. However, the Federation's space and place in governing social housing cannot ignore the importance of its support for other activities. Promoting the expertise of associations in providing for 'specialist' housing needs, as one way of separating them from local government and the private sector, continued. Housing for older people still took a prominent place in annual reports throughout the 1960s, associations specifically set up to provide for older people by now accounting for nearly one-third of the membership.[66] In the 1970s, associations began to respond to different specialist needs. Special funding took some associations into the provision of hostels for single people, people leaving prison and others with support needs which became an important activity. In 1976 the Federation employed a special projects officer.[67] Whilst the issue of housing for older people did not appear so frequently in the annual reports, it remained key and the Help the Aged Charitable Trust was established by the Federation in 1977.[68] Co-operative housing also became a focus after the

[66] Eg, 1965: 401 out of total membership of 1316; 1966: 447 out of 1530; 1967: 490 out of 1775—sources, NFHS annual reports.

[67] National Federation of Housing Associations (NFHA) *1978 Annual Report*, which reported that the post had been funded by one of the Sainsbury trusts.

[68] NFHA, *1982 Annual Report*, 17.

publication of the Campbell report[69] and a Department of the Environment (DoE) circular encouraging local authorities and housing associations to do more to support co-ops.[70]

Such specialist niches were used as a demonstration of the sector's innovation, flexibility and entrepreneurial spirit. Arguably, housing associations' specialism was in their ability to respond where funding was available, and then the Federation became of crucial importance in negotiating improved forms of funding. However, the associations carrying out these activities were often small, with few staff and therefore more reliant on the Federation for support. As the sector grew, this disparity between the resources of the larger and smaller associations increasingly became an issue in the way the Federation could organise its work; smaller associations needed more support, were important in maintaining an image of a sector that was community and need focused, but at the same time they contributed less in fees to the Federation's finances. It seems these specialist posts were generally funded by other trusts; for example, the new post of Adviser, Housing for the Elderly, which was set up in 1984 and funded by Age Concern. Nevertheless, these specialisms were an important asset to the sector, indeed for some its only asset.[71]

Geographical Tensions and Expanding the Regional Agenda

The Federation was increasingly forced to respond to tensions arising from geography. The regional organisation is now a significant factor in its ability to influence the political agenda; this has not always been the case. The need for a strong regional base grew out of threats to the housing association sector.

Regional organisations grew out of specific local needs. London organised as a region from the 1960s, largely as a means of influencing the London County Council. Merseyside, which had the largest concentration of housing association properties outside London, set up the Merseyside Voluntary Housing Group 'very early on because the Nat Fed didn't give us anything locally'.[72] This was an informal grouping which had to bring in a chair from outside the sector to smooth out inter-association rivalries. The Federation provided an officer to service the committee, but it was not formed into an official committee of the Federation until sometime later. Wales, like Scotland, had its own office, with a director. In 1975, the Scottish office was closed and the Scottish Federation of Housing Associations was formed. A Northern Ireland office was also established

[69] Department of Environment committee chaired by Howard Campbell MP.

[70] NFHA, *1975 Annual Report*, 6; Shelter's magazine, *ROOF*, was not particularly supportive of co-operative housing, questioning whether this was a diversion irrelevant to the housing crisis: *ROOF* editorial, vol 1 (March 1976) 34.

[71] J Hills, 'The Voluntary Sector in Housing: The Role of British Housing Associations' in E James (ed), *The Non-Profit Sector in Internationals Perspective* (New York, Oxford University Press, 1989).

[72] Interview with Barry Natton, above n 61.

in 1975. The Federation gradually created a network of regional officers supported from the centre, each with a fair degree of autonomy to pursue local agendas and set up appropriate local structures. In 1980, the Federation introduced a new constitution (the first major change since its formation) which formally introduced regional councils and allowed for a 'heavy representation' from these councils on the national Council.[73] Parallel to this structure, associations were pooling resources at a regional level to collectively train their rapidly growing staff teams.[74] In addition, other less formal arrangements were set up, such as the Northern Housing Associations Group (NorHAG), a grouping of large associations.[75]

The threat of funding cuts to the housing association sector that came in the 1980s gave strength to regional identity: 'the north–south divide, only became apparent when the pot of money was limited'.[76] The Government's review of the Housing Needs Index (HNI), the basis for allocating Housing Corporation funding to each region, ignited divisions. For many years, the Corporation's need to spend its budget had meant that grants were allocated as much on grounds of ability to spend allocations effectively as on any assumptions about relative housing need; a relationship of trust between associations and the Corporation. However, increasing homelessness in London and the South East of England was one catalyst for a government review of the rationale for allocating funds.

In early 1989, the DoE and the Corporation announced a review of HNI, initially without the Federation, who were subsequently brought in. A policy statement agreed by the Federation's council, demonstrated its dilemma in representing associations nationwide:

— Dealing with worst housing conditions and providing housing for those in greatest need . . . the role of stock regeneration must not be downgraded … .
— Increased resources to solve the problems of homelessness in London.
— Increased resources to solve the problems of housing shortage, especially in the southern parts of the country outside London.
— A no detriment policy so that no individual region lost actual homes as shares varied between regions.[77]

For northern associations, the HNI review could have meant losing grant allocations to fund increased spending in the South. Despite the Federation's attempts, 'there was a very strong feeling that the North didn't have a strong enough voice. [So] housing associations in the North actually formed themselves into a kind of battle battalion'.[78] A need to *resist* changes that were moving resources and initiatives more and more towards London and the South East of

[73] NFHA, *Annual Report 1980*, 5.
[74] Interview with Andrea Titterington (28 October 2003).
[75] Inteview with Eric Armitage (22 September 2003).
[76] Interview with David Bebb, above n 62.
[77] NFHA, *1989/90 Annual Report*, 7.
[78] Interview with Andrea Titterington, above n 73.

England strengthened the regional structures. It made the Federation's regional committees work closely with their local authorities to defend regional resources and, in the North, it made regions co-operate in a 'super-region'.

Transformations 2: Private Finance and Voluntary Transfer

The 1974 Act funding meant that the 1970s was a period of rapid expansion for many associations. Rapid growth brought new difficulties: adapting to the demands of larger budgets, bigger building programmes and managing many more dwellings. For the Federation came new opportunities to guide and steer the sector. The embodiment of the Federation's thinking came from a working party report, *Growing Pains: Coping with the Problems of Growth in Housing Associations*.[79] It advocated that the voluntary management committees should hand over administration to employed staff, leaving them free to oversee and monitor the activities. Expertise was now to be bought, voluntary board members were no longer to directly provide services to tenants; a shift to professionalisation that was a significant culture change for the sector.

1979 was a significant turning point in many senses. Margaret Thatcher's neo-conservative ideology aimed to confront the political power of local government. Traditional understandings of interdependency between central and local government were challenged[80] and housing became a central battleground. The Housing Act 1980 introduced the 'right-to-buy' for council house tenants, and central government resorted to coercive powers and 'rigorous surveillance'of local authorities to ensure that local authorities *actively* engaged in selling council properties.[81] Central government also sought to enforce change through the local authority subsidy system:[82] councils could neither afford to repair council housing, nor were allowed to build new.[83] Housing subsidies were withdrawn in order to enforce increases in council house rents, helping to force the privatisation of council housing.[84]

[79] NFHA, *Growing Pains: Coping with the Problems of Growth in Housing Associations* (London, NFHA, 1977).

[80] See, eg, JAG Griffith, *Central Departments and Local Authorities* (London, Allen & Unwin, 1966); M Loughlin, 'Restructuring of Central–Local Relations' in J Jowell and D Oliver, *The Changing Constitution* 4th edn (Oxford, Oxford University Press, 2000); M Loughlin, *Legality and Locality: The Role of Law in Central–local Government Relations* (Oxford, Clarendon Press, 1996).

[81] See *Norwich City Council v Secretary of State for the Environment* [1982] 1 All ER 737 and D Cowan, *Housing Law and Policy* (Basingstoke, Macmillan, 1999) 345 for commentary.

[82] Loughlin, 'Restructuring of Central–Local Relations', above n 79.

[83] M Loughlin, 'Law, Ideologies and the Political–Administrative System' (1989) 16(1) *Journal of Law & Society* 21–41, 27.

[84] I Cole and B Goodchild, 'Local Housing Strategies in England: an assessment of their changing role and context' (1995) 23 *Policy & Politics* 40–60.

The 1980s brought funding cuts for the housing association sector as well. Unlike local authorities, however, association development continued and many focused resources on politically favoured initiatives such as shared ownership.[85] Concerned that public funding would not continue at existing levels, threatening both the ability of associations to tackle housing need and their expansion, the Federation began to consider the potential for supplementing public funds with private loans. In 1984, it was funding from the Nationwide Building Society (to support the shared ownership programme) which enabled the Housing Corporation's development programme to continue at respectable levels.[86] So began a shift back again, away from a total reliance on public finance. The critical event was the acceptance by the Treasury that housing associations counted as private organisations, so that funding raised from private sources would not count against the Public Sector Borrowing Requirement.[87] Once again, associations were to cross the public–private divide in pursuit of funding.

Reintroducing private funding split the sector; for some it was the only way to continue development, for others it would make rents unaffordable to the associations' traditional client group. Negotiations took place away from the public gaze of the sector. The DoE proposals were contained in a White Paper and consultation paper in 1987.[88] The Federation's 'cautious welcome' demonstrated once again dilemmas in representing a diverse sector:

— Will we house the same people as under the 1974 Housing Act arrangements?
— Will we continue to work in the same places on agreed housing priorities?
— Will tenancy terms be appropriate?
— Will we continue to be partners with local authorities?[89]

Like the 1974 Act, the resultant Housing Act 1988 was a key to fundamental change. Allowing associations to borrow from private lenders led some in local government to consider the status of their own council housing. Transfer to an association became attractive as it meant freedom from central government controls; freedom to carry out repairs; freedom to build new homes. The first transfer of a local authority's housing stock took place in 1988, as an initiative not from central government but local government officers.[90] Other transfers followed, mostly in rural, Conservative authorities. When the New Labour

[85] Sometimes called 'equity share', households bought a percentage share in homes produced under these programmes, with the remaining portion retained by the association and a rent paid for it.

[86] J Coulter, 'Associations face cut in programme' *ROOF* (September/October 1984) 7.

[87] See below, ch 6.

[88] Department of the Environment (DoE), *Finance for Housing Associations: The Government's Proposals* (London, HMSO, 1987); DoE, *Housing: The Government's Proposals* (Cm 214, 1987).

[89] NFHA, *1988 Annual Report* (London, NFHA, 1988).

[90] Chiltern District Council set up Chiltern Hundreds Housing Association to take over the council's entire housing stock.

Government was elected in 1997, it adopted the large-scale voluntary transfer programme as a major platform of its housing policy,[91] and now large urban authorities have followed.

Transfer of council housing not only changed the delivery of social housing; it changed the shape of the sector and so the Federation. It brought both a significant increase in the Federation's income and a new group of large associations whose staff (and possibly tenants) came with different backgrounds and understandings of 'voluntary housing'. The impact on what now seem to be 'traditional' associations has been the change of scale. Many factors, including the threat of competition from private developers who became eligible for social housing funding in the Housing Act 2004, has meant that size seems all important to the sector. Associations merged, taking on new names so that they were no longer identified with a locality or a region. For the Federation, a significant increase in membership fees brought new threats as well as possibilities, for size meant that the originating rationale of a 'federation' may have seemed inappropriate to the largest associations, which saw themselves as large enough to perform all the functions the Federation offered. With the break-up of housing associations' monopoly of the social housing grant came the end of the 'regulatory community' housing associations had become accustomed to. The Cave report on the regulation of social housing brought new forms of governing.[92]

The sector now has a new Housing and Regeneration Act, which came into force in July 2008. The Act dissolved the Housing Corporation replacing it with a system that separates funding from regulation. The Tenant Services Authority has taken over regulation of the sector and a new funding body (the Homes and Communities Agency) has been created from the amalgamation of parts of the Corporation and English Partnerships.[93] These are significant changes, not just in organisational form, but in normative values too. In the new funding regime, the ethos of English Partnerships of 'doing deals' is likely to predominate over the Corporation's bureaucratic handing out of allocations, a system that will suit those geared up for the intense competitive mode.[94] On the regulation side, the Federation saw serious threats to the independence of associations in the powers granted to the new regulator set out in the Housing and Regeneration Bill,[95] calling it the 'greatest threat ever'.[96] Intensive lobbying achieved 'substantial

[91] Department of the Environment, Transport and the Regions/Department of Social Security (DETR/DSS), *Quality and Choice: A Decent Home for All* The Housing Green Paper (London, HMSO, 2000) paras 7.9–7.38.

[92] M Cave, *Every Tenant Matters: A Review of Social Housing Regulation* (Communities and Local Government Publications, Wetherby, Yorks, 2007) and www.communities.gov.uk/index.asp?id=1511391.

[93] English Partnerships; the National Regeneration Agency. See: www.englishpartnerships.co.uk/.

[94] Discussion with James Tickell (12 June 2008).

[95] Housing and Regeneration Bill 2007–08.

[96] National Housing Federation (NHF), (February 2008) 135 *The Bulletin* 3.

changes' but they lobbied for more. The Federation's engagement with this Housing Bill was very different from previous times. Here they were no longer working with civil servants and ministers to achieve a framework that was in part their own making; this time, it felt more as if the Federation was just one among many arguing for specific interests.

Conclusion

There is a tendency to map one part of twentieth century history onto the whole, to see the story of an organisation, sector or domain as no more than a microcosm of the society's politics. In this chapter I have resisted the temptation to constantly refer back to a more general British political history. I have wanted to tell the Federation's story from its own point of view, for to do otherwise would have been to obscure many important features of everyday patterns and battles that have shaped the present. But, of course, every story is told in its own way for a particular end. Certain battles and victories have become important because they tell a story and set up a particular set of power relations. So the battle for domination over the 'fee-grabbers' put those on the winning side on the moral high-ground, setting standards for the behaviour of housing associations in future decades. There is also an inevitability in the way the actors tell their stories; given their commitments to meeting homelessness and particular housing needs, the only course available to housing associations was continual expansion. And so the route to private funding, and its domination of the daily practices of present-day associations, is also presented as inevitable.

However, there would be a validity in relating the Federation's history to the history of a certain slice of British society, for in housing associations we have always been able to see a fair representation of the political classes. Indeed, the Federation might be seen as a certain distillation of a stratum of British society, with its lords (and occasionally ladies) on its council, representatives of military and ex-military and retired civil servants. It has used its social/political connections, as much as its claims to expertise, to promote the cause of the housing association sector. When social connections alone could no longer suffice, it turned associations professional. When 'managerialism' and business values became the dominant political mode, housing association accountants made their asset base (developed out of *public* funding) intelligible to private funders.[97] They became private organisations once again; although, this time, not private charities but businesses.

Housing associations once saw themselves as part of a 'voluntary housing movement'; for a brief moment in the 1960s and 1970s their actions seemed to place them in a position of resisting hegemonic trends. In this new century, they

[97] See below, ch 6.

hold themselves up as a model, as forerunners of the public–private partnerships that seem to be the only tool available to political programmers. The Federation has now, perhaps, become no more than another trade body.

3

Unacceptable Boundaries of Charity Regulation

Introduction

PHILANTHROPY AND CHARITY have motivated housing associations since almshouses were established in the twelfth century. The Victorian era, that great age of philanthropy, saw the formation of housing trusts that have remained key players in the housing association sector. From a historical perspective, charity seems to form the environment in which much of the sector rests, and philanthropic motives have, at times, seemed to provide the sector with a set of values (acknowledging, of course, the existence of many, overlapping sets of values). The story that forms the centre of this chapter is one in which regulatory forms of charity become highly problematic. The pivotal point occurred when homelessness became identified as a social issue of national importance. In 1966, the homelessness charity Shelter was launched and a transformation of the housing association sector began. As associations attempted to react to new understandings of housing need, the Federation tried to reshape the space of charitable regulation to support this transformation. When the charitable sphere proved inflexible, associations turned away from charity as a regulatory mode.

This chapter has two aims. First, to examine the space in which state regulators of the charitable sphere—the Charity Commission and the fiscal authorities of the Inland Revenue and local government—have sought hierarchical control through the production of particular regulatory practices.[1] We see the regulatory space of charity as also a *social* space, in which actors from the housing

[1] Here I draw upon Henri Lefebvre, *The Production of Space* (trans D Nicholson-Smith) (Oxford, Blackwell, 1991). Through *spatial practice* actors appropriate social space and make it their own; spatial practice is what holds social space together, 'ensures continuity and some degree of cohesion' (33). The idea of 'spatial practice' contains in it both (a) the relations that connect people (and create a from others)—so in this story, for example, these are the relations of class, education and upbringing that place Lewis Waddilove in a certain retaliation to Charity Commissioner Lewis, create certain levels of understanding and knowledge, and (b) their everyday practices, such as the routine acts of inspection and surveillance by the Inland Revenue officers.

association sector could utilise social relations to appropriate and shape charitable space. However, attempts to impose a particular normative view led not to domination and control, but a rejection of those norms and the usefulness of the charitable form as a mechanism of control. The story becomes important not simply for what it tells us about charity, but about how different modes of governing impact on the subjects of governing.

Despite this break, charity has remained important for some in the housing association sector, and so the second aim is to consider how charity has continued to be used: first, as a defence against neo-conservative governments' attempts at privatisation; and secondly, as a potential model for the development of the broader 'third sector'. For whilst housing associations found a different regulatory framework to expand their sector in the 1970s, the contemporary focus on a 'third sector' as provider of welfare services in fields beyond housing, leads policy makers to look for appropriate models. To some, the housing association sector is a success story; to others it appears as a cautionary tale.

Charity Law and the Housing Association Sector: A Historical Introduction

For housing organisations, charity has been an ambivalent label, fraught with tensions. We might see it as a flag of convenience flown by associations to gain access to tax and other fiscal benefits. We can also see it as a 'chartermark',[2] a badge denoting trustworthiness that opens doors to resources: financial donations and volunteered time to run associations; grants from public bodies (in particular local authorities); and support from those others who themselves carry badges of respectability, the lords (and very occasionally ladies) who would sit on the boards of associations—who (as this story shows) in times of crisis, can be called on to defend associations' charitable assets from the designs of a privatising Conservative government.

Charity and philanthropy get used fairly interchangeably. Seventeenth and eighteenth century England saw charity as originating in religion, but philanthropy as secular activity; indeed, state action could be philanthropic, while religious institutions provided charity as a voluntary action.[3] Whilst Victorian philanthropy espoused the principle of 'laissez-faire' (seeing in philanthropy the restoration of the principle of self-help, enabling individuals to take charge of

[2] As in the Chartermark introduced by *The Citizens' Charter, Raising the Standard* (Cm 1599, 1991).

[3] H Cunningham, 'Introduction' in H Cunningham and J Innes (eds), *Charity, Philanthropy and Reform* (Basingstoke, Macmillan, 1998) 2.

their own situation),[4] charity and philanthropy have always been highly interventionist. Philanthropists (mostly moneyed and upper-class) calling into question the conduct, values and culture of 'the poor', would use their philanthropy as the means to impose regulation and seek to change the behaviour of their beneficiaries.[5] From the seventeenth century, intervention increased, driven by a 'sense of danger to the social order and by an Enlightenment confidence that, given the appropriate environment, people's lives could be reshaped'.[6] The approach of philanthropy and charity was to distinguish between the deserving and undeserving poor. The 'poor' as deserving, could be worked on and made useful to capitalism; 'paupers', on the other hand, meant social unrest and mob rule and pauperism had to be eliminated.[7]

Central to the organisation (and order) of philanthropy in the nineteenth century was the Charity Organisation Society (COS). Under their rules, support would only be given to the 'deserving' poor, those who were 'doing all they can to help themselves'. Those who had 'thrown themselves out of employment' or were 'of drunken, immoral or idle habits' could not count on charitable support.[8] The COS strongly objected to state intervention in the 'social work' role they allotted themselves. Its secretary, CS Loch, complained that in such circumstances 'the essential nature of philanthropy would not survive';[9] and Octavia Hill, another central character in the COS in providing housing for the poor, objected to the role the London County Council came to play in providing housing for the poor which, she said, would discourage private enterprise.[10] Antagonism to state

[4] J Clarke, A Cochrane and C Smart, *Ideologies of Welfare: From Dreams to Disillusion* (London, Routledge, 1987).

[5] A Hunt, *Governing Morals: A Social History of Moral Regulation* (Cambridge, Cambridge University Press, 1999) ix.

[6] Cunningham, above n 3 at 4, fn 51.

[7] S Woolf, *The Poor in Western Europe in the Eighteenth and Nineteenth Centuries* (London and New York, Methuen, 1986) 18; see also G Procacci, 'Social economy and the Government of Poverty' in G Burchell, C Gordon and P Miller (eds), *The Foucault Effect: Studies in Governmentality* (London, Harvester Wheatsheaf, 1991) examining the eighteenth and nineteenth centuries in which a discourse of *social economy* operated alongside political economy. Here, the distinction between 'poverty' and 'pauperism' was central. Pauperism was associated with social danger and mob rule, particularly in the urban environment. Paupers did not signify an extreme level of poverty, but a category of persons who could not be brought into use for the development of wealth, and therefore pauperism had to be eradicated. Poverty and 'the poor', on the other hand, 'figure in the scenario only as virtuous exemplars of renunciation of pauperism and adhesion to the values of well-being' (at 159). The 'poor' can be worked on, made 'better' because they aspire to a state of well-being or happiness. Their aspirations for a state of well-being can be brought into play to advance the cause of capitalism and wealth creation; the labour of the poor and their capacity to consume the products of capitalism to improve their state of well-being, requires the conservation of poverty, not its elimination. In the terminology of the twenty-first century, antisocial behaviour performs a similar mode of division, allowing social landlords to exclude certain categories of people because of their unacceptable behaviour—see the discussion of nomination agreements at the end of ch 4, below.

[8] Charity Organisation Society Form No 28, reproduced in K Woodroofe, *From Charity to Social Work* (London, Routledge & Kegan Paul, 1962) 41.

[9] G Finlayson, 'A Moving Frontier: Voluntarism and the State in British Social Welfare 1911–1949' (1990) 1(2) *Twentieth Century British History* 183–206, 156.

[10] D Owen, *English Philanthropy 1660–1960* (London, Oxford University Press, 1965) 387.

intervention led some housing charities to eschew state subsidies. The Guinness Trust, opposed to any attempt by the central or local state to govern its affairs, only built one scheme with central government subsidy in the years before the Second World War.[11]

Charity had become tainted by the image of the workhouse and the Poor Laws and was considered by many to be anachronistic, patronising, 'odious and superfluous'.[12] By the late 1940s, the majority of public opinion thought that philanthropy had little to do in the modern world.[13] Nevertheless, the intervention of the welfare state had similar moral overtones to the Victorian version of philanthropy[14]—the Beveridge report proposed social security not as an alternative to individual responsibility, but 'to leave room and encouragement for voluntary action by each individual to provide more than that minimum for himself and his family'.[15]

What then of the historical connection of housing associations with charity? Charitable housing in the form of almshouses has been in existence since the twelfth century.[16] Victorian philanthropy, which led to the establishment of charitable trusts such as Peabody, Rowntree, William Sutton and Guinness, was also tied up with creating a moral order: a concern to address the perceived 'moral evil' of the slums.[17] This was a space of 'moral regulation':[18] thus, for example, Octavia Hill, an inspiration to many of the organisations that set up the Federation in the 1935,[19] had a programme which was not just about providing housing; she wanted to instil 'the habits of industry and effort' into her tenants.[20] Her methods involved the 'instruct[ion of] tenants in methods of hygiene and

[11] P Malpass, *Housing Philanthropy and the State: A History of the Guinness Trust* (Bristol, Faculty of the Built Environment, University of the West of England, 1998).

[12] M Taylor, 'Voluntary Action and the State' in D Gladstone, *British Social Welfare, Past, Present and Future* (London, University College Press, 1995) 219; *cf* R Titmuss, *The Gift Relationship: From Human Blood to Social Policy* (London, Allen & Unwin, 1970).

[13] PL Garside, 'Reassessing Voluntary Action in English Housing Provision post 1900' (2001) 30 *Journal of Social Policy* 613–36, 625, referring to a survey carried out in 1948.

[14] Finlayson, above n 9 at 192–93.

[15] W Beveridge, *Report on Social Insurance and Allied Services* (London, HMSO, 1942).

[16] B Bailey, *Almshouses* (London, Robert Hale, 1988) 15.

[17] S Morris, 'Private Profit and Public Interest: Model Dwelling Companies and the Housing of the Working Classes in London 1840–1914' (unpublished PhD thesis, University of Oxford, 1998).

[18] Hunt, above n 5.

[19] The influence of her views on philanthropic ideals of the Federation's first chairman, Reginald Rowe, can be seen in the 'Foreword' he wrote in E Moberley Bell, *Octavia Hill: A Biography* (London, Constable, 1942). Here he described how Hill had helped with the establishment of the Improved Tenements Associations, 'set[ting] our scheme on its feet' (at xii) and provided the service of one of her 'rent-collecting managers'. He was, he says 'fully convinced that the best of all that is now being done for the better housing of the poor has had for its origin and inspiration the life-work of this remarkable Englishwoman' (at ix).

[20] P Malpass, *The Work of the Century: The Origins and Growth of the Octavia Hill Housing Trust in Notting Hill* (London, Octavia Hill Housing Trust, 1999) 11.

household management, including financial management';[21] an approach to housing management which was adopted by many in the emerging voluntary housing sector.

The value-laden, moral overtones of charity could spill over into argument between members of the Federation. In 1945, a rather strange debate took place in the pages of the Federation's *Quarterly Bulletin.* One association, Oxford Cottage Improvement Society, felt it had been accused of 'acting in an anti-social manner' and 'tax-dodging'[22] because it had chosen to become a registered charity. A letter from the Federation's chairman had warned of the dangers of societies 'posing' as charities.[23] Another housing society argued that the tax rebates received by charities were not in fact *charitable* resources, but resources from government and therefore belonged to tax-payers. Whilst conversion to a charity might be in keeping with the letter of the law, this correspondent argued, it 'is not the spirit of charity; it is so easy to be charitable with other people's money'.[24]

Charity as a Legal Form

The power of charity and philanthropy, however, can be seen to be in the authority of law, through the creation of the charitable legal form. This is despite the lack of a statutory *definition* of charity until the Charities Act 2006. From the seventeenth century, charity had worked with a list of purposes considered to be charitable set down in the *Preamble to the Statute of Charitable Uses 1601.*[25] This list had been interpreted and reinterpreted by the courts and 're-categorised' into four main groups by Lord Macnaghten in *Commissioners for Special Purposes of Income Tax v Pemsel.*[26] Lord Macnaghten's four 'heads of charity' were: the relief of poverty; the advancement of education; the advancement of religion; and other purposes beneficial to the community. In addition to falling within one of the four categories already mentioned, the objects of a charitable organisation had to demonstrate a 'public benefit', a requirement that acknowledges 'the particularly privileged place charities enjoy in contemporary society'.[27] This

[21] M Brion and A Tinker, *Women in Housing: Access and Influence* (London, Housing Centre Trust, 1980) 60.

[22] *OB* 36, 1945, 12.

[23] *Ibid.*

[24] *OB 37,* March 1946, 5.

[25] The Statute was apparently a response to a fear of, and an effort to quell social unrest and institute a tight programme of social reform; see W Holdsworth, *History of English Law* vol 1 (London, Methuen & Co, 1922); GH Jones, *History of the Law of Charity 1532–1827* (Cambridge, Cambridge University Press, 1969) and more recently: A Dunn, 'Demanding Service or Servicing Demand? Charities, Regulation and the Policy Process' (2008) 71 *Modern Law Review* 247.

[26] *Commissioners for Special Purposes of Income Tax v Pemsel* [1891] AC 531.

[27] SR Moody, 'Self Giving in "Charity": The Role of Law' in C Mitchell and SR Moody (eds), *Foundations of Charity* (Oxford, Hart Publishing, 2000) 80.

seventeenth century form has remained largely unchanged. Even the Charities Act 2006, which was supposed to be a transformation, has done little more than codify the list.

To be charitable, housing providers have generally had to demonstrate that their functions fall under the first heading, *the relief of poverty*. As will become clear in what follows, it has been the definition of 'poverty' that has been problematic. The Federation attempted to encode 'relief of poverty' into model housing association rules by making it an object of an association that it must house people 'of limited means'. Later, when this proved insufficient to the regulators, revised rules referred to people 'in necessitous circumstances'.[28] Further difficulties arose because a charitable organisation also had to demonstrate that its rules 'restrict the application of its assets to *wholly* and *exclusively* charitable purposes'.[29] It is perhaps hardly surprising that frequent conflicts have arisen between charity regulation and the wider purposes of housing associations. As associations have sought to meet changing needs over the past century, they have given both 'poverty' and 'housing' a wide interpretation and have been encouraged to build not just for the poorest households, but for 'mixed communities'. Whilst practitioners in these charitable associations might have considered their work to be of 'public benefit', it has been the need to ensure that activities were directed *exclusively* at relieving poverty that has been the problem.

The Charities Act 1960 was intended as a modernisation of charitable regulation.[30] The Act established a register of charities to be administered by the Charity Commission. This device of the register, the Federation hoped, would create the certainty that case law had so far not produced, for it would

> establish conclusively that any organisation which is on the register is a charity at law and thus no question could arise as to eligibility for charitable privileges, for example, exemption from Income Tax.[31]

As we shall see below, this expectation turned out to be somewhat optimistic.

The Act appeared as a symbol of changing attitudes towards the need for supporting a 'third sector', one that was neither state nor motivated by private profit. Within the housing association sector there was a renewed interest in charity; charity could be both a source of funds and a motivation for the formation of new housing associations. In 1960, the Federation set up its own charity, the Housing Societies Charitable Trust (HSCT) as a means of raising funds for the sector. The remit of the HSCT was to:

(1) allocate by way of grant or interest free loan, funds from charitable bodies

[28] Geoffrey P Hall, Director of the National Federation of Housing Societies (NFHS) writing in the Federation's new journal: 'Charity entails obligations' (1969) 1 *Voluntary Housing* 370.

[29] P Luxton, *The Law of Charities* (Oxford, Oxford University Press, 2001) para 8.219; emphasis added.

[30] Owen, above n 10.

[31] *QB* 97, April 1961, 3.

who prefer to use the Trust as their agent, rather than receive applications from individual Housing Associations, and

(2) operate an interest free loan fund which it has itself built up over a period of time, in support of Associations.[32]

An awareness of homelessness, a new wave of philanthropy, the formation of the homelessness charity Shelter in 1966 and the establishment of new associations, all led to the legal charitable form gaining a new significance. There were a number of reasons for this. First, Shelter was enormously successful in its charitable fundraising,[33] but only charitable bodies could benefit from these funds. Secondly, charitable associations could gain access to tax concessions. But the most critical factor was probably the need for a recognised identity: charitable status was a badge of trustworthiness and one that was seen as the object of control. The trustees of charitable associations could not simply choose to dissolve their associations and take the assets, they were subject to the control of the Charity Commissioners (and ultimately, the courts). For local authorities in the 1960s who were looking to invest in non-municipal rented housing, the political risk was high following the Rachmann affair.[34] This regulatory aspect of charitable status led some local authorities (in particular, the London County Council/Greater London Council) to insist that any association they funded was a registered charity in order to protect their public subsidy.[35] 'Charity' was the chosen vehicle, in spite of the image problems inherent in the notion.

However, these new philanthropic associations were frequently in tension with the regulatory space of charity, the subject of the next section. In particular, it was the fiscal regulation of charities that brought the most significant challenges to the charitable framework. Here, the National Federation's role was not simply as mediator; since its formation the Federation had supported new associations in setting up by offering model rules. One strategy employed by the Federation was to renegotiate these model rules with the Charity Commission, the Inland Revenue and the Registrar of Friendly Societies, to meet concerns that associations' objects might not be charitable.[36] However, the Charity Commission's files show that revised rules did not stop challenges from officers of the Inland Revenue. For the Revenue rules were only part of their concern: it was not simply *form* that determined whether an organisation was charitable, but the everyday, mundane activities of choosing tenants and providing a housing service.

[32] National Federation of Housing Societies (NFHS) *1969 Annual Report.*

[33] See below, ch 7.

[34] Rachman was a private landlord who became notorious for his exploitation and harassment of tenants. See, eg, D Cowan, *Housing Law and Policy* (Basingstoke, Macmillan, 1999) 63–64.

[35] L Waddilove, *Housing to Let by Non-Profit Organisations* (1970) TNA HLG 118/1390.

[36] NFHS, *1967 Annual Report*, 4.

Housing Associations Challenged

Challenges to the activities of housing associations concerned disputed interpretations of 'for the relief of poverty'. The Inland Revenue made two specific challenges to the procedures of associations. The first related to associations set up by the Catholic Housing Aid Society (CHAC) and Father Eamon Casey. These associations had established housing policies within a moral framework that pursued the continuation of values recognised by the Roman Catholic Church among young people. These housing policies were aimed at

> . . . young people who are contemplating marriage and who intend to live in the centres of our large cities. . . . If they must live where housing is expensive . . . he [Casey] promises them a flat when they marry in return for an undertaking that between them they will save a given sum each week before marriage and will continue to pay an agreed sum in addition to the rent after their marriage. Then within a year he is able to advise them how to use their accumulated capital to buy a house . . . His view is that three out of four couples whom he helps in this way would otherwise within a very limited time be coming to him as 'welfare cases'.[37]

For the Inland Revenue, a tenant's ability to save a sum of money each week called into question whether they were 'in necessitous circumstances'. The Federation adopted what seems to be a common tactic in disputes with the Revenue (from the evidence in the Charity Commission file)[38] and sought the help of the Charity Commission. Lewis Waddilove, the Federation's chairman, entered into discussions with Charity Commissioner Lewis. Lewis suggested that part of the problem was that associations simply adopted model rules, rather that amending these rules to accurately reflect their particular objectives. By doing so they could take themselves out of the problematic domain of defining 'poverty' and demonstrate their charitable status under another of the charitable categories. So, for example, in this particular case he suggested using a heading of '"gifts or trusts for the care, upbringing and establishment in life of children and young persons" with a sub-heading for "trusts for the promotion of marriage"'.[39] Lewis sought to work within the constraints of an archaic charity law to find a solution to new problems.

It was the Inland Revenue's second challenge to the ongoing activities of associations that proved most problematic, for this was a fundamental clash between fiscal priorities and the values of associations. The Revenue's view was that it was not sufficient for an association simply to ensure that tenants were 'in poverty' when offered a tenancy. Their status of poverty should be kept continually under review, with the implication that tenants who could no longer be classified as 'in poverty' should be evicted. This was a far more fundamental

37 TNA CHAR 11/205: letter from Lewis Waddilove to Charity Commissioner Lewis (16 September 1968).

38 TNA CHAR 11/205.

39 *Ibid*: letter from WEA Lewis to Lewis Waddilove (8 October 1968).

challenge to the operation of housing associations, which could, said Waddilove, lead to 'all but a very small sector of the voluntary housing movement [coming] to an end'.[40] In intervening here, Charity Commissioner Lewis demonstrated an understanding of the practicalities of running an association, along with a desire to make charitable regulation work for associations. It was his view that associations 'should not be obliged to eject' tenants once they ceased to be poor, a view he acknowledged that 'is most likely to trouble the Inland Revenue'.[41]

The difficulties raised by the fiscal regulators appeared at first to Lewis and Waddilove as the actions of an over-zealous local bureaucrat. However, when Waddilove attempted resolution with the local Inland Revenue office, he revealed a systematic regime of regulation carried out by the Revenue:

> Once any housing association has applied for re-payment of income tax because of its charitable status the Department then includes it on a list so that in due time an examination may be made of the principles on which the charity operates.[42]

Waddilove noted that he 'thought this general review was the function of the Charity Commissioners'.

Having failed to deal with the matter informally, Lewis and Waddilove agreed that the Federation should make a formal approach to the Charity Commissioner. Lewis expressed the hope that a common response agreed with Inland Revenue lawyers could be provided. The notes of Lewis and Waddilove's meetings reveal an interesting operation of governing conducted at the level of the personal, a 'social connectedness' and the operation of social relations. The Charity Commissioner's enthusiastic intervention was to bring legal knowledge into play creatively, not restrictively. The two had shared understandings and (at this point) a common goal for the transformation of charity law in a manner that embodied the concerns of housing organisations. Waddilove raised wider issues of redefining charitable status to meet current thinking about the provision of housing, which Lewis termed

> 'community housing' . . . the idea that if a large Trust is developing a very large estate by way of housing it is sociologically undesirable that all buildings on that estate should be intended to be occupied by people of the same low income group.[43]

Waddilove was also a member of a government committee, the Central Housing Advisory Committee[44] in which

> persons closely involved in the past in council housing have drawn attention to the very unfortunate state of affairs developing in places like Tower Hamlets where almost the

[40] *Ibid* (19 March 1969).

[41] *Ibid.*

[42] *Ibid*, notes of Waddilove's meeting with Inland Revenue Office (Bootle, 5 May 1969).

[43] *Ibid.*

[44] The Central Housing Advisory Committee (CHAC) was set up by the Housing Act 1935, as a committee of 'experts' to advise the Minister on a range of housing issues.

> whole borough consisted of council housing with the result that professional and well-to-do people were not living there at all. This they deplored.[45]

In a creative application of his lawyer's expertise, Lewis suggested a mechanism for pursuing 'community housing' through charity law. The development of an estate that provided both commercial and residential properties, where housing was let at market rents as well as reduced rents could, he argued, come within 'the spirit of the preamble of the Elizabethan statute by analogy with bridges and causeways'. This seemingly bizarre analogy makes sense when one understands the *process* of charity law-making. Over the centuries, the courts have developed the meaning of 'charity' through a process of analogy; first by finding an analogy with the preamble to the statute of 1601 (through which the construction of bridges and causeways had become a charitable activity) and then by analogy with some other activity already deemed charitable.[46]

Lewis wrote to the Inland Revenue, enclosing the Federation's letter, stating his concern that 'we and your department should not in public be taking a different line on these problems'. The Revenue's response is not on file, but its tone must have been as unyielding as that of the local office. On receiving Lewis's draft reply, Waddilove wrote that he was 'disappointed that there is not to be a review of the boundaries within which charitable housing associations have to work'. Finally, Lewis resorted to a Charity Commission response without agreement from the Inland Revenue. By this point Waddilove had decided to 'avoid any attempt to redefine charitable status in relation to housing. The consultations which you kindly initiated have shown how sterile this to be', he concluded in a letter to Lewis in October 1970. He confided that he had been asked by Peter Walker, Minister for Housing, to prepare a paper

> on principles that might be included in a Housing Bill dealing with the Voluntary Housing Movement [..] on the basis of the advice you have given I propose to suggest that in any new legislation, voluntary housing bodies, which have charitable status, shall simply be empowered to house persons who do not fall within the 'poverty' requirements of charity provided that they do not benefit from the bounty of charity.[47]

[45] TNA, above n 38 at fn 57; this concern about one tenure estates raised as it was in the 1960s has echoes of present-day concerns about social exclusion. The 'marginalisation and residualisation' thesis became important in academic thinking about housing when raised by Ray Forrest and Alan Murie in *Selling the Welfare State: The Privatisation of Public Housing* (London, Routledge, 1988) with concerns about one tenure estates particularly in inner cities where high numbers of unemployed and homeless households were 'funnelled' (at 160).

[46] *Scottish Burial Reform and Cremation Society Ltd v Glasgow City Corporation* [1968] AC 138, quoted in R Pearce and J Stevens, *the Law of trusts and Equitable Obligations*, (2nd ed) (London, Butterworths, 1998): 457–58.

[47] TNA, above n 38.

Reflections on the Rejection of Charitable Space

So what is the significance of this rejection of the charitable form by the housing association sector at the end of the 1960s? And what does this story tell us about the role of the Federation and other political actors in shaping the housing association sector? What followed was the Housing Act 1974, which in effect set up a state regulator and funder (the Housing Corporation)[48] for the housing association sector. The story of the Federation's role in the making of the 1974 Act is told in chapter five.[49] For the purposes of this chapter, the Act's importance was in providing associations with their own regulatory regime that meant they no longer needed to seek charitable status. The Housing Corporation was given statutory powers to set up a register of housing associations, provide grants to registered associations and a duty to monitor and supervise registered associations, including controlling the disposal of housing association assets. The Corporation could even reimburse associations for Corporation tax paid on surpluses, until this was withdrawn in the 1990s. As regards housing associations that were also charitable, the Act required the Charity Commissioners to consult the Housing Corporation on certain matters, for example, for the disposal of land.[50]

So, for many associations, charity law could be ignored. Arguably, however, it was not charity law that had failed, but the regulatory space that charitable status had produced. It was inhabited by regulators whose knowledge was competing and had very different objectives: the Charity Commission wanted to make charity law work, because that was its *raison d'être*; the Inland Revenue was only concerned that the State was not 'cheated' out of tax revenues. These competing regulatory agencies argued that their knowledge was 'expert' and authoritative. But eventually the housing associations' expertise in housing enabled them to argue for regulation that would facilitate the transformation they and other political actors were seeking.

Regulatory Regimes

Waddilove's observation that attempts to redefine charity law were 'sterile' was not simply a comment on law, but on the regulatory *regimes* that had become responsible for implementing charity law. 'Regime' is a useful concept here, for it embodies the idea of a relatively ordered and systematic set of practices that

[48] Established in 1964 for the limited purposes of promoting cost-rent and co-ownership housing societies: see above, ch 2.

[49] Also see M McDermont, 'Territorializing Regulation: A Case study of "Social Housing" in England' (2007) 32(2) *Law & Social Inquiry* 373–98.

[50] Housing Act 1974 s 2(3).

emerge from particular forms of knowledge.[51] These forms of knowledge, arising from common training and education, social background and class, enable sets of values to be accepted as 'common sense'. The practices that develop produce relatively stable institutional environments, which then can lead to the development of new practices.[52]

In this story, two branches of the central state, the Charity Commission and the Inland Revenue, had interpreted the same body of legislative and case law from two very different perspectives: they had developed radically different practices arising out of different normative values and different understandings of their roles as regulators. This rather undermines claims to a unitary nature for law. Rather, law is complex and hybrid, increasingly colonised by forms of knowledge and expertise that are non-legal.[53] Here, the resulting clash of value systems was arguably a factor in Waddilove's eventual rejection of charity. Each of these regulatory regimes had developed their own 'framing',[54] which I explore next. In the end, these competing ways of seeing created conditions where a dis-connection with charity law was the only way forward.

(i) Charity Law and the Charity Commissioners

Concerns for charitable trusts to be publicly regulated had brought about the formation of the Charity Commission in the Charitable Trusts Act 1853. From the beginning there was a presumption that their role would be principally *legal,* a majority of the commissioners had to be legally trained. The powers of commissioners to investigate endowed charities were 'fairly generous', but primarily limited to curbing 'certain varieties of administrative malpractice'.[55] For most major decisions they were required to seek the permission of the courts (for example, to appoint new trustees, or to take action to resolve the problem of obsolete trusts), but they have the courts' powers when determining whether an organisation has charitable status.[56] They are 'quasi-judicial' in function,[57] their

[51] 'Regimes of practices' and 'regimes of government' arise out of the governmentality literature. Mitchell Dean usefully identifies that such regimes 'can be known along four independently varying but related axes: fields of visibility; forms of rationality; techniques and technologies; and identities and agencies': M Dean, *Governmentality: Power and Rule in Modern Society* (London, Sage, 1999) 21 and also ch 1.

[52] Dean, *ibid* at 20–22. Michael Power shows how the regime of accountancy and audit has powerfully shaped mechanisms of governing a diverse range of activities, from social work to parks management, education to museums, since the 1980s: M Power, *The Audit Society: Rituals of Verification* (Oxford, Oxford University Press, 1997).

[53] N Rose and M Valverde, 'Governed by Law?'(1998) 7 *Economy & Society* 541–51, 543.

[54] K Hawkins, *Law as Last Resort: Prosecution Decision-Making in a Regulatory Agency* (Oxford, Oxford University Press, 2002) 52–59.

[55] Owen, above n 10 at 202.

[56] Charity Commission, *Framework for the Review of the Register of Charities* (London, Charity Commission, 1998) Annex D.

[57] Eg, see, National Audit Office (NAO), *Monitoring and Control of Charities in England and Wales,* Report by the Comptroller and Auditor General, 380 (London, HMSO, 1987) 4.

form of thinking is 'reminiscent of judicial law making' and like judges, they use their own decisions as precedent to extend, clarify and define charity law.[58] Nevertheless, when it came to controlling the best endowed of charitable housing trusts, the William Sutton Trust, it was the Chancery Court that took charge, directed by officials at the Local Government Board.[59]

However, statute also required the commissioners to provide advice to charities and it was this that they appeared to consider a central function and indeed prioritised it over other responsibilities. In this role, too, they could steer and control the domain. However, as audit and regulation made probity and value for money key, the provision of advice came to be considered a low priority for a regulator.[60] A National Audit Office (NAO) report criticised the 'serious deficiencies in the management information produced by the Commission',[61] noting that the monitoring of charities and in particular their financial position, received little attention.[62] In 1987, only eight out of 330 Charity Commission staff were employed exclusively in examining charities' accounts, none of them professional accountants.[63] In any case, only a small proportion of charities submitted annual accounts and the Charity Commission resources were so limited that they could not afford the postage to send out reminders.[64] The Commission was described as 'living up to their self-imposed image of benevolent family solicitors … [perhaps giving] too much to their legal duties as opposed to the responsibilities in other spheres'.[65]

Legalistic and paternalistic as they were, the commissioners operated in an environment of dialogue between regulator and regulatee. The mode of regulation operated by the Inland Revenue was very different.

(ii) Financial Regulation: The Inland Revenue and Local Government

The different approaches to charitable regulation operated by the Charity Commissioners and the Inland Revenue were identified by the National Audit Office's 1987 report:

[58] PW Edge and JM Loughrey, 'Religious Charities and the Juridification of the Charity Commission' (2001) 21 *Legal Studies* 36–64, 36–37.

[59] Garside, above n 13 at 613–36; and PL Garside, *The Conduct of Philanthropy: The William Sutton Trust 1900–2000* (London, Athlone Press, 2000).

[60] See, eg, P Day, D Henderson and R Klein, *Home Rules: Regulation and Accountability in Social Housing* (York, Joseph Rowntree Foundation, 1993). By the late 1980s, the Housing Corporation considered it could not afford to service the advice function for housing associations.

[61] Above, n 57, para 1.26.

[62] Above n 57 at 380.

[63] *Ibid*, para 1.24: the NAO's concern for financial accountability was entirely consistent with the rationale of the NAO itself, which was required to carry out 'value for money' audits: see Power n 52.

[64] J Irvine, 'Adopting a Long Term View' (1988) 102(1132) *Accountancy* 92–93, 92.

[65] House of Commons Select Committee on Expenditure, *Annual Report session 1974–75*, quoted in NAO 1987, n 62, para 1.22.

> Inland Revenue are notified of all charity registrations. Proposals to accept a charity for registration are referred by the Commission to Inland Revenue to prevent, as far as possible, disagreements on a body's status once it has been registered. Disagreements over what is charitable occasionally occur in borderline cases because the Commission tends gradually to extend the boundaries of what is considered charitable, whereas the Inland Revenue have to consider whether tax relief is legally due to the body concerned.[66]

Charitable regulation has frequently co-existed uneasily within these two regulatory frameworks, the legal and the fiscal. In terms of fiscal regulation, it has been not only the Inland Revenue, but the treasurer's departments of local authorities, that have had an interest in what is, or is not, charitable. Such bodies, considering themselves 'guardians' of public funds, have contested definitions of what counts as charitable activities. So, for example, the Guinness Trust, established as a charitable trust in the nineteenth century, was taken to court by West Ham Borough Council for its practice of investing in stocks and shares, as well as letting out land or property for profit. The local recorder agreed with the council that this was a profit-making activity, making the Guinness Trust ineligible for relief from local rates.[67] Significantly for housing associations and other charitable trusts, Guinness successfully overturned this judgment,[68] when the Court of Appeal took a wider view of charitable activities:

> The making of profit by the Guinness Trust is part of the machinery by which it achieves its charitable purposes. The making of profit, which can never be distributed, is not an object or purpose of the Trust. It is a means for the expansion of the sphere of charity.[69]

The legal frame here took a broader view of activities that could be considered appropriate for charitable organisations. Like Charity Commissioner Lewis in the above account, the Court was concerned with the practical operations which enabled charitable organisations to carry out their functions as part of a broader structure of welfare, rather than imposing narrow understandings that only served to restrict the ability to claim fiscal benefits. Nevertheless, despite winning court and other battles, and the somewhat paternalistic, but nevertheless facilitative attitudes of the Charity Commissioners, housing associations frequently found themselves up against the Inland Revenue. Revenue officers were inculcated with concerns that taxes must be paid where 'the law' required and technologies of governing that enabled them to take invasive and punitive action where 'the law' (as judged from their 'expert' perspective) was transgressed. Such is the position of the tax authorities in the popular imagination that a book

[66] NAO, *ibid* n 62, para 2.13(a).

[67] Rating and Valuation (Miscellaneous Provisions) Act 1955: s 8(1)(c) enabled organisations that were neither 'established for profit' nor 'conducted for profit' to obtain relief from local rates.

[68] *Guinness Trust v West Ham Borough Council* [1958] 1 WLR 541.

[69] Reported in *QB* 89, April 1959, 31.

studying the British tax system had the title *The Power to Destroy*.[70] The resources of surveillance and oversight that the Revenue could bring to bear were substantial. In 1965, 60,000 people were employed by the Inland Revenue (not all, of course, working on charities) in a highly decentralised bureaucracy,[71] whereas in 1987 the Charity Commission only employed 330 staff. The Revenue's position in the corridors of power was well-established. Such was the importance of taxation to economic policy that the 'Board [of the Inland Revenue] are constantly in consultation with the Treasury, the Department of Economic Affairs and other economic departments'.[72] The Revenue was (and is) an environment that is 'highly formalized and highly bureaucratized'.[73]

The story told above provides a practical example of the stark difference in the way the two organisations saw their regulatory role: the Charity Commissioners as facilitators, the Inland Revenue as the authoritative power not open to question. Their differing conceptions of 'common sense' caused charitable organisations enormous frustration, at times threatening to freeze their operations. A letter in the National Archives from Waddilove in his capacity as Director of the Joseph Rowntree Memorial Trust (JRMT)[74] to Charity Commissioner Lewis, provides a demonstration. It is worth quoting from this at length for it brings into sharp relief the impact the Inland Revenue's regime could have on the housing trust:

> I am very exercised in my mind about the relations between your department and the Inland Revenue. We have suffered bitterly from this because the powers of the Trustees in relation to housing as defined by the Joseph Rowntree Memorial Trust have greatly restricted the work of the Trust and are as a result of 'advice' given by Revenue authorities and in conflict with the views of Counsel and the Chief Commissioner at that time. None of these arguments prevailed however, and we were told that if the Bill passed into law in the form then approved the charitable status for taxation purposes of the whole of the Trust's endowment would be withdrawn, and this would be so even if Parliament passed the Act on the assumption that it was creating a charitable instrument. Nor could this advice be challenged because it was made clear that if the case went against us our charitable status would be lost and that without remedy. Bearing in mind the Trustees' large responsibilities, Counsel had to advise them that they had no alternative but to accept the Inland Revenue advice. *It thus comes about that if the Trustees obeyed the law their large housing estate would gradually become peopled with the*

[70] DR Myddleton, *The Power to Destroy: A Study of the British System* (London, Johnson, 1969).

[71] A Johnston, *The Inland Revenue* The New Whitehall Series No 13 (London, George Allen & Unwin Ltd, 1965) 12.

[72] *Ibid.*

[73] CC Hood, 'The British Tax Structure Development as Administrative Adaptation' (1985) 18 *Policy Sciences* 3–31, 29.

[74] JRMT was one of the three trusts created by Joseph Rowntree in 1904, originally established to administer Joseph Rowntree's model village, New Earswick, York. Quote from Joseph Rowntree: 'I do not want to establish communities bearing the stamp of charity but rather of rightly ordered and self-governing communities'—taken from the website of the Joseph Rowntree Foundation: www.jrf.org.uk/centenary/.

> *old, the poor and the handicapped, many of whom would be unsuitably housed, and a thriving and vigorous community with schools and other things would disappear. We make no secret of the fact that we simply ignore the law.*[75]

Nevertheless, the Revenue's attempt at regulating housing associations did not result in acceptance of the domination of its authority. Rather, an alternative regime was chosen.[76] The Federation recognised the need for the housing association sector to be seen to be regulated, but also the need for an alternative to charitable regulation because it simply was not working *for* the sector. So the move was a pragmatic one, but it was also *symbolic*. Waddilove and others recognised the need to create a new identity for the housing association sector. The placing of those who saw it as their mission to provide housing for the poor had not been simply a pragmatic placing, driven by fiscal regulation; the sector had a long tradition in the *ideology* of philanthropy. There was a feeling among some in the housing association sector in the late 1960s that the old charitable trusts were out-dated, 'outmoded and an anachronism', as Waddilove described them in his evidence to the Cohen Committee.[77] Arguably, simply updating charity law (even if it had proved a possible project) would not have facilitated a break with the past, and a re-placement of housing associations in a new, dynamic, less patronising space.

Returning to the pragmatic perspective, continued regulation in the charitable sphere would have proved problematic for visions of a housing association sector expanding to become the 'third arm' of social housing.[78] It is doubtful that the Charity Commission could ever have performed the role that was required for a much expanded housing association sector. As discussed, the NAO was highly critical of the way the Charity Commission carried out its duties. In particular, its lack of resources devoted to chasing up charities to submit accounts (a requirement of the Charities Act 1960) and exercising any monitoring and oversight of the use or mis-use of charitable funds,[79] would inevitably have caused problems for a sector that came to rely on large amounts of public funding. The Federation was looking to charitable regulation to perform the function of providing a symbol of trustworthiness. This symbolic value would have been severely diminished by a regulator that could not exercise effective control over financial affairs.

75 TNA CHAR 11/205: letter dated 27 August 1968.

76 Teubner's 'regulatory trilemna' is called to mind here. Teubner would say that charitable regulation and fiscal regulation were different *systems*, each cognitively open but normatively closed. If one system should try to control another, the result is the 'regulatory trilemna': either the intervention will be ignored by the system, or it will destroy the system's traditional norms, or the intervening system will itself be destroyed: see G Teubner, 'Substantive and Reflexive Elements of Modern Law' (1983) 17 *Law and Society Review* 239–85.

77 TNA CHAR 11/205.The Cohen Committee was a sub-committee of the Central Housing Advisory Committee set up in 1968 to review the activities of housing associations. See Cohen Committee, *Housing Associations* (London, HMSO, 1971).

78 L Waddilove, 'Developing a Third Arm' (1967) (26 December) 219 *The Spectator* 7279.

79 NAO, above n 62, paras 1.13–1.17.

The Housing Association Model and Third Sector Transformation

From 1974, housing associations had their own national regulatory body and, perhaps most critically, a centralised funding system. Many housing associations considered themselves to be public bodies until at least the mid-1980s, tied as they were into state priorities (though not without conflict particularly with local government, as discussed in chapter four). Even those who still remained as charitable, including the older charitable trusts, increasingly became vehicles of public service delivery. There was, however, one point at which the legal and ideological status of charity came to be used as a powerful defence against the Thatcher Government's (equally) ideological promotion of home ownership. The Housing Act 1980 brought in the right-to-buy for local authority tenants and some housing association tenants. Early in the progress of the Bill, the National Federation of Housing Associations successfully lobbied for charitable housing associations, mutual housing co-operatives, accommodation for the elderly, hostel schemes and homes on leasehold and other projects to be excluded from the proposals.[80] With a large proportion of the sector's tenants excluded, a second, and this time much more serious attempt, was made by the Conservative Government to reintroduce the right-to-buy. Clause 2 of the Housing and Building Control Bill 1982 proposed that tenants of *all* properties financed with grants under the 1974 Act should have a statutory right to buy.

For the Federation, it was important to carefully construct its engagement with politics, given its presented image of an independent sector, outside politics. Such sensitivities were noted in its 1982 annual report in the comment that '[i]t is inevitable that a highly individualistic and independent Movement, and the Federation that represents it, will find itself occasionally in conflict with the government of the day', whilst making clear its 'appreciat[ion for] the support we have received during 1982 from the Ministers responsible for our work'.[81] The Federation launched a campaign aimed at defeating the proposals, a lobbying campaign that brought into action those many members of the House of Lords who were connected with the charitable housing sector. The second reading of the Bill in the House of Lords was almost entirely a debate about clause 2.[82] Successive speakers spoke of their long involvement with charitable associations: 'I have been a trustee of the Guinness Trust for half a century' was Lord Moyne's opening statement.[83] These trustees and board members were joined by others not necessarily affiliated to the housing association sector, many of them Conservative peers, outraged at what they saw as the Government's attack on the

80 NFHA, *1980 Annual Report*.

81 NFHA, *1982 Annual Report*, 9.

82 The debates are reported in Hansard HL vol 437 cols 712–13 (16 December 1982) and vol 441 cols 21–851 (11 April 1983), committee stage of Housing and Planning Bill.

83 Hansard HL vol 437 col 712.

independence of the charitable sector. Here, charity's legal and ideological status became powerful weapons, as these lords and ladies argued that the proposals undermined the principles of 'giving' and the independence on which charitable organisations were based; were illegal in terms of the existing law of trusts; and acted retrospectively, and so contrary to the 'rule of law'.

The campaign led to the defeat of clause 2 in the House of Lords committee stage by 96 to 182 votes, 'possibly still the largest defeat by the Lords of a Conservative government proposal', Richard Best, Director of the National Federation of Housing Associations (NFHA) claimed in 2002.[84] Like the success in the Housing Act 1974, this victory is one that has gained immense significance in the folklore of the Federation, a symbol of its effectiveness in shaping the 'voluntary' housing environment. The effective weapon was, once again, the Federation's ability to rally support in the House of Lords. That very traditional of institutions was brought in to defend the traditional values of charity against an intrusion from the radical ideology of the neo-conservatives.

The Third Sector, the 'Third Way' and the 'Service Pull'[85]

The stories in this chapter can give us insights into the conditions that have made possible the housing association sector as it exists in the twenty-first century. Can they also tell us anything about the trajectory of other voluntary, 'third sector' or charitable organisations?[86] For the housing association sector, the Conservative Government's antipathy towards local government meant that they continued to be supported for the delivery of what became known as 'social housing'. The Housing Act 1988 enabled associations to move away from public grants and they increasingly became reliant on private loans. For other third sector organisations, the 1990s meant a shift in attitudes reminiscent of the shift towards housing associations in the 1970s, as third sector organisations were increasingly pulled into public service delivery.[87] The Thatcher Government's introduction of quasi-market principles into public service provision[88] offered new opportunities for voluntary and community as well as 'for-profit' organisations to deliver services under contract to public sector 'purchasers' (mostly local government). Although

[84] Richard Best interview (12 August 2002); by this time he too had become a member of the House of Lords.

[85] See Dunn, above n 25.

[86] To use the term 'third sector' in the singular is admittedly something of a mis-use, for the organisations that make up the 'third sector' are immensely diverse. A number of terms tend to be used interchangeably: not-for-profit sector; charitable sector; third sector. Like housing associations, third sector organisations are not necessarily charitable, but their lack of other funding options meant charity remained dominant.

[87] This part of the chapter draws on a paper given at the ARNOVA Annual Conference in Denver, November 2003, written jointly with Marilyn Taylor. My thanks to Marilyn for allowing me to have the benefit of her understanding of and research into the third sector.

[88] J Le Grand and W Bartlett (eds), *Quasi-markets and Social Policy* (Basingstoke, Macmillan, 1993).

these and other changes saw a considerable increase in state funding for the voluntary and community sector,[89] the move to a 'contract culture'[90] was greeted with much more suspicion by these organisations than housing associations had ever done. They feared that, by entering into service agreements and contracts with the State, they would simply become its agents.[91]

New Labour's election victory in 1997 seemingly brought with it a renewed commitment to charities and voluntary sector organisations as delivery vehicles for public services. In New Labour's ideology, the sector offered a solution that avoided the 'worst excesses' of both the market and government, according to Anthony Giddens, architect of 'third way' politics.[92] The new Government's stated commitment to tackling social exclusion, to radical service reform and to civic renewal all offered the sector significant new opportunities.[93] However, as with the housing association sector in the 1970s, existing structures were considered unsuitable to enable charities to become key players; new instruments were needed and some saw housing associations as a model for these instruments.[94] Government instituted a number of reviews, aimed at 'helping the sector achieve its full potential',[95] specifically examining the financial capacity and legal framework for third sector activity. A Treasury 'cross-cutting review'[96] placed emphasis on enabling the voluntary sector to take on more roles in public service delivery. Out of this review came 'Futurebuilders', a £150 million fund backed by the Cabinet Office that provides loans and grants to the voluntary and community sectors.[97] For the housing association sector, the asset base that they had built up, mostly as a result of the very generous funding that came out of the Housing Act 1974, was key to the strength and expansion of the sector. Futurebuilders is, in part, aimed at supporting voluntary organisations to build up assets, through

89 L Hems and A Passey, *The Voluntary Sector Almanac* (London, NCVO Publications, 1998); J Kendall, *The Voluntary Sector* (London, Routledge, 2003).

90 6 and P Kendall and J Kendall (eds), *The Contract Culture in Public Services: Studies from Britain, Europe and the USA* (Aldershot, Arena, 1997).

91 See, eg, R Gutch, *Contracting: Lessons from the United States* (London, NCVO, 1992); D Billis and M Harris, 'Taking the strain of change: UK local voluntary organisations enter the post-Thatcher period' (1992) 21 *Nonprofit and Voluntary Sector Quarterly* 211–25; J Lewis, 'What does contracting do to voluntary agencies?' in D Billis and M Harris (eds), *Voluntary Agencies: Challenges of Organisation and Management* (London, Macmillan, 1996); M Taylor and P Hoggett, 'Quasi-markets and the transformation of the independent sector'in W Bartlett, C Propper, D Wilson and J Le Grand, *Quasi-markets in Public Services: The Emerging Findings* (Bristol, School for Advanced Urban Studies, 1993); J Lewis, 'Reviewing the Relationship Between the Voluntary Sector and the State in Britain in the 1990s' (1999) 10 *Voluntas* 255–70.

92 A Giddens, *The Third Way: The Renewal of Social Democracy* (London, Polity Press, 1998).

93 Kendall, *The Voluntary Sector*, above n 89.

94 Richard Best interview, above n 84.

95 Cabinet Office, *Private Action, Public Benefit: A Review of Charities and the Wider Not-for-profit Sector* (The Cabinet Office, London, 2002) 7.

96 *The Role of the Voluntary and Community Sector in Service Delivery: A Cross Cutting Review* (London, HM Treasury, 2002).

97 See, eg, Futurebuilders England, *Investment Plan 2007–08* (April 2008); and an interview with the chief executive of Futurebuilders in A Benjamin, 'Loan star' *Guardian* (4 July 2007).

funding the purchase and refurbishment of buildings.[98] However, the scale is very different. The £150 million for Futurebuilders is a small fraction of the billions invested in the housing association sector throughout the 1980s.

Other developments have drawn on the housing association experience. The Public Management Foundation (an independent think-tank based at the same address as the National Housing Federation, with connections to New Labour politicians) floated the idea of the 'public interest company' in 2001. Their argument for the Public Interest Company was that

> [w]e need to create an organisational form that is based upon entrepreneurial trading for public service, but that will do so without the need to generate profit for external distribution.[99]

They referred to the housing association form as 'an important development' in the area of charitable organisations in their ability to raise capital in the money markets, many of them now treated as 'very good risks'.[100] The concept was adopted by government, but unsurprisingly (given New Labour's ambivalent relationship with the public) was renamed 'community interest company' by the time it was introduced in the Companies (Audit, Investigation and Community Enterprise) Act 2005.[101]

Other statutory changes are also shifting the field for a wide range of charitable organisations. The Charities Act 2006 further strengthens the bond between 'charitable purposes' and public policy, 'extending from urban and rural regeneration in areas of social and economic deprivation, to the relief of unemployment, the promotion of community building, the efficiency of charities and use of their resources, to the promotion of human rights'.[102] Increased linkage between government priorities and charity can be found in recent decisions of the Charity Commission, for example in awarding the Restorative Justice Consortium[103] and an organisation concerned with waste recycling[104] charitable status.[105]

Concerns about independence predominate across the charitable and housing association sectors. The proposed powers for the new social housing regulator contained in the Housing and Regeneration Bill led the Charity Commission to warn of their 'dire consequences for housing associations, undermining their independence and forcing them into activities which could ultimately lead to the

[98] Futurebuilders, *ibid*, para 2.4.

[99] *The Case for the Public Interest Company: A New Form of Enterprise for Public Service Delivery* (London, Public Management Foundation, 2001) 6.

[100] *Ibid*, 11.

[101] Also Community Interest Company Regulations 2005, SI 2005/1788.

[102] Charities Act 2006, s 2; see Dunn, above n 25 at 252.

[103] Decision of the Charity Commissioners, 30 May 2003: www.charitycommission.gov.uk/Library/registration/pdfs/rjcdecision.pdf.

[104] Decision of the Charity Commissioners, April 2002: www.charitycommission.gov.uk/Library/registration/pdfs/rio.pdf .

[105] Dunn, above n 25 at 252.

loss of their charitable status'.[106] Across the voluntary and charitable sectors, many fear that the Government's desire to use charity in service delivery is a significant threat to the independence:

> [T]he recent crosscutting review of the voluntary and community sector (Treasury 2002) appears to emphasize yet again government's interest in the service delivery role of the voluntary and community sector, possibly, in doing so, closing the partnership window somewhat.[107]

Conclusion

This chapter has told the story of housing associations' relationship with regulation through charity. The story has demonstrated that contested meanings of charitable objects, the *relief of poverty*, eventually led to the breakdown of the charitable form for the housing association sector. In re-telling the story of disputes between various arms of the State responsible for the regulation of charities, the Charity Commission and the Inland Revenue, we see that different regimes seemingly operating in the same regulatory space can have dramatically contrasting ways of understanding the task of regulation. Such differing ways of thinking about and instrumentalising regulation, in this particular story, made the regulatory space unusable when the need came to transform and expand the organisations that were the subject of regulation.

In the 1970s, there was a new 'policy paradigm' in government that saw a different way of delivering housing policy, one in which the housing association sector could play a major role. This enabled the sector to find a new framework for regulation that facilitated transformation and expansion, as the subsequent chapters will show. However, the charitable form has continued to be important for some associations and for many 'third sector' organisations. The second part of this chapter showed how old traditional forms can be used as a defence, when charitable housing associations effectively fought off a neo-conservative government's attempt to impose the right-to-buy. The discussion then moved to consider whether the housing association model could be an effective vehicle for a 'third sector' transformation into major public service providers. However, here we see a concern among other charitable organisations that the sector may, by seeking dramatic expansion, have compromised its identity as an independent organisation. In the final chapter of this book, I return to the puzzle that this creates, in a consideration of the meaning of 'independence' to the housing association sector.

[106] 'New Bill creates "serious implications" for housing associations' *Charity Times* (12 February 2008).

[107] G Craig, M Taylor and T Parkes, 'Protest or Partnership? The Voluntary and Community Sectors in the Policy Process' (2004) 38(3) *Social Policy and Administration* 221–39, at 238; also see D Morris, 'Charities in the contract culture: survival of the largest?' (2000) 20 *Legal Studies* 409–27.

4

Governing Locally: Housing Associations and Local Government

Introduction

> The existence of such a Federation is, in my view, not merely desirable but necessary if we are to secure full and harmonious co-operation between housing societies and local authorities.[1]

THIS WAS KINGSLEY Wood, Minister of Health, writing in the first *Official Bulletin* of the National Federation of Housing Societies in March 1936. His statement is more than a message of support; it is also an indication that the housing association–local government relationship needed to be worked on. This was, possibly, the frustration of a government minister who felt his powers to influence the relations between housing associations and local authorities were limited, and was looking for another to assist.

Despite Wood's endorsement of the newly-formed Federation, it was rare to find evidence of its intervention in governing relations at the local level in the pages of the Federation's *Bulletin*. The Federation was (and is) a national organisation, based in London, that 'naturally' looks to relations with central government to shape the housing association environment. Nevertheless, the relationship between local government and housing associations has always been critical because of the myriad roles played by local government that interacted with the role of associations as housing providers.

This chapter explores the relationship between housing associations and local government through the lens of the *nomination agreement*—arrangements by which local government can require associations to house tenants of its choosing. Nomination arrangements have always been problematic and provide an insight into the difficulties in the relationship between the two parties. The story told in this chapter shows housing associations beginning in a relationship of dependency on local government, controlled by agreements tied to local authority

[1] National Federation of Housing Societies (NFHS), *Official Bulletin* No 1, April 1936, 4.

funding. Then as associations gained confidence and increased financial resources, in part through the success of the charity Shelter, they came to challenge local authority domination of housing policy. A period of relative autonomy within the regulatory and funding environment of the Housing Corporation followed, until dwindling resources and spiralling homelessness forced associations and local authorities into partnership; nomination agreements became a critical and contested site of housing policy. As housing associations were required to house increasing numbers of homeless households, they sought to regain control over allocations policies. They created new understandings of community as they sought to exclude the risky tenant, perceived to threaten the viability of associations through non-payment of rent and anti-social behaviour.

This chapter is also a mechanism for exploring the legal plurality that is an essential element structuring relations at the level of local government. Local rules and agreements interact with legal obligations and duties provided by parliamentary statute and central government guidance has more recently become overlaid with rules and regulations of the global sphere of financial markets. This interaction of legal spheres is explored in the next section, before moving on to the day to day detail of local relations and the ways in which national–level relations have shaped the sphere.

The Technicalities of Governing Locally

Relationships at the local level can seem to be structured by many *different* legal understandings. This arises from the nature of local government's legal status, as corporations established by statute to undertake specified functions, always constrained by a requirement to establish legal authority for all their actions.[2] This abbreviated explanation does not reflect the totality of local government's relations with central government, but it does explain why local government will often look to *law*, whether it is statute or guidance, as a means of structuring its relations with others. Therefore, when housing associations consider their relationship at the local level, they may see different forms of law operating on them at the same time; a *plurality* of legal forms frequently in tension. They look to local government for resources (land, or money) and planning permission and other approvals to enable new housing to be developed and tenants to be housed; all these are bounded by various forms of statute, guidance and local agreements. At the same time, housing associations are subject to law operating at the

[2] M Loughlin, 'Restructuring of Central-Local Relations' in J Jowell and D Oliver, *The Changing Constitution* 4th edn (Oxford, Oxford University Press, 2000); H Elcock, *Local Government: Politicians, Professionals and the Public in Local Authorities* 2nd edn (London, Methuen, 1982) 1.

national level, a relationship now governed principally by the state regulator[3] but in previous eras exerted direct from central government through ministers and civil servants. More recently, a third level of legal structuring has appeared: the rules and regulations to which housing associations operating within (frequently global) financial markets must adhere. The term *interlegality*[4] describes this intersection of a plurality of legal orders and is helpful in understanding the fluidity of fields that the housing association sector operates within.

However, the range of processes and procedures through which law operates at the level of local government often appears to be more administrative and bureaucratic than legal. At the local level, the concern is for *minute detail.* Here, instead of a focus on large-scale programmes, political ideologies and budget allocations, governing frequently occurs through understanding and controlling the number of houses, the size of each house, the number of households, the size of each household and even such detail as the size and orientation of a bathroom or the age of a child (as will be shown later in this chapter). Knowledge at this local level is particular and specific; it focuses on the ways in which housing associations and local government interact, in a technical sense, around resources and expertise.

The wide variety of roles allocated to local government by statute are all intimately tied up with expertise and professional knowledge: the housing role; the social services role; the planning role; the land-banking role; and the 'banker' role, have allowed local authorities to govern associations. These appear to be little connected by rationale or logic, but more as a set of functions arbitrarily assigned to the local sphere.[5] For housing associations, however, they are functions connected by a pragmatic reality: they are key resources required by associations for the development and management of housing. Indeed, one of the reasons why local government has played such an important role in governing for much of the last century has been because of its significance as a site of resources. They are resources for which local authorities act as gatekeepers. In one sense this is the central state 'governing at a distance';[6] local government operating the powers allocated to it by statute, acting as central government's 'surrogate regulator'.[7]

[3] Now the Tenant Services Authority, previously the Housing Corporation; the role of the Housing Corporation, and its relationship with housing associations, is discussed in chs 2 and 5.

[4] B de Souza Santos, 'Law: a map of misreading. Toward a postmodern conception of law' (1987) 14(3) *Journal of Law and Society* 279–302.

[5] M Valverde, 'Seeing like a city: legal tools of municipal order' paper to the Law and Society Association Conference (Pittsburgh, June 2003) has referred to the legal governance operated by municipal authorities as 'pragmatically connected sets of precedents, that is, administrative habits [..that] ubiquitous antitheoretical knowledge format: the unprioritized list' (at 5).

[6] N Rose and P Miller, 'Political Power beyond the State: problematics of government' (1992) 43 *British Journal of Sociology* 173–205.

[7] That parties other than central government can act as regulators has been extensively explored in the regulation literature; however, this has particularly been in relation to governments using *private* sector organisations to control the terms of access: see, eg, J Black, 'Enrolling Actors in

Local government, however, cannot be regarded simply as agents of central government:

> Central government may pass a law, provide money, inspect and, on occasion, directly provide a service but, for the most part, it needs the co-operation of other bodies to meet its electoral promises.[8]

Statute may have defined *how* they could use these resources but the resources are seen very much as *belonging* to the local (local land, local subsidies available from local rates and the sale of local assets) and even if statute delineates the types of arrangements they can make, local authorities enter into arrangements of their own choosing. Local authorities are political actors in their own right, democratically-controlled bodies that have sought to use the resources at their disposal to implement their own political programmes within the boundaries of law.[9] This is *interlegality* in action, interactions that flow between different legal orders that are essential for the processes of governing. The freedom of local government has been partly defined by this practical reality; the central state has needed local government to put into practice its political programmes. For much of the twentieth century, the central State's reliance on local government's implementation meant that the central–local relationship allowed arguments and antagonisms as a necessity for both parties to maintain interdependence and control.[10]

This relationship of mutual reliance between central and local government did not last the election of Margaret Thatcher's New Right government in 1979. The 'crisis' in the relationship between central and local, as ministers sought to increase control over local government,[11] led to arguments being transposed to the courts; the relationship became not just highly-charged ideologically, but juridified.[12] However, housing associations were beneficiaries as the Conservative

Regulatory Systems: Examples from UK Financial Services Regulation' [2003] *Public Law* 63–91, 70–71; J Braithwaite, *Restorative Justice and Responsive Regulation* (Oxford, Oxford University Press, 2001) 113–16; J Braithwaite and P Drahos, *Global Business Regulation* (Cambridge, Cambridge University Press, 2000) 618–19; N Gunningham and P Grabosky, *Smart Regulation* (Oxford, Clarendon Press, 1998) 408–13; R Kraakman, 'Gatekeepers: the Anatomy of Third Party Enforcement Strategy' (1986) 2 *Journal of Law, Economics and Organization* 53–104.

8 RAW Rhodes, *Beyond Whitehall and Westminster* (London, Allen & Unwin, 1988) 3.

9 For an example of a local authority using resources for political ends that fell outside the legal boundaries, see the Westminster City Council 'Homes for Votes' scandal, discussed in D Cowan, '"Rage at Westsinster": Sociolegal Reflections on the Power of Sale' (2003) 12 *Social & Legal Studies* 177–98.

10 See JAG Griffith, *Central Departments and Local Authorities* (London, Allen & Unwin, 1966) 506.

11 G Jones and J Stewart, *The Case for Local Government* 2nd edn (London, George Allen & Unwin, 1985). Also see M Loughlin, 'Law, Ideologies and the Political–Administrative System' (1989) 16(1) *Journal of Law & Society* 21–41; M Loughlin, *Legality and Locality: The Role of Law in Central–Local Government Relations* (Oxford, Clarendon Press, 1996); and above, ch 2

12 See Loughlin, 'Restructuring of Central-Local Relations', above n 2.

Government chose non-elected agencies and supposedly non-political bodies as their chosen 'policy instruments'[13] and delivery vehicles. Local authorities were to become 'enablers'.

Nevertheless, local government retained many functions important to housing associations and so, even today, the relationship with local government remains vital to associations.

The Roles of Local Government

(i) The Housing Role

From 1919 until recently, it was local authorities that were dominant in housing provision,[14] their role perceived as providing for those in 'housing need'. However, the concept of 'need' is by no means clear;[15] the word 'need' does not appear in any of the legislation setting out local government's housing powers and duties, rather they have been required only to give 'reasonable preference' to particular groups, reflecting housing policy priorities as well as the history of central–local relations.[16] Local authorities had a limited responsibility to provide for people who were 'destitute' and homeless under the Poor Laws; the National Assistance Act 1948 produced little improvement. They frequently split up homeless families into single sex, dormitory-style accommodation and children were sent into care.[17] Although the Housing (Homeless Persons) Act 1977 required local authority housing departments to provide accommodation for persons accepted as homeless, the legislation erected significant obstacles for homeless people and allowed local authorities to continue operating highly discretionary criteria.[18] The local authority's housing waiting list (sometimes termed the 'housing register'), intended to reflect housing needs broader than homelessness, was similarly operated through broad discretion.

The housing powers and duties of local authorities have meant that they have had considerable control over housing associations if the latter were seeking subsidies or loans from the authority for the housing scheme, and increasing power over who gets housed. More recently, however, some associations have turned the nomination arrangements around. Associations have dispensed with their own waiting lists and only housed tenants from the local authority waiting

13 *Ibid*, 215.

14 P Malpass and I Murie, *Housing Policy and Practice* 5th edn (Basingstoke, Macmillan, 1999) 143.

15 For a discussion of 'housing need' see: D Cowan and M McDermont, *Regulating Social Housing: Governing Decline* (London, Glasshouse, 2006) ch 3.

16 E Laurie, *The Enduring Appeal of Reasonable Preference* (unpublished PhD thesis, University of Southampton, 2002).

17 See P Somerville, 'Homelessness Policy in Britain' (1994) 22 *Policy and Politics* 163–78, discussed below in ch 7.

18 See: D Cowan, *Housing Law and Policy* (Basingstoke, Macmillan, 1999) ch 7.

list/register. Whilst this reduces the association's administrative running costs, it places the association in a condition of dependency on the local housing authority.

(ii) The Social Services Role

Whilst a housing association's principal relationship would be with the housing department, social services departments have also been a source of funding. Particularly since the NHS and Community Care Act 1990, which placed housing at the centre of community care planning, housing associations have played a role in providing for people with disabilities in the community. Under the Act, social services authorities were allocated the lead responsibility for implementation through joint planning, purchasing and providing and conducting care management and assessment. However, health authorities had a 'lead implementation' role,[19] which left a somewhat messy and confused environment for associations to operate in. Research carried out ten years after the Act reported that 'efforts to integrate housing with community care services continue to be dogged by problems associated with joint working'.[20] For a number of associations,[21] providing housing with a range of care elements is a principal part of their operations, meaning that social services (and health) links become crucial.

(iii) The Planning Role

Housing associations, like other developers of housing, require approval from the planning authority for most new developments. Through planning powers, local authorities can control the location and layout of housing developments as well as the type of housing (which has a bearing on the type of tenants that can be housed). Large-scale developments can also lead to requirements for facilities such as shops, play areas, even schools and accessible public transport. Building control and environmental health powers also provide authority to regulate building standards. Of particular importance has been the legal obligations placed on private developers to provide 'planning gain', now under section 106 of the Town and Country Planning Act 1990. Local authorities will often require private developers to enter into a 'section 106 agreement' (as they have become known) as a condition of obtaining planning approval. Frequently, the 'planning

[19] C Allen, 'The policy and implementation of the housing role in community care—a constructionist theoretical perspective' (1997) 12 *Housing Studies* 85–110, 97.

[20] A Cameron, L Harrison, P Burton and A Marsh, *Crossing the Housing and Care Divide* (Bristol, Policy Press/JRF, 2001).

[21] See, eg, Sanctuary Housing Association, which has two subsidiaries, Sanctuary Care and Sanctuary Home Care which provide specialist care homes and home care: see www.sanctuary-housing.co.uk/homepage.html; Anchor Trust, the largest provider of housing, care and support services in England: see www.anchor.org.uk/about_us.html.

gain' required is to undertake to provide affordable housing. If this is to be housing for rent at below economic rents, this often requires the local authority to link the developer with an association that can access grant to fund the housing. In this way, 'section 106 agreements' can provide some additional resources for associations' developments.

(iv) The Land–Banking Role

Local authorities have powers to acquire and hold land for a number of reasons; for example: road building, leisure facilities and building housing. The local authority as a 'land-bank' became particularly important from the 1980s, when central government policies meant housing departments no longer had the subsidies available to build their own housing and so sold land to associations for housing developments. Frequently, land would be sold at nil cost, in effect acting as a local authority subsidy to the association's development. These schemes gave local government increased control over the development, regularly resulting in the housing department nominating 100 per cent of the tenants on first letting. Local government could also be a source of individual street properties for associations to purchase and renovate. This was particularly important in the 1970s and 1980s in those authorities that developed strong urban renewal strategies: the local authority would compulsory purchase long-term empty properties[22] and would then sell them on to housing associations for improvement and/or conversion using Housing Association Grant.[23]

(v) The 'Banker' Role

It was the function of 'banker', however, that most provided both sides with the possibility of formally structuring the relationship and led to nomination arrangements being put in place. It was the Housing Act 1935 that first required (section 27) that local authorities put in place agreements with housing associations as a condition of granting subsidy. The Act simply specified that these agreements must detail the types of houses and rents at which they were to be let. It was left to the discretion of the local authority to include other terms it 'may think expedient in view of the needs of their district in relation to the housing of the working classes'.[24] Part of the impetus for these powers came from local government itself; in 1934, the London County Council asked the Minister of Health to consider extending controls over associations in receipt of loans from

[22] Eg, under the Housing Act 1974 s 43(1), local authorities, with the approval of the Secretary of State, had powers to acquire land, including dwellings, through compulsory purchase or by agreement.

[23] See: MS Gibson and MJ Langstaff, *An Introduction to Urban Renewal* (London, Hutchinson, 1982).

[24] S 27(2).

local authorities. The council was concerned that early repayment of loans it provided to associations would mean that associations were no longer bound by conditions on rent levels and requirements that dwellings should be let to the 'working classes'.[25]

The Federation, however, saw in these agreements not simply a hierarchical mechanism by which local authorities could regulate associations; here they saw the possibility of intervening to exercise power over this relationship. The Federation negotiated a model form of agreement with the Ministry of Health, which it urged associations and local authorities to adopt.[26] Some associations saw the legal form as a means of securing their position with the local authority. At a 1937 Federation conference, a representative 'urged on all Societies the desirability of sealed agreements with Local Authorities, in respect of arrangements concerning subsidies'.[27] Government departments, he said, insisted on sealed agreements and the Ministry should put pressure on local authorities to do the same. Associations appeared to assume that their uncertain position and subordinate status could be made more certain through the use of binding contracts. These legal agreements were also the first attempts to structure what has become one of the most contentious elements of the local authority–housing association relationship, the nomination of households for tenancies in housing association properties. For local authorities, the need was to ensure that at least some of the dwellings which their subsidies provided remained under their control. In these early agreements, as in later relations, it was the nomination of tenants to association properties that was the principal cause of resistance between associations and councils. In structuring the relationship through the mechanism of the nomination agreement, attention becomes focused on the minute detail of day to day working arrangements between local government and associations. And so, whilst the *nomination agreement* comes into focus at various points at the level of national relations, at the nation-state level (the level at which the Federation operated) the concern was, for the most part, with the broad-brush concepts of 'meeting housing need' and reducing homelessness budgets. The relations of concern in this chapter occur at the level of *region* and *local*. This left the Federation largely absent, its regional structure only appearing in 1946.[28]

25 Minutes of the LCC Housing and Public Health Committee (18 April 1934).
26 *OB* 2, July 1936, 1.
27 *OB* 5, July 1937, 8.
28 See above, ch 2.

Nomination Agreements: Contestation and Partnership

Background

Nomination agreements arise in a contested environment. It is the local authority that has the statutory obligation to provide a permanent housing solution to those households deemed to be in 'housing need' (the definition and statutory requirements having changed over the time covered by this study). In most cases, the local authority holds a housing waiting list (or register) for the district, and elected councillors will frequently see themselves as being in the firing line if housing needs in the area they represent are not met. It is therefore unsurprising that local authorities have sought routes for accessing housing association properties through the formalising of nomination arrangements. However, the nomination agreements that result from this formalisation are often regarded by housing associations as compromising their independent, self-governing status. Hence, the Federation has sought to intervene in order to provide associations with expertise, examples of good practice and other means by which associations themselves can have control over the nominations process. Nevertheless, whilst nomination agreements act at the local level, they are *always* contextualised by central/local government relations, even though these may be obscure to local actors.

The 1940s and 1950s: Nomination and Subsidy/Loan Agreements

Commenting on the model agreement it had negotiated with central government under the 1935 Act arrangements, the Federation noted that a 'valuable feature of the model form of agreement is the selection of tenants by means of a joint tenancy committee, elected by the local authority and the housing association'.[29] By 1946, the Ministry of Health had drawn up a new agreement; this one, however, appears not to have been negotiated with the Federation.[30] The terms included: types of dwellings to be built; a requirement for a fair wages clause in all building contracts; arrangements for the fixing of rents; and notification of vacancies to, and nomination of tenants by, the local authority.[31] Again, it is the nominations clause that appears as the arena of contestation; the Federation's *Bulletin* comments:

[29] See above, n 26.
[30] *OB* 39, September 1946, 4.
[31] *National Federation of Housing Societies* (NFHS) (London, NFHS, 1946) 11.

> It is not meant to be hard and fast, and the Ministry has agreed to some insertions, in some cases, in the clause which deals with the nomination of tenants.[32]

The suggestion of contestation is, perhaps, unsurprising. The Housing Act 1935 had deemed certain categories of persons to be in greater need and therefore entitled to 'reasonable preference' in council housing; but beyond this, local authorities had complete discretion. They were free to decide who was eligible to join their housing waiting lists and to allocate housing according to their own priorities.[33] For associations, their choice of tenants went to 'the general character of the estate . . . [and] the building of a happy contented community'.[34] Controlling the allocation of housing was a means of ensuring that more risky tenants (for example the antisocial, or less likely to pay rent) were not admitted. Nomination agreements controlled the associations' freedom to decide whom they housed. Since legislation did not specify the methods of selecting tenants or the proportion of local authority nominees, local authorities could be seen to have the upper hand. The Federation warned that

> [m]utual agreement on the *proportion* is a matter for careful and tactful arbitration between the housing society and the local authority, as the latter may exercise its right of nomination for the *full*.[35]

This issue of the *Bulletin* sought to provide associations' housing managers with expertise similar to local authorities by recommending how to set up a points scheme for allocating tenancies.[36]

Sometimes local authority attempts to control associations seemed to be almost direct rule, seeking to take control of the allocations process. For example, Tynemouth County Borough nominated the three *chairmen* of their finance, health and housing committees as its representatives on the joint committee for the selection of tenants with the Square Building Trust, appearing keen to exert control through the authority and status of elected officials.[37]

The ability of the Federation's (or associations') to alter these early agreements frequently seems minimal compared with that of local government. One association, Oxford Cottage Improvement Society,[38] sent a deputation to discuss a proposed scheme with Ministry officials, but found civil servants would only

[32] See above, n 31.

[33] See Malpass and Murie, *Housing Policy and Practice*, above n 14 at 68.

[34] *OB* 39, September 1946, at 1.

[35] See above n 31 at 1.

[36] The priorities set out by the suggested points scheme is itself an indication of the norms of the time. Such a scheme would allocate 10 points to those who provide '*Value to community* (ie, helps out in key position)' something akin to today's 'key-worker', to those living separated from their family, or with urgent needs for accommodation, such as a notice to quit; 6 points to people with war service or government service; and only 2 points on medical grounds; *OB* 39, September 1946, 2.

[37] Archives of Square Building Trust: letter from Co Borough of Tynemouth to Secretary of Square Building Trust dated 17 November 1947; there is evidence on file of similar arrangements in place from 1942.

[38] The Minutes of the Directors of OCIS, (2 November 1936).

agree to informal discussions. It was made clear that societies should agree terms with the local authority first, before approaching the Ministry. The Ministry was not even prepared to intervene on the issue of the rents, which it considered 'on the high side' but acceptable if the council agreed to them.

Control meant overseeing the minutiae. This was particularly true for London, where the London County Council and its successor the Greater London Council (GLC) were significant funders of housing associations.[39] Council committees expressed opinions about minute detail. One scheme was approved 'subject to consideration being given to the arrangement of bathroom fittings so as to provide easy access to the window';[40] in another, 'a further report on the wages and conditions of domestic staff' was required.[41] Scheme approvals were given via a legal agreement, which always included 'substantial nomination rights',[42] as well as giving the Council considerable control over association rents and levels of rent increases.[43]

Changing Environment, Changing Relations

In the 1960s, the expansion of the housing association sector (funded by Shelter[44] and, particularly in London, by the London County Council/GLC)[45] led to the sector's growing self-confidence. In 1970, the London Housing Association Council sought to challenge the local authority domination over what constituted 'housing need'. Councils, they said, were putting forward 'unsuitable tenants':

> It has not been found satisfactory for the Council simply to nominate the families at the top of the waiting list who . . . may well be facing less severe housing difficulties than many others known to a housing association for whom there is no hope of decent accommodation for many years.[46]

As associations became more confident of their own 'expertise', so they sought to contest local authorities' expert knowledge in the assessment of housing need. As chapter seven demonstrates, those associations that linked themselves to Shelter

[39] LCC/MIN/7552 and 7553 Housing and Public Health Committee (29 May 1935) Item 14 (held at the London Metropolitan Archives).

[40] *Ibid.*

[41] LCC/MIN/777 Housing Committee (8 July 1964).

[42] GLC/DG/SCR/1/3 Housing Department Report to Chair of Scrutiny Committee (held at the London Metropolitan Archives).

[43] LCC/MIN/7767 Housing Committee (5 February 1964). The report proposed that the committee delegate approval of rent increases for improvements to dwellings permissible under the Housing Act 1961 to the Director of Housing. It was predicted that the number of applications for rent increases would rise, given that the majority of dwellings owned by HAs came from agreements put in place before the Second World War.

[44] See below, ch 7.

[45] See chs 2 and 7.

[46] London Housing Associations Committee (LHAC), *Report on Housing Associations in London: 1970* (held at the London Metropolitan Archives, ref: P28–81 LON).

saw their role as championing the needs of the most vulnerable households, one of many indications of changing relationships between associations and local government. Later, as we shall see, roles are again reversed, with associations becoming focused on financial risk, seeking to avoid the risks of housing large numbers of homeless households.

The Housing Act 1974, which gave the Housing Corporation powers to regulate as well as fund a wide range of housing association activity, was critical in re-positioning associations to centre-stage in housing policy (as will be discussed in chapter five), as well as realigning central–local relations. For local authorities, the 1974 Act signalled an attenuated role in overseeing and regulating housing association activity, which from now on would be the domain of the Housing Corporation;[47] and as local authority funding diminished and Housing Corporation funding increased, associations and the Corporation became shapers of housing policy. The dependency on local government had been broken; housing associations could now be regarded as alternative providers to local government (and the private sector) and left open the possibility for more central direction of housing policy through government control over the Corporation.

Moreover, central government sought to marginalise local government through changing the housing subsidy system. Since the 1950s, the subsidy system had recognised the interdependency of central and local government through the principle that the 'bulk of grant-aid should take the form of general or block grant',[48] leaving decisions concerning the balance of service provision to local authorities. From the 1980s onwards, this understanding was altered. Central government imposed direct control over local authority spending on housing, helping to force the privatisation of council housing.[49] Housing subsidies were withdrawn, forcing increases in council house rents; budgets for the repair of council housing became one of the principal casualties of this manipulation of the subsidy system. Grant aid became increasingly identified with meeting specific central government objectives, through directed programmes such as supplementary credit approvals and the Single Regeneration Budget.[50]

Whilst much of the realignment of central–local relations took place in the public arena of the courts,[51] quieter battles were being fought at the more mundane level of bureaucratic control over local housing programmes by local authorities anxious to maintain their role. The 1974 Act had begun the marginalisation of local authorities' ability to exercise control over housing association

[47] As discussed below in ch 5, a powerful 'regulatory community' of the Housing Corporation, the Federation and associations, began to form.

[48] Loughlin, 'Restructuring of Central-Local Relations', above n 2 at142.

[49] I Cole and B Goodchild, 'Local Housing Strategies in England: an assessment of their changing role and context' (1995) 23 *Policy & Politics* 40–60.

[50] See: P Malpass, 'Policy Making and Local Governance: how Bristol failed to secure City Challenge funding (twice)' (1994) 22 *Policy and Politics* 301–12.

[51] Eg, *Norwich City Council v Secretary of State for the Environment* [1982] 1 All ER 737; for commentary see: Cowan, *Housing Law and Policy*, above n 18 at 345.

activities. Whilst the Federation continued to advise that there should be 'close co-operation with the local authority in determining the type of needs to be catered for and in the selection of tenants',[52] there was little or no role for local authorities in decisions about the allocation of Housing Corporation funding. This led, as the GLC suggested in evidence to a review of Housing Corporation practices, to

> housing associations operating in an area … feel[ing] that it is *their* responsibility to decide the amount, location and type of housing needed by the local community as a whole.[53]

The GLC proposed that local authorities should be able to influence programme agreements between the Corporation and associations, a suggestion that was ignored. The Housing Corporation would impose housing associations on local authorities without consultation and, until the 1990s, funding to associations continued to be made with little, if any, reference to the local authority. Programme agreements were a reflection of Corporation perceptions of an association's ability to meet targets rather than local housing need;[54] and as chapter five shows, the housing association sector was itself able to shape these understandings.

Local Government and Associations in Partnership

As central government increasingly constrained the discretion of local government, local government officers saw their power eroded and shifted to 'boundary actors'[55] such as voluntary organisations and housing associations. Eventually, this was to be a factor in encouraging housing authorities to 'opt out' of central control, through the large scale voluntary transfer (LSVT) programme. The idea of *partnership* also became a key element in the local authority–housing association relationship at this time. The 1987 Housing White Paper[56] set out a 'new' role for local government: local housing authorities should 'increasingly see themselves as enablers who ensure that everyone in the area is adequately housed; but not necessarily by them'.[57] The idea of enabling was not new;[58] since the

[52] NFHA, *Housing Management Practice in Housing Associations: A Code of Conduct* (London, NFHA, 1975) 24.

[53] Greater London Council (GLC), *GLC Response to the National Federation of Housing Associations' Report of September 1979 on Project Control* (held on file at the London Metropolitan Archives: ref GLC/DG/SCR/1/3).

[54] C Wolmar, 'Corporation critics' *ROOF* (September/October 1982) 12–14, 13.

[55] D Cooper, 'Local Government Legal Consciousness in the Shadow of Juridification' (1995) 22 *Journal of Law & Society* 506–26, 508.

[56] Department of the Environment (DoE), *Housing: The Government's Proposals* (Cm 214, London, HMSO, 1987).

[57] *Ibid*, para 1.16.

[58] See: R Goodlad, *The Housing Authority as Enabler* (London, Chartered Institute of Housing and Longman, 1993).

middle of the nineteenth century, local authorities had possessed powers to assist others in improving housing conditions. Now, however, enabling was not a matter of choice for local government.

Nevertheless, local housing authorities retained a statutory responsibility towards homeless households. Interest rates spiralled, repossessions soared and homelessness was ever-increasing. By 1989, London local authorities were accepting responsibility for twice as many homeless households as in 1979.[59] With their stock of housing reducing through the right-to-buy and no powers (or funds) to build new housing, authorities came to rely increasingly on housing associations to accommodate homeless households. 'Partnering' became a new buzzword. For local government, driven by the need to take homeless households out of expensive temporary accommodation into more cost-efficient alternatives, nomination arrangements became critical. Local government looked to statute for authority: the Housing Act 1985, section 72 required that, where a housing authority requested a housing association to assist them in carrying out statutory duties towards homeless households, the association should 'cooperate in rendering such assistance . . . as is reasonable in the circumstances'.[60] This made the nomination agreement between the local authority and the housing association into a crucial tool for putting this 'duty to co-operate' into action (though Housing Corporation guidance stated that 'absence of a nomination agreement does not exempt an association from duty').[61]

From the association perspective, the need for partnership arose from the inadequacy of Housing Corporation funding. Housing associations increasingly needed local government resources, either as grants funded from local authorities' capital receipts from the right-to-buy, or their land holdings. So, we see associations moving from a position of dependency (from the 1930s to the 1960s) to relative autonomy and rebellion against local authority control (in the 1970s) to partnership in the 1980s. Local law, in the form of partnership agreements, allowed each party certain freedom to negotiate their own affairs.

However, the nomination agreement once again became the site of contest. The proportion of properties that an association should make available to a local authority became a principal issue. As far back as 1972,[62] government circulars had made it a requirement of all local authority loans to associations that the latter make 50 per cent of properties available; at this time there was no requirement that schemes funded by the Corporation should allow nominations for the local authority. However, in 1974 Department of the Environment

[59] D Levison and I Robertson, *Partners in Meeting Housing Need—Local Authority Nominations to Housing Associations in London: Good Practice Guide* (London, NFHA, 1989) v.

[60] See, eg, J Alder and C Handy, *Housing Association Law* 2nd edn (London, Sweet & Maxwell, 1991) 355–57.

[61] This Housing Corporation guidance was contained, *Access to Housing Association Homes: A Guide to Tenant Selection* (apparently not issued using statutory guidance powers) is referred to in Alder and Handy, *ibid*, 356.

[62] See: CV Baker, *Housing Associations* (London, The Estates Gazette Ltd, 1976) 419–22.

circular 170/74 suggested that local authorities should get 'a significant proportion' of nominations on Corporation schemes. By 1989, Housing Corporation guidance[63] stipulated that, for publicly-funded schemes (local authority and Corporation-funded) a formal agreement between the association and the local authority should be entered into which would 'normally' allow for 50 per cent of first and subsequent lettings to be allocated to local authority nominees. Where the authority had provided cheap land or other additional subsidy, this percentage could rise.[64] Most developments on local authority land had requirements that the majority (often 100 per cent) of properties should be available for local authority nominated tenants. In addition, demands from homeless households meant that local authorities also sought access not only to properties on new developments, but *all* existing housing association accommodation. Despite the requirements of statute and guidance, housing associations continued to be criticised for playing only a limited role in the relief of homelessness.[65]

The response of the London Housing Association Council, the Federation and the London local authority associations to these tensions was to commission research into the existing nomination arrangements and produce a code of practice for associations and councils. Published in 1989, *Partners in Meeting Housing Need*,[66] contained 'recommendations of good practice ... taken from examples set by housing associations and council housing departments who work well together'. The intention was to produce 'a fairer and more efficient nominations system'.[67] *Partners* has been described as a 'landmark document'.[68] It was an attempt to use bureaucratic structures to implement a normative agenda: associations should be housing those in greatest housing need (as determined by the local authority) and should not be able to pick and choose tenants in order to minimise their management problems. It 'recognised that each housing association will have its own selection criteria ... [but] recommend[ed] that housing associations should generally accept the local authority's prioritisation of housing need'.[69] It acknowledged that housing association management systems required home visits to all nominees prior to allocation but stipulated that the purpose of the visit was purely to check the information supplied by the authority and give information to the nominee, '*not* to make assessments of the housing need or to check housekeeping standards'.[70] Associations should only reject a nominee for

[63] Housing Corporation Circular 48/89.
[64] *Ibid*, paras 5.1 and 5.2.
[65] See, eg, Audit Commission, *Housing the Homeless: The Local Authority Role* (London, HMSO, 1989).
[66] Levison and Robertson, above n 60.
[67] *Ibid*, v.
[68] H Pawson and D Mullins, Changing Places: Housing Association Policy and Practice on Nominations and Lettings (London, The Housing Corporation, 2003) 4.
[69] Levison and Robertson, above n 60 at 25.
[70] *Ibid*, emphasis in original.

specific reasons, limited to changes in the circumstances of nominated households, unsuitability of the property to the household's needs, or inaccuracies and changes in the information supplied by the council.[71]

Partners became adopted by London boroughs and, in the absence of other models, was used in partnership arrangements throughout the country. It could be criticised for attempting to put a straightjacket on housing association activity whilst the housing selection and allocation processes of local government still operated within very broad areas of discretion.[72] Indeed, the report's approach and concept of partnership was soon challenged, as associations sought to reassert their independence and freedom to govern their estates. This new challenge came through a re-identification of associations with their capacity to build communities.

'Building for Communities' or Ruling through Community?

It was the report, *Building for Communities: A study of New Housing Estates*[73] (which became known simply as the 'Page Report') that provided a serious challenge to *Partners* when published in 1993. The report was described by the Federation's deputy chief executive as producing a 'paradigm shift' in housing associations' thinking. It took a very different stance from *Partners* on housing associations' responsibilities as key providers of what had become known as *social* housing. It was highly critical of the direction some housing associations had taken in building large estates in 'remote and difficult locations'[74] which would house 'a segregated income stratum of uniformly poor tenants' and would 'almost certainly be difficult to manage and . . . likely to gain a reputation as a "poor" housing estate'.[75] It brought a perception of an impending crisis in the sector (alternatively, the crisis had already arrived). Its impact was far-reaching, but it was neither a product of the Corporation or the Federation, but of the Joseph Rowntree Foundation.[76] Its instigator was Ken Bartlett, previously Director of Paddington Churches HA (one of the 1960s new inner-city based associations funded by Shelter) and Associate Director of the Federation, who moved on

71 *Ibid*, 26.
72 Eg, Cowan, *Housing Law and Policy*, above n 18.
73 D Page, *Building for Communities: A Study of New Housing Association Estates* (York, Joseph Rowntree Foundation, 1993).
74 *Ibid*, 13.
75 *Ibid*, 12.
76 The Foundation's position as a seemingly neutral funder of research, together with its ability to attract media and political attention meant that the report had influence far beyond its readership, a point that Ruth Levitas has made about the Foundation's 1995 Inquiry into Income and Wealth (R Levitas, *The Inclusive Society? Social Exclusion and New Labour* (Basingstoke, Palgrave, 1998) 41). In fact, *Building for Communities* was not research and the Joseph Rowntree Foundation had not intended it as such. It was a 'position statement' by the Foundation, an organisation that had played a central part in shaping housing policy for the whole of the twentieth century, carrying on the legacy of Seebohm Rowntree and his inquiry into poverty in York.

to work for the Housing Corporation from 1979 to 1992. On leaving the Corporation, he suggested to the chief executive, Anthony Mayer

> that housing associations were creating slums. By acquiring large estates and packing them with people who all were on very low incomes and some of them had very difficult lifestyles . . . this was undesirable and we should alter it. Anthony clearly understood the point but was not at all keen on the Housing Corporation suggesting that there might be something basically flawed with the pattern of HA development. So I then wrote the outline brief which Rowntree adopted and which led to the Page Report.[77]

The Page Report could be said to be the rediscovery by housing associations of the idea(l) of community. It proposed that associations should return to those areas of expertise to which they had laid claim in the 1940s. It advocated that they should either return to building smaller developments or to buying up and improving street properties 'using skills they have developed over the last century'.[78] Alternatively, if large estates had to be built they should mix rented housing with housing for sale or shared ownership, producing 'balanced communities' with 'renters and owners living in adjoining houses'.[79] It was, in effect, proposing a form of social engineering in the building of 'balanced communities'.

However, in creating inclusive communities, the need to exclude those who could not be expected to conform to the community norms becomes paramount: 'community is not simply the territory within which crime is controlled; it is itself the *means* of government'.[80] The Page report advocated attention to estate security,[81] which led to involving police officers in assessing design layout, and a 'Secure by Design' certificate from the police authority in order to meet Housing Corporation requirements. Significantly for the housing association–local authority relationship, it advocated that associations should exercise *exclusionary practices* in order to ensure the security of their estates. Criticising the approach of *Partners*, the report advocated that 'housing associations ... have a good and valid reason to enquire about the tenancy history of each applicant and to refuse a nomination from a local authority where the nominee is known to have a history of seriously disruptive behaviour'.[82]

But it was not only the security of members of their newly-made communities that associations were concerned to ensure. As will be discussed in chapter six, the funding of housing associations had been transformed at the end of the 1980s. The Housing Act 1988 had enabled associations to raise a proportion of their development capital from private lenders. Associations became focused on controlling financial risk and in particular the need to ensure that tenants paid

77 Interview with Ken Bartlett (30 June 2003).
78 Page, above n 74 at 50.
79 *Ibid.*
80 N Rose, 'Government and Control' (2000) 40 *British Journal of Criminology* 321–39, 329.
81 See below, ch 6.
82 *Above* n 74 at 36.

their rents which serviced private loans. In this context, the allocations process presented 'a critical opportunity to weed out bad payers'.[83] From this perspective, nomination arrangements of the kind proposed by *Partners* became a straight-jacket. Dependence on private funders created the need for associations to distance themselves from local authorities' power in nomination agreements so that they could meet the requirements of their new partners.

Stock Transfer, Coercive Practices and the Recurring Problematic of Nominations

Central government has restructured central–local relations in many ways over the last thirty years or so, employing a range of techniques to alter the framework in which local government could manage its own affairs. By reshaping the responsibilities of local government and the subsidies and grants made available to it, the behaviour of local authorities could be altered. Much of this restructuring, first begun by Margaret Thatcher's Government, has been applied across the public sector; her 'New Public Management' programme aimed to bring the values and practices of the private sector into public services.[84]

One significant effect has been to make many local authorities transfer their housing stock to housing associations. The process of transferring part or the whole of a council's housing stock to a housing association, known as large scale voluntary transfer (LSVT) was discussed in chapter two and earlier in this chapter. The New Labour Government's promotion of LSVT has meant that stock transfer has become, for most local authorities, the *only* option for dealing with significant disrepair in their housing stock which is a result of years of under-funding. More recently, the option of setting up an arm's length management organisation (ALMO) has been taken up by some 'high performing' authorities,[85] as a means by which the management but not the ownership of the housing is transferred.

The transfer to housing associations of *all* a council's housing stock can have a particularly dramatic effect on nomination arrangements if the outcome is that one association becomes a near monopoly provider in a particular area. Recent research has shown that stock transfer creates new tensions in the local

83 D Cowan, C Pantazis and R Gilroy, 'Social housing as crime control: an examination of the role of housing management in policing sex offenders' (2001) 10 *Social & Legal Studies* 435–57, 411.

84 There is a considerable literature on New Public Management: see, eg, C Hood, 'A Public Management for All Seasons' (1991) 69(1) *Public Administration* 3–19; E Ferlie, L Ashburner, I Fitzgerald and A Pettigrew, *The New Public Management in Action* (Oxford, Oxford University Press, 1995); J Newman, 'Beyond the New Public Management: Modernising Public Services' in J Clarke, S Gewirtz and E McLaughlin (eds), *New Managerialism, New Welfare* (London, Open University/Sage, 2000). On the effect of New Public Management on housing, see: D Mullins and A Murie, *Housing Policy in the UK,* (Basingstoke, Palgrave Macmillan, 2006) ch 7.

85 Office of the Deputy Prime Minister, *Guidance on Arm's Length Management of Local Authority Housing* (London, ODPM, 2004).

authority–housing association relationship.[86] The research with local authorities and housing associations confirms that, seventeen years after *Partners in Meeting Housing Need,* this aspect of the relationship remains problematic.

Nomination agreements, as they are now operated by many local authorities, function through classic New Public Management techniques: a public service provider and local authority tied together under a quasi-contractual arrangement, enforced through techniques of performance monitoring. The *process* of monitoring performance by local authorities becomes problematic: local authority and housing association argue over categories, whether a property should have been offered to the authority for nomination or fell outside the agreement, as well as the accuracy of the Council's statistics.[87] Critically, the relationship also turns on concerns about freedom and control. Housing associations' policies on *excluding* households they considered problematic remain a point of contestation between local authority and association.[88] One association in the case study was concerned that it had spent considerable amounts of funding improving and upgrading the housing, which they did not want 'wrecked' by tenants they labelled as antisocial. They also justified exclusions along the lines of the Page report:

> [T]here was the general duty that RSLs [associations] had to their local community of occupiers, who were conceived of as effectively having rights in the nominations process.[89]

For another association, this was coupled with the business interests of the association:

> The exclusions policy doesn't require anybody to behave in any way that they wouldn't be required to behave as a tenant. So from that point of view it is absolutely about protecting communities, but it is also about protecting business interests. Why would you allocate the tenancy to somebody that you're then going to have to spend a whole load of time and effort dealing with the consequences of that?[90]

So, for the association, the argument comes down to protecting the interests of the communities in which it works and, significantly, of its *business* interests. Indeed, other research indicates that the understanding of housing associations as *businesses* is strong in the board members of these new associations set up to

[86] What follows is based on research carried out by D Cowan, M McDermont and K Morgan at the University of Bristol Law School, funded by the Economic and Social Research Council (grant ref no RES-00–22–1930). The research methodology, key findings and final report 'Problematic Nominations' can be found at www.bris.ac.uk/law/research/centres-themes/nominations/index.html.

[87] *Ibid,* 5–6.

[88] *Ibid,* 10–11.

[89] *Ibid,* 11.

[90] D Cowan and K Morgan, 'Trust, Distrust and Betrayal: A Social Housing Case Study' (2009) 72(2) *Modern Law Review* 157–181; D Cowan, K Morgan and M McDermont, 'Nominations: An Actor–Network Approach' (2009) 24(3) *Housing Studies* 281–300.

take the housing stock from local authorities.[91] The association's business plan and the priorities of private funders, weighs heavily in the decision-making processes of the board.[92] We see a significant realignment of the meaning of 'community' from earlier understandings, now to be understood in terms of *financial* viability.

For local authorities, however, the story was different. The local housing authority retained the statutory responsibility towards homeless households in priority need. In particular, where a local authority had transferred all its housing stock to an association, and that association operated tight policies on exclusions, the authority was left with households which they could not re-house, stuck in temporary accommodation for which the local authority had to pay. [Moreover, local authorities are also ruled by targets and performance monitoring; central government has tied future allocations of subsidy into the authority's ability to reduce use of bed and breakfast and other expensive temporary housing. Indeed, housing association and local authority staff argue that central government's performance targets were part of the problem.[93] Meeting targets dominates the agenda for local authorities, making it very difficult for local authorities and associations to tackle homelessness. Once again, it is the central–local government relationship that dominates in the relations between organisations that now see themselves as all being 'social housing' providers. However, the housing associations have now begun to dominate the agenda with their arguments for restructuring nominations processes using 'business' models. Housing association borrowing is now tied into global financial markets, which begin to interact with national-level law (statutory duties imposed on local authorities) and the local law of nomination agreements and performance standards.

Conclusion

At the end of the day, the local authority representatives and the housing association actors find themselves arguing that it is not the technicalities of nomination arrangements that are failing, nor is it local level relations that are at fault. The problem is lack of resources; there are just not enough social housing properties.

However, closer examination of the identities of the actors calls into question the 'we are all on the same side' argument. Sitting on the metro of a large city in England, one can see an advert for an organisation that is all about regeneration;

[91] D Cowan, M McDermont and J Prendergast, *Governing and Governance: A Social Housing Case Study* (Centre for Market and Public Organisations, University of Bristol, Working Paper No 06/149, June 2006): www.bristol.ac.uk/cmpo/publications/papers/2006/wp149.pdf.

[92] M McDermont, D Cowan and J Prendergast, 'Structuring Governance: A Case Study of the New Organisational Provision of Public Service Delivery' (2009) 29(1) *Critical Social Policy* 677–702.

[93] Contributions from a South West Homelessness conference held in November 2007 where the research report, *Governing and Governance: A Social Housing Case Study*, above n 92, was presented.

you have to look hard and know the context before you can 'see' the housing association behind this advertiser's façade. This is not 'merely' advertising but a matter of location. How do we 'locate' this organisation? Within the local, as a provider of social housing or within the 'market', as profit-maker and competitive entrepreneur? Place is all important once again. The local authority does not have this choice of relocating its place. Its decisions *must* be based on its location in the *local.* As sociologist Zygmunt Bauman has noted, politics is located in the local and does not have the capacity to relocate, whereas capital is based in the market and has the choice to move to another place.[94] The possibility of relocation means local technicalities, the nomination agreement in this particular story, can be ignored; organisations can take cover in the market and in meeting other housing requirements and 'needs'. There are plenty of examples of housing associations redefining their sense of place, some already referred to in this book. There was, for instance, North Housing, which began life as the North East Housing Association: a body set up by central government to deal with the specific housing issues of the North East. When North Housing became the first association to experiment with private funding in the 1980s, it looked not to its home base but the prosperous South East to set up its 'innovative' schemes for, in finance terms, it was only in these regions that they could be made to work.[95]

As with all the regulatory spaces associations occupy, it is the needs of the private funding markets that become the dominant factor. But, as Jones and Stewart argued in *The Case for Local Government:*

> Local government is no passing value. It should be the guardian of fundamental values. It represents, first and foremost, a spread of political power.[96]

Their argument is even more relevant today: the global demands of the financial markets will continue to dominate unless local government is allowed into the power relations. This means that housing associations' engagement with the local must recognise the importance of this spread of power, of local government as a counter-balance not only to the nation state, but to the global policies of funders that have little concern for localities. However, for some in the housing association sector, maintaining competitiveness means spanning counties, regions, even countries; the sense of the local diminishes out of sight. For others, however, the connection with the local, so important to associations in their past claims of expertise over bureaucratic local government, remains an essential element of the housing association identity. The danger is that the competitiveness of the former squeezes out the latter.

[94] Z Bauman, *The Individualized Society* (Cambridge, Polity, 2001) ch 14.
[95] See above, ch 2.
[96] Above n 11 at 5.

5

Territorialising Regulation: Creating a National Regulatory Community

Introduction

ON OCCASIONS, a single Act of Parliament becomes pivotal. What becomes pivotal is not simply the text, but the power relations arising out of the *process* of the making of the Act. The Housing Act 1974 was just such a piece of legislation. For housing associations it was their 'landmark' legislation;[1] it created mechanisms to control and regulate an emergent housing association sector, thus legitimising the sector as a 'third arm' of government housing policy. In the longer term, it created conditions that allowed housing associations to become *the* dominant providers of social housing. In this chapter, I explore the formation of the regulatory community that arose out of the 1974 Act, a community made up of housing associations *and* the Housing Corporation as state regulator. I employ the concept of 'territorialisation' both in its literal sense, as an area delineated by boundaries used to control access, and as a metaphor, invoking ideas of 'jurisdiction' or 'authority over'.

The central argument in this chapter is that through an understanding of the way in which the making of the Housing Act 1974 (and subsequent events) carved out a new *regulatory territory* and led to the creation of a *regulatory community*, we can better understand the centrality of housing associations in UK housing and regeneration policy today. It challenges an understanding of law and regulation as top-down, replacing it with a more nuanced, three-dimensional understanding of how all actors in a regulatory community produce the norms and 'common sense' that guides and rules them. Indeed, the argument opens up questions of the subject-position of actors within a regulatory system: the position of regulated organisations as being subject 'to' the control of a regulator

[1] National Federation of Housing Associations (NFHA), *1974 Annual Report*, 6.

is only part of the story; at the same time they make themselves subjects 'of' a regulatory system through shaping their own identity and the identity of other actors around them.[2]

In the first section, I provide some thoughts and observations, in a general sense, on how regulatory territory is constructed. In the following sections I tell the story of the construction of the 1974 Act and of a housing association regulatory community. The Act was about attaining legitimacy for a major paradigm shift in housing policy, from local government-led social housing towards state-funded urban renewal via a 'third' sector. To make this shift, boundaries had to be redrawn and battles had to be won; in government, the Department of the Environment (DoE) had to take control of the agenda over other departments and agencies and, in the housing association's Federation, the question of the sector's identity was fought out in a battle for leadership. Then, new gateways into the territory had to be created through the mechanism of a registration system, through mundane practices and social relations. In occupying this territory, housing associations were enabled to exercise considerable control.

The story, however, has a postscript, one that shows that all dominant forms are contingent. Concerns about the ability of the social housing system to deliver public policy are, at this very moment, disturbing the territorial space of social housing. The boundaries of the regulatory territory had already been breached by the Housing Act 2004, which had allowed private developers into the territory. The Housing and Regeneration Act 2008 will bring about the breakup of this community, through the dissolution of a single regulator *and* funder for the sector, to be replaced by a funder that 'does deals' in the private sector mode, and a regulator operating rules that no-one is as yet quite certain about. The Act has the potential to be as much of a landmark as the 1974 Act; the tight-knit regulatory community to be replaced by a social housing 'domain'.[3]

Regulatory Space, Regulatory Territory

If UK housing academics pay attention to the 1974 Act, it is usually to discuss its importance in 'ushering in a different approach to urban renewal';[4] alternatively

[2] See M Foucault, 'Afterword: The Subject and Power' in H Dreyfus and P Rabinow (eds), *Michel Foucault: Beyond Structuralism and Hermeneutics* 2nd edn (Chicago, University of Chicago Press, 1983) 208–26.

[3] M Cave, in his review of social housing regulation, *Every Tenant Matters: A Review of Social Housing Regulation* (Communities and Local Government Publications, Wetherby, Yorks, 2007) and www.communities.gov.uk/index.asp?id=1511391 frequently uses the phrase 'whole domain of social housing': see, eg, Recommendations S1 and S2, at 24.

[4] MS Gibson and MJ Langstaff, *An Introduction to Urban Renewal* (Hutchinson London, 1982) 108.

it is to consider the 'charter' for housing associations[5] which the new funding system was said to have created. Whilst acknowledging the importance of both these aspects, the focus here is on the *regulatory* systems that emerged. A new scheme of funding, which channelled grants through the state regulator, the Housing Corporation, was a crucial element in these systems. The extremely generous funding arrangements enabled housing associations to move to 'centre stage' of housing policy.[6] The sector expanded from 200,000 dwellings in 1970, to 519,000 in 1989,[7] when the system changed again. Academics make the link between funding and central government control but tend to view this as one-way, hierarchical control: '[t]hrough the Housing Corporation and its accountancy controls central government was able to exert a considerable influence over what housing associations did'.[8] Similarly, the registration system introduced by the Act, which required associations to register with the Housing Corporation in order to be eligible for state funding, is seen as central government insisting on top-down control:

> [T]he introduction of registration as a condition of receipt of subsidy was a reflection of a long established, and well founded, suspicion within government circles that voluntary housing organisations could not always be trusted to act in a completely disinterested way.[9]

Such a top-down view of the regulatory systems that the Act produced is only part of the story. These mechanisms were not just expressions of government concerns; rather they were tools that the housing association sector and its allies in government saw as essential for the expansion of their *territory.*

Organisations that are subject to regulation (and housing associations are no exception)[10] always feel that regulation is something being done *to* them. They portray a process by which external bodies, usually the State, impose on them systems of control; all they can do is work within such systems. Research tells a different story. For example, a twenty-year study of the UK Health and Safety Executive showed that its systems of regulation operated as much using the knowledge and expertise of the companies as of the health and safety inspectors.[11] This chapter, and indeed the book as a whole, shows this process in operation in the housing association sector. The starting point for analysis here is

[5] Department of the Environment (DoE) Circular 170/74.

[6] MJ Langstaff, 'Housing Associations: A Move to Centre Stage' in J Birchall (ed), *Housing Policy in the 1990s* (London, Routledge, 1992).

[7] P Malpass, *Housing Associations and Housing Policy: A Historical Perspective* (Basingstoke, Macmillan, 2000) 161.

[8] D Hughes and S Lowe, *Social Housing Law and Policy* (London, Butterworths, 1995) 35.

[9] Malpass, *Housing Associations and Housing Policy*, above n 7 at 161.

[10] An NHF recent publication said that associations 'are one of the most regulated groups of organisations in existence': National Housing Federation (NHF), *The Regulation of Registered Social Landlords* (London, NHF) 3.

[11] K Hawkins, *Law as Last Resort: Prosecution Decision-Making in a Regulatory Agency* (Oxford, Oxford University Press, 2002).

the understanding that the way we *appropriate* the spaces we occupy, whether they are metaphorical or physical spaces, is intimately connected with thoughts and ideas about how we govern.[12] The way we divide up space (for example, into public or private) and the ways we occupy and use it for different functions, means that space has become an organising principle for thinking about the exercise of power.[13] Seeing law spatially can help develop new insights into how we constitute social life and the terms, conditions and consequences of social change.

This description of the relationship between ways of governing and ways of seeing space has already been considered in chapter one. There, I discussed the work of Hancher and Moran who coined the term 'regulatory space' as an analytical construct.[14] The range of issues subject to public decision, they argue, defines regulatory spaces. The regulatory space metaphor has focused thought away from hierarchical, top-down concepts of regulation onto the fragmentary and dispersed nature of regulatory power; away from the regulator to the organisations that are (purportedly) regulated. It identifies that the resources of the various occupants of the space are critical in holding 'regulatory space' together.[15] These create interdependencies between the actors as resources (be they personnel, property, funding or ideas) can be exchanged and bargained as part of the functioning of power.[16] The idea of space, as Hancher and Moran point out, 'encourages us not only to examine relations between those who enjoy inclusion, but also to examine the characteristics of the excluded'.[17]

In this chapter, I show how the *construction* of such spaces is fundamental to the operation of subsequent power relations. Regulatory space cannot just be seen for what it is now; it has history. It is *territory* that has to be carved out of existing space, there are boundaries to be defined and redefined, indeed fought over. 'Territorial battles and tribal disputes' is how Dezalay[18] described the complex power relations between accountants and lawyers in the rapidly expanding international consultancy market. In the housing association sector, battles over territory that took place prior to the making of legislative boundaries were

[12] Eg, P Bourdieu, 'Social Space and Symbolic Power' (1989) 7 *Sociological Theory* 14–25; B Latour, 'Visualisation and Cognition: Thinking with Eyes and Hands' (1986) 6 *Knowledge and Society: Studies in the Sociology of Culture, Past and Present* 1–40; H Lefebvre, *The Production of Space* (trans D Nicholson-Smith) (Oxford, Blackwell, 1991).

[13] Although it perhaps took the 'law and geography' scholars to point this out: see, eg, N Blomley, D Delaney and RT Ford (eds), *The Legal Geographies Reader: Law, Power and Space* (Oxford, Blackwell, 2001); also D Cooper, *Governing Out of Order: Space, Law and the Politics of Belonging* (London, Rivers Oram Press, 1998).

[14] L Hancher and M Moran, 'Organising Regulatory Space' in L Hancher and M Moran (eds), *Capitalism, Culture and Economic Regulation* (Oxford, Clarendon Press, 1989).

[15] C Scott, 'Analysing Regulatory Space: Fragmented Resources and Institutional Design' [2001] *Public Law* 329–53.

[16] *Cf* B Latour, 'The Powers of Association' in J Law (ed), *Power, Action and Belief: A New Sociology of Knowledge?* Sociological Review Monograph 32 (London, Routledge & Kegan Paul, 1986).

[17] Above n 14 at 277.

[18] Y Dezalay, 'Territorial Battles and Tribal Disputes' (1991) 54 *Modern Law Review* 792–809.

just as important in creating new regions of governing as legislative divisions. Within new territorial borders rules, values and laws of governing were created to make the space *within* safe and productive for those who occupied it. However, rules that create security for some, at the same time exclude others. The re-making of the regulatory space of social housing, to allow private developers a way in and the means to flourish, is the business of the Housing and Regeneration Act. In what follows, the focus first is on the carving out of territory from existing space.[19]

Making the Housing Act 1974: Defining Territory

The Crisis in Social Housing Provision

Access to financial subsidy has always been critical to providers of housing for poor households. Chapter two discussed how attempts to make the voluntary, non-profit sector of housing societies, trusts and associations into a central pillar of housing policy had failed in the 1930s, in the making of the Housing Act 1935. However, out of this failure emerged a national representative body for the housing association sector, with the Housing Act 1935 providing the National Federation of Housing Societies with funding. The Federation then took on the role of lobbying for increased subsidy for the voluntary associations, and continued to receive government support as the principal strategy against a local authority monopoly of rented housing.

By the beginning of the 1960s, the non-profit housing association sector was still insignificant and local authorities owned over a quarter of the housing in Britain.[20] Nevertheless, this was a period when existing modes of housing provision were being called into question. Local communities, as well as Conservative governments, were critical of the role of municipal authorities as providers of rented housing.[21] In 1961, ministers attempted to reinvigorate a non-municipal rented sector by promoting a new type of housing society to

[19] This process has much in common with Lefebvre's 'production' of 'social space' (above n 12). 'Each mode of production' he says, 'produces its own space' (at 31). The way that a society, or a group, occupies and lives in a space, their practices within that space 'propounds and presupposes it . . . produces it slowly and surely as it masters and appropriates it' (at 38). Contained in this concept, it seems to me, is a sort of iterative idea; social space is both carved out by the group and at the same time shapes and re-shapes the community itself. Social relations, or 'spatial practices', are the central element in this shaping process.

[20] In 1961: public rented = 27%; owner occupied = 43%; private rented (including housing associations) = 31%; D Mullins and A Murie, *Housing Policy in the UK* (Basingstoke, Palgrave Macmillan, 2006) 36 table 2.5.

[21] The concern that local government should not have a monopoly of new rented housing was not new. In 1953, Harold Macmillan (as Minister of Housing and Local Government) had set up a committee to study the alternative of establishing a new form of housing association delivering 'co-ownership and co-partnership' housing (letter from Macmillan to RA Butler, Chancellor, 11 June

develop housing at cost (or economic) rents. They also sought to promote home ownership through setting up co-ownership societies.[22] These new housing societies were to be significantly different from existing voluntary housing associations. Their committee members, architects, lawyers and contractors, were able to gain financially from any work generated, in exchange for time put in to manage these organisations. The Government called this 'enlightened self-interest' but to some this was a displacement of the philanthropic motive that had driven the sector for so long. These associations became known as the cost-rent and co-ownership housing societies, and the Federation became the Government's channel for funds to these new societies.[23] This was a Conservative government that only wanted 'arm's length' control over attempts to upset local authorities' monopoly on rented housing. It was not only the Conservative Government that was trying to re-map housing provision.[24] A new wave of philanthropically motivated associations was emerging as a response to community concerns about the inadequacy of housing. These associations, established by local people, church groups, vicars and priests, received considerable funding from charitable donations and, in particular, the newly established homelessness charity, Shelter.

The first battle for the territory of social housing was *internal* to the housing association sector. The cost-rent and co-ownership societies and the new philanthropic housing associations, set themselves up as opposing 'camps' in the struggle for control of the Federation and housing association territory. This was a battle about the *identity* of the sector[25] and there was much at stake, given the Conservative Government's concern to find a 'third arm' of housing policy that could provide rented housing. Battle lines were drawn: around the type of housing to be provided—new build (by the cost-rent societies), or rehabilitated street properties (by the new philanthropists); and the type of tenant—those who could afford economic rents, or the poorest, marginalised households. More fundamentally, lines of difference were drawn around values and images of trustworthiness. The new philanthropists called into question the motivations of people running the cost-rent societies, referring to them as the 'fee-grabbers'. In

1953, TNA T 227/806) reported in P Malpass, *Housing and the Welfare State: The Development of Housing Policy in Britain* (London, Palgrave, 2005) 80.

[22] Members of co-ownership societies were the people living in the society's dwellings. They paid a proportion of the construction costs, the rest of the costs being covered by a mortgage. Members were considered as owner-occupiers for tax purposes (Malpass, *Housing Associations and Housing Policy*, above n 7 at 136–37).

[23] Those I interviewed about this time were concerned that I understood the terminology; these organisations were housing *societies*, it was the philanthropic organisations that were to be termed the housing *associations*. Labelling as ever was important in creating divisions as well as identity.

[24] See chs 2 and 7.

[25] Thanks to Sharon Gilad for her astute observations; also see S Albert and DA Whetten, 'Organizational Identity' (1985) 7 *Research in Organizational Behavior* 263–95.

turn, the cost-rent associations referred to the Shelter associations as 'the brown rice and sandals brigade', who could not be trusted to run their operations in a 'commercial-like way'.[26]

In chapter three we saw how charitable regulation had largely failed to support attempts to expand the housing association sector. This failure arose in part because the technical means of governing through charity and taxation law placed limits on housing associations that meant they could not fulfil what they perceived as their role in the housing system. Failure pointed to a need for a new framework and different technical means, ones that could accommodate an expanding housing association sector whilst at the same time providing funders with reassurances of trustworthiness. The Federation's chairman, Lewis Waddilove, had played a pivotal role in attempting to work with charitable regulation; he was also to play a pivotal role in seeking alternatives. Waddilove had been asked by the Conservative Housing Minister, Peter Walker, to prepare a paper 'on principles that might be included in a Housing Bill dealing with the Voluntary Housing Movement'.[27] Waddilove's *modus operandi* was not to enter into battles. He was a Quaker, a consensus-seeker and a person who commanded widespread respect among all sides in the Federation. Nevertheless, he had an able general's feel for strategy. In 1970, he invited those from the sector who were 'associated individually with a variety of housing trusts, associations or societies'[28] to what proved to be a decisive meeting. The older charitable trusts, the cost-rent/co-ownership societies and the new philanthropists, the Shelter-based charitable associations, were all represented. The purpose of the meeting was to discuss a paper, prepared by Waddilove, which set out his proposals in response to Walker's invitation. They were 'the principles which should be included in any new legislation designed to establish a vigorous growth of organisations providing dwellings without profit'.[29]

Waddilove's paper was 'wholly supported' by all those who attended the meeting.[30] This consensus was surprising, given the divisions within the housing association sector, and highly significant, given the proposals contained in the paper:

[26] From interviews with Richard Best (now Lord Best) (12 August 2003), Director of the Federation from 1973 to 1988; and Eric Armitage (22 September 2003), member of the Federation's council and chairman; from 1973 he worked for North British Housing Association, one of the associations branded as the 'fee grabbers'.

[27] TNA CHAR 11/205; see above, ch 3.

[28] L Waddilove, *Housing To Let by Non-Profit Organisations* (1970) (copy held by author and at the National Archives: HLG 118/1390) para 27.

[29] Taken from a letter to Peter Walker, Secretary of State for the Environment, TNA CHAR 11/205; in ch 3, we saw that Waddilove (in his correspondence with Charity Commissioner Lewis) had referred to an invitation from Peter Walker to write this paper.

[30] National Federation of Housing Societies (NFHS), *34th Report of the Council of the National Federation of Housing Societies* (London, NFHS, 1970).

(1) A single definition for a housing association, based on letting without profit, in an attempt to end the distinctions between types of associations.
(2) Public aid only to be available to those associations who were registered with a Housing Commission, which would control disposals of assets by registered associations.
(3) Rent pooling and fair rents, and rent allowances to tenants, to be encouraged.
(4) Recognition of the need for increased private investment by permitting the Housing Commission to raise loans direct from building societies and other lenders, on the security of a government guarantee.[31]

It is both Waddilove's thinking and his technical solutions that are of interest, for this paper also addressed the question of the sector's identity.

Where previous legislation had created division, his first concern was to create unity:

> It is important to avoid the kind of situation which arose following the 1961 and 1964 Housing Acts, when a particular category of housing was created which remains in isolation, operating under separate rules and having separate sets of accounts.[32]

In carving out a new territory for the housing association sector as an alternative to local government, unity would provide strength. The sector had to be seen as sufficiently well resourced to take on what was to be a major role; it also avoids different parts of the territory being separated off and either dominated or absorbed within enemy territory. In inviting members of opposing 'camps' within the Federation to this meeting, Waddilove was attempting to secure this unity in his troops. The Federation's annual report, usually silent on all internal divisions, admitted with uncommon frankness that 'it was a surprise' that all those who attended the meeting supported the paper.[33]

Despite receiving approval from all sides, Waddilove's proposals were by no means neutral. The first embodied a tactic meant to mark out a territory capable of being governed, to which I return below. His second reflected a concern that the value of *trustworthiness* had to be embodied in the sector's identity. It was critical to overcome concerns that 'voluntary housing organisations could not always be trusted to act in a completely disinterested way',[34] expressed in particular in relation to the cost-rent associations where the 'enlightened self-interest' of committee members might lead *self-interest* to dominate. The concern to control the disposal of assets was a direct response. Such safeguards were already built into charitable regulation: the public's trust in charities was in part because their assets could not be disposed for private gain, only in a manner approved by the Charity Commissioners. However, as charitable regulation

[31] TNA HLG 118/1390.
[32] Waddilove, above n 28 at para 24.
[33] NFHS, *34th Report*, above n 30.
[34] See text associated with n 9 above.

proved a barrier to expansion, a new system had to achieve the same end without charity's constraints. The third proposal also reflected the concerns of the Shelter-based associations that the prime motivation of the sector had to be in housing the poorest households; prior to any form of state housing benefit, rent pooling, fair rents and allowances to enable low-income tenants to claim a rent rebate from the association embodied this objective.

Waddilove and others were looking to effect a transformation of the sector; to bring into being a new politics based on philanthropic motives whilst at the same time expanding the sector into a significant force. Waddilove's proposals marked out a territory for an expanded housing association sector by identifying it with a certain set of values. This vision for expansion was in opposition to what was now the 'old guard' in the Federation, the cost-rent and co-ownership societies who sought expansion for those who could afford economic rents. In part, it was also in opposition to the (much older) charitable trusts who, while being concerned with housing the poor, were accustomed to performing a limited role and did not see themselves as entrepreneurial or expansionist.[35]

However, Waddilove's attempts at building unity did not last. The opposing rationales (and egos) of the two camps were in an uneasy truce. Just as values are associated with organisational identity, so too are the figureheads and leaders. Before the new territory for housing associations could be carved out, the leader of the sector, in the form of the Director of the Federation, had to be changed. Waddilove offered Geoffrey Hall (who had been the Government's choice for Director to run the cost-rent pump-priming programme) retirement and he was replaced by Richard Best, one of the new philanthropists. When it came to the battle for the Federation's president, both camps had their candidates; Waddilove found a compromise candidate acceptable to both sides and the battle for the sector's identity was complete.[36] The dominant values were to be for a dynamic and innovative sector, motivated by philanthropy not financial gain.

(Re)-defining the Territory within Government

The housing association sector had begun to redefine its boundaries.[37] Victory in the Federation's leadership battle meant that the spokespersons and figureheads of the Federation were now either the new philanthropists or, like Waddilove, speaking the same language as ministers and civil servants who were also looking

[35] John Coward, told of how he was considered a 'hot-headed upstart' for his aspiration that Notting Hill Housing Trust should be developing hundreds of new homes each year: from interview with John Coward (30 June 2003).

[36] This story is told in ch 2 above.

[37] Much of this section is based on papers found in the file TNA HLG 118/1370 held at the National Archives.

to achieve transformation. A paradigm shift[38] was taking place in housing policy, away from strategies of demolition and the relocation of communities to outer city high-rise dominated by local government, towards urban renewal, in which the locally-based associations would 'rehabilitate' older housing, preserving communities. The local authority territory of 'social' housing was being eroded but there were still many battles to be won.

Waddilove's paper had arisen out of dialogue with civil servants.[39] Discussions revolved around two issues: *funding* the expansion of the housing association sector and *controlling* the sector through a regulatory body and registration system. In 1964, the Government had set up the Housing Corporation to fund cost-rent and co-ownership housing societies and subsequently given it powers to fund fair rent (that is below economic rent) schemes. This embodiment of the Corporation saw its primary role as promoting the cost-rent and co-ownership societies. It appears to be little involved in discussions about revitalising the housing association sector as a whole and indeed DoE civil servants suggest it was hostile to change. Although Waddilove envisioned a different organisation as regulator/funder (in his paper he called it the Housing *Commission*), it was the existing Housing Corporation that was transformed by the Housing Act 1974, given new powers and functions to fund and control the whole sector. And like the Federation, the Corporation too was to undergo leadership transformation.

Meanwhile, the DoE had its own battles within government to fight. We often talk of the State as a unified entity, but this is a mirage. The DoE may have been convinced of the housing association sector's role in transforming housing policy but this was only one element of the State's response to the housing crisis. The various interests of *other* government departments and agencies posed obstacles to be confronted or circumvented before transformation could be effected.

Perhaps the most critical battle was with the Treasury over mechanisms for subsidising a developing sector, for a new subsidy system was central to expansion. The associations argued for a central funding system; experience of negotiating local authority funding had been problematic, producing geographically differentiated results. They also claimed that existing mechanisms were inadequate to deal with the high cost and risks of rehabilitating older property. Shelter research[40] showed a funding gap between the costs of acquiring and improving older property, and the rental and subsidy income that could be generated under existing systems.[41] As DoE officials anticipated, the Treasury opposed Waddilove's proposal for government guaranteed loans, so they proposed a system of capital grants, a subsidy mechanism novel within the housing

[38] On the importance of ideas in policy-making and the way in which ideas can structure decision-making just as much as institutions, see: PA Hall, 'Policy Paradigms, Social Learning, and the State: the Case of Economic Policymaking in Britain' (1983) 25 *Comparative Politics* 275–96.

[39] Marginal notes in the DoE files from the early 1970s: TNA HLG 118/1370.

[40] See below, ch 7: it was Shelter's aim from the outset to ground its claims in empirical research.

[41] From an interview with David Bebb (11 August 2003), who became a housing director with Shelter in 1971.

system, which could be contained within cash limits. Significantly, the architect of this new system was an 'outsider' to the DoE, a civil servant who had previously worked in the Department of Transport.[42] Indeed, this carving out of new territory was associated with changes in personalities at many levels, discarding tradition and bringing in the 'new'.

The Treasury would always be the ultimate authority in matters of public funding; its concerns had to be accommodated within any newly defined territory. With other government departments and agencies, however, DoE civil servants could be more cavalier in ensuring that *their* regulator controlled any new system of regulation. Some housing associations were companies registered with the Department of Trade. The new proposals required that associations should adopt a restricted range of objectives. This, it was anticipated, might meet resistance, for 'trying to stop a company from altering its objects would be a radical change in company law, which would be apt to upset the Dept of Trade'.[43] Here the solution was simple: a 'housing association' could not be a company under the new definition.

The situation was similar with the Registrar of Friendly Societies.[44] At the time, the Registrar controlled the objects and rules of associations set up as Industrial and Provident Societies (which included all the Housing Corporation promoted cost-rent and co-ownership societies and many of the older societies). Waddilove suggested that there would no longer be a need for registration with the Registrar. Civil servants ruled out removing the Registrar's entire role, fearing to contest established territories and re-draw boundaries prescribed by previous legislation: 'by leaving housing associations and societies under the Industrial and Provident Societies Act umbrella we avoid the need for much complicated legislation repeating the provision of that Act'.[45] *Legal* boundaries were hard to move but *practicalities* could be changed, so under the 1974 Act the Registrar had no supervisory role, with the Housing Corporation conducting investigations into associations registered as Industrial and Provident Societies. Retention of registration with the Registrar appears to have been principally a tactic to avoid battles on too many fronts.[46]

Attempts to exclude the role of the Charity Commission were less successful. In a discussion about who should authorise the transfer of assets of a charitable housing association, civil servants complained about not having yet 'settled the score with the Charity Commission':

[42] From an interview with John Baker (11 September 2003), civil servant then deputy chief executive at the Housing Corporation 1974–78. Also see below, ch 6.

[43] DoE memo: TNA HLG 118/1390.

[44] The Registrar (now Registry) of Friendly Societies registers all mutual societies, maintains their public records and has a limited monitoring role.

[45] DoE, 'Comment' on Waddilove's paper, in TNA, above n 43 at 2.

[46] However, the Financial Services and Markets Act 2000 (ss 334 and 335) transferred responsibilities of the Friendly Societies Commission and the Registry of Friendly Societies to the Financial Services Authority to no audible complaints.

> [B]ut if they object too strongly to a dissolved charity's assets becoming the property of the Corporation, we might fall back on the idea of providing that in the event of a charity's dissolving the Corporation would transfer its assets to another housing charity.[47]

In the end, the 1974 Act was entirely silent on the procedures for winding up ailing charitable housing associations, as it was on the matter of the investigation of charitable associations that did not meet the required regulatory standards. Section 2(3) simply required the Charity Commissioners to 'consult' with the Housing Corporation before agreeing to the disposition of land held by charitable associations.

A New Territory of Regulation

In effect, a new territory for social housing had been created, a territory where new alliances would arise and new forms of expertise would become dominant. Changes across the range of public services over the past three or four decades have created many new governable spaces into which 'expert communities' have been easily able to insert themselves. Those who come to make up such communities can share vocabulary, ethical principles, mutually explanatory logics and commonly accepted facts.[48] New alliances of expertise and governing, and the social practices the allies develop, both *constitute* the new regulatory territory and enable the newly created 'regulatory community' to *appropriate* and *control* it.[49]

In the case of housing association regulation, the community was (more or less) self-forming. The regulatory body, the Housing Corporation, though based on an existing form, was essentially a new organisation with greatly expanded powers of regulation and funding. There was a transfer of personnel from the DoE to the Housing Corporation. Nevertheless, new expertise was needed to govern this space, a vacuum that the housing associations (the regulatees) were able to fill. Housing associations laid claim to expertise as managers of housing and of urban renewal. This co-location of expertise was crucial because the Housing Act 1974 was primarily designed to establish policies and practices for the renewal of existing urban environments and housing, replacing previous policies of demolition and rebuild. This meant that the new philanthropists who had taken control of the housing association sector and begun its transformation had to form alliances not only with the DoE, but with the 'old' philanthropists, the traditional (often Victorian) housing trusts labelled by some (including Waddilove) as 'dinosaurs'. These charitable trusts and the housing societies

[47] TNA HLG 118/1390.

[48] *Cf* N Rose, *Powers of Freedom: Reframing Political Thought* (Cambridge, Cambridge University Press, 1999) 28.

[49] Lefebvre, above n 12 at 35.

formed earlier in the twentieth century not only had political connections (including considerable numbers in the House of Lords) but could lay claim to historical expertise in the field of urban renewal. This expertise, and the recent experience of the new Shelter associations, allowed the sector to challenge the domination by the local authorities of social housing as they were considered to lack the necessary skills and experience in rehabilitation.[50] In turn, this expertise was vital to the formation of alliances with civil servants looking for a solution to the increasing concerns of government ministers with the state of inner city housing.

Such commonality of needs moulded the regulator and regulatees into a strong community. Such a community has a capacity for self-governing, as community members become disciplined and responsiblised, adhering to a new common sense. It is certainly true that the actors in the present-day space of housing associations believe that associations 'are one of the most regulated groups of organisations in existence'.[51] Nevertheless, in the new territory of governing created by the Housing Act 1974, the expertise of the associations enabled them to exert a significant degree of control by carving out new territory (from old). Expertise and alliances were utilised as mechanisms for both inclusion and exclusion. Claims to expertise ensured the inclusion of housing associations in the redefinition of social housing and also acted to exclude local authorities from certain areas of housing policy. Expertise created advantage for the associations; in effect it was utilised as a technology of domination, one that had continuing relevance.

Securing the Borders, Creating Gateways: The Registration Process

One example appears in the Federation's influence over the system of registration with the Housing Corporation, which was to become a principal mechanism for controlling associations. It could exclude outsiders and at the same time provide associations with authority. The requirement to register with the Housing Corporation restricted access to public funding to those organisations whose objectives complied with the Act. Registration was combined with scrutiny by the Corporation of all new housing schemes developed by associations. Prior to the enactment of the 1974 Act, this second mechanism appeared to have had only secondary significance to the DoE.[52] Their aim was to govern 'at a distance', to

[50] ADH Crook and M Moroney, 'Housing associations, private finance and risk avoidance: the impact on urban renewal and inner cities' (1995) 27 *Environment and Planning A* 1695–1712. However, The London Boroughs Association, when consulted about the Housing and Planning Bill 1974, expressed their doubts 'as to whether Has have the ability or the resources to fulfil the role expected of them by government': memo (22 April 1974) from LBA to DoE: TNA HLG 29/1115.

[51] NHF, *The Regulation of Registered Social Landlords*, (London, NHF) 3.

[52] Though once the Act was in place and the Housing Corporation had taken over the function of allocating grants, the DoE still insisted on scrutinising associations' scheme development; ie, how the

create a sector of a small number of strong associations which could be left to get on with the process of development with little scrutiny, as this internal memo reveals:

> Mr Waddilove in recent discussion preferred his idea on the ground that the Corporation ought to keep a minute control over associations, but surely meticulous control over accounts etc. is in place only for the weak associations who have to be helped at every turn, whereas the ideal is to encourage a smaller number of big strong associations in place of a multitude of small, weak ones.[53]

Certainly, if the exercise had simply been to create an easily governable territory, admittance would be limited to certain types of organisation that could be trusted to comply with the new norms. Rules would be put in place to enable associations to expand their activities of meeting housing need, whilst ensuring that they could deliver the type and standard of housing required to meet national policy objectives. However, it is dangerous to assume uni-directionality and coherence in new political programmes. Rather, new forms emerge from pre-existing ones, which may well be competing and contradictory.[54] The historical reality was that the housing association sector was made up of a large number of small, independent organisations, each run by a management committee of volunteers. It had always been argued that diversity was one of the sector's strengths. Associations claimed that they could 'do' inner city renewal better than municipal authorities precisely because they were diverse, local, responsive and on the ground.

The new system attempted to accommodate these competing and contradictory demands. What emerged from the registration process was *not* a streamlined sector of large strong organisations but a continuation of diversity. That continuation largely arose from the influence the associations and the Federation were able to exert over the design of the registration system. The rhetorical argument for a registration system may have been that it would ensure the protection of *public* resources; the struggle for control of the Federation (between the 'fee grabbers' and the new 'brown rice and sandals' philanthropists) had been partly a battle about who could be entrusted with the new resources. Nevertheless, when it came to system design, the Federation succeeded in influencing a number of strategic decisions concerning both the principles and the processes of the registration system. Hence, both 'camps' were allowed to enter the new territory. The 1974 Act had created a Housing Associations Registration Advisory Committee (HARAC) to advise the Corporation on registering associations. Its first key decision was the nature of the 'gate' that would allow associations into the

money was spent. This led to 'double scrutiny' by both the DoE and Corporation and was the subject of considerable criticism from the associations (see N Lewis and I Harden, 'The Housing Corporation and "voluntary housing"' in A Barker (ed), *Quangos in Britain* (Basingstoke, Macmillan, 1982).

[53] DoE memo: TNA HLG 118/1390.

[54] Eg, see, D Garland, *The Culture of Control: Crime and Social Order in Contemporary Society* (Oxford, Oxford University Press, 2001).

territory; in effect a mechanism to determine how many associations would be registered. The Cohen Committee[55] had concluded that there were too many associations[56] and one view in the Corporation was that two hundred was about right. At the time, there was in excess of 2000 housing associations that were members of the Federation, so a decision to register only one-tenth of these would have been disastrous for the Federation[57] as well as the associations. Federation supporters on HARAC were able to persuade the Committee that

> it wasn't terribly sensible to lop out these very well meaning voluntary outfits doing very good work not taking much public money. They can make far more trouble for anybody, galvanised to oppose this, than they could ever be trouble.[58]

The Federation had succeeded in protecting *all* its members; the threat that some of the approximately 26,000 committee members of housing associations might cause trouble in the media or with MPs was a strong incentive for the Corporation to take the line of least resistance. The logic of an efficient system became overlaid by political imperatives.

The registration system, in effect, provided a gateway to the new housing association territory, albeit one that would allow most of the existing members through. However, the emerging territory was principally framed by the dominant grouping in the Federation, which used its network of social contacts to ensure that the Advisory Committee's policies would exclude those associations controlled by the 'fee grabbers'. The Corporation adopted a policy that no more than half of an association's management committee should have a financial interest in the association.[59] Nevertheless, research into the operation of the registration system reveals that local mechanisms limited the impact of this. Even though central criteria were established, officials in regional offices were given wide discretion, enabling them 'to exempt associations from the full force of the criteria with little or no justification'.[60]

The primary function of the registration system was to create a symbol of quality and trust. When the sector had been small, local relationships with municipal authorities, landowners and others had been sufficient guarantors of trust. However, if the sector was to expand, the activities of its members would begin to cross these local boundaries and local memory would be insufficient. The housing association sector was to be bureaucratically mapped by the Corporation; rules, monitoring and supervision provided a form of certainty

[55] A government committee which reported in 1971 on the future of the housing association sector.

[56] Cohen Committee, *Housing Associations: A Working Paper of the Central Housing Advisory Committee* (London, HMSO, 1971) 75.

[57] The NFHA was, by this time, reliant on subscriptions from associations for its income.

[58] From an interview with Richard Best, above n 26, who also supplied other information about the operations of the Housing Associations Advisory Committee used in this section.

[59] M Noble, 'From rules to discretion: the Housing Corporation' in M Adler and S Asquith (eds), *Discretion and Welfare* (London, Heinemann, 1981) 175.

[60] *Ibid.*

necessary for the continuation of trust. Bureaucratic mechanisms removed understandings of trustworthiness from the vagueness of memory and the changeability of social connections.[61]

It may well be that the registration system was not intended to re-shape the existing housing association sector. Indeed, even the aim of creating trust in the sector was compromised by accusations that only the '"obvious crooks" had been caught by the registration net and many "rogues" had slipped through'.[62] It was not intended to exclude the 'fee-grabber' associations but presumably to enable their transformation to fit in with the accepted value systems.[63] However, the emerging technologies of registration certainly enabled some restructuring as some Corporation officers saw the opportunity to use law to change the geographical map of the housing association sector. The rules of registration could be used to limit the area of operation of a housing association or to encourage associations to spread their wings and work regionally or even nationally.[64]

Registration turned out to be an exclusionary practice in another sense: it effectively excluded local authorities from decisions about which associations would work within their locality. In consultations with local authorities on the Bill that became the 1974 Act, both the Association of Metropolitan Authorities and the Greater London Council argued for a statutory duty on the Corporation to consult with local authorities about whether to register an association.[65] Whilst civil servants would concede the principal of consultation, they were not prepared to put this into statutory form.[66] They may well have advised the Housing Corporation to consult local authorities about registration, but pragmatic realities told a different tale; the Corporation became more concerned with supporting those associations that could spend the funds allocated than to the niceties of local consultation.[67]

[61] Alain Pottage makes a similar point about the land registration system: A Pottage, 'The Measure of Land' (1994) 57 *Modern Law Review* 361–84.

[62] D Noble, 'Policing Voluntary Housing' (July 1979) *ROOF* 122–23, 122, reporting on statements made by several directors of housing associations and also by staff in the Housing Corporation and the NFHA.

[63] Mostly these associations stuck to new-build rather than becoming embroiled in the difficulties of urban renewal. Some of these associations have now become the biggest players in the sector: eg, North British Housing Association which (according to Eric Armitage, who was the chief executive from 1983, had difficulties registering with the Corporation) is now, as People for Places, calls itself 'one of the largest property management and development companies in the UK': www.placesforpeople.co.uk/aboutus/index.aspx.

[64] Malpass, *Housing Associations and Housing Policy*, above n 7 at 165–66.

[65] TNA HLG 29/1115: letter from AMA to Mr Lazarus, DoE (3 May 1974); letter from Director of Housing, GLC, to Mr Pickup, DoE (4 June 1974).

[66] Notes of meeting held with AMA (13 May 1974) TNA HLG 29/1115.

[67] C Wolmar, 'Corporation Critics' (September/October 1982) *ROOF* 12–13.

Controlling Assets: Mappings of Property in Space

Property interests open up possibilities for making space both 'countable and accountable'.[68] The mechanisms for controlling property interests introduced by the Act were important both for trust-making and for shaping the sector. Associations' most valuable assets were the homes they owned; their freedom to dispose of land and property had to be controlled, recognition that withdrawing the availability of homes from those in need could threaten the legitimacy and authority of the whole sector. It would seem that the 'fee grabbers' label had been successfully attached to the cost-rent and co-ownership housing societies; the 'enlightened self interest' of professionals running them was called into question. To guard against fears that the founders of these societies would choose personal gain by disposing of the assets, associations would not be able to dispose of property interests without obtaining the consent of the Housing Corporation.

The outcome was a new regulatory framework which required registered housing associations to exchange the freedom to dispose of property as they wished for certain privileges (access to public funds, subsidy and loans) and exemption from tax liabilities. Thus, those who sought to deal with associations registered with the Housing Corporation could be assured that their investment would be as secure as if the body was covered by charity law. Indeed, there is a hint that the DoE officials thought that even charity law was not strong enough in this respect, as evident in their correspondence with the Charity Commission: 'it is a prime purpose of the proposed legislation to stop up any leaks in the control of equity of housing associations'.[69]

In another respect, property interests also shaped the nature and values of the emerging housing association sector. It was considered that controlling the old co-ownership societies (organisations where occupiers had an ownership interest) was too problematic. Organisations were governable whilst individuals were not easily so. The 1974 Act, therefore, restricted the definition of a registered association to organisations that provided only housing for *rent*. Control at a distance did not seem possible for those organisations that provided other forms of tenure and so it was easier to exclude them altogether. This understanding of the role of the housing association sector (indeed it became seen as part of the mission) as providers of rented, not owner-occupied housing, more or less remained as a central tenet until public funding for rented housing began to diminish in the mid-1980s under a government with an agenda of privatisation and marketisation.

[68] N Blomley and J Sommers, 'Mapping Urban Space: Governmentality and Cartographic Struggles in Inner City Vancouver' in R Stamdych (ed), *Governable Places: Readings on Governmentality and Crime Control* (Aldershot, Dartmouth, 1999) 266.

[69] TNA HLG 29/1097.

Defining Contours: Making Rules

This new regulatory community was effective because it functioned at the micro, as well as the national, level. Here, governing occurred through the making of 'local rules' by the community, for the community. These were rules that regulated the everyday activities of housing association development teams, finance staff, housing management offices and special needs hostels. In the context of local rule-making, local knowledge comes into play; those who have daily knowledge of building construction, the costs of management and the necessity for maintenance programmes become vitally important. Local knowledge of housing association staff, of putting policies into practice on a daily basis, enabled them and the Federation to play a central role. It was association finance directors who mapped out the system of allowances that set funding levels available for daily management and maintenance of properties. When the funding system changed again, it was the Federation that brought together the business plans from a small survey of associations and 'cobbled these figures together'[70] to produce a matrix of figures that made up the funder's formula for grant allocations.

This informality of decision-making was not just at the day to day level. In the 1970s, an informal grouping of three, the Deputy Director of the Federation, the chief executive of the Corporation and the head of the housing associations division at the DoE, set in motion a number of important initiatives. This group came up with a new grant for improving properties on a short term basis and a scheme funded by the Housing Corporation, intended to literally plant people from other sectors into the new housing association world the 1974 Act had created (they became known as the 'flower-pot men'). Again, 'outsiders' assumed critical roles in the new territory.

Conclusion

In this chapter, I have told a story of how law reform in the housing association sector set in train a process of territorialisation. In carving out new territory, the 'traditional' and the 'old' ways of doing things make way for the new. New alliances are forged which can lead, as this story shows, to the formation of close-knit regulatory communities. From the ways in which the regulatory community comes to occupy this territory, a new 'common sense' emerges: accepted and unchallenged modes of operation. These are Scott's 'interpretive communities',[71] in which not only new ideas and rules are able to arise out of informality but the informality between regulator and regulatee becomes central

[70] Interview with Stephen Duckworth (13 November 2002), the Federation's Finance Director, who had also been a housing association Finance Director in the 1970s.

[71] Scott, above n 15 at 341.

to communication in the regulatory process. We are going beyond ideas of 'regulatory capture';[72] indeed 'capture' in regulatory space makes little sense, since all actors occupy the same space and cannot be 'captured' from the outside.[73] Just as the initial battles to claim domination over the new territory sought to exclude others, so too did subsequent events.

However, all forms of domination are contingent. For the actors in the social housing regulatory community, their territory and its particular forms of common sense are in the process of being disturbed. The Housing Act 2004 changed the rules for Social Housing Grant, which up until then had been available only to housing associations registered with the Housing Corporation. The 2004 Act removed the *not*-for profit requirement, making it possible for private developers to access this grant, so breaching a fundamental boundary of the regulatory territory. Then followed the Cave review,[74] a wide-ranging government review of the delivery of the 'sustainable communities' agenda, which proposed sweeping changes in the system of regulation. The funding and regulatory roles of the Housing Corporation are to be separated, thereby changing another unwritten rule that had enabled the Corporation to regulate through threats of withdrawal of subsidy. The 'investment' (funding) part of the Corporation has been merged with another quango, English Partnerships, which is responsible (according to its website) for delivering 'high-quality, well-designed, sustainable places for people to live, work and enjoy'.[75] The regulatory role is now to be carried out by the Tenant Services Authority, its new regulatory powers defined by the Housing and Regeneration Act 2008. These changes, according to David Orr, the Federation's present chief executive, were inevitable:

> [I]f you look at the history of Housing Associations since the Corporation was created and particularly since the '74 Act, while it is true that housing associations have had a very close relationship with the Housing Corporation, it's equally true that the Housing Corporation had no reason to exist without housing associations. ... The Corporation came along, the partnership worked extremely well, but the umbilical link was broken by the 2004 Act. And it in the end had a more profound impact on the Housing Corporation than it has on housing associations. I think.[76]

The words 'I think' were no doubt connected to the debate about the role and powers of the new regulator contained in the Housing and Regeneration Bill. The Federation became involved in a frantic lobbying exercise to influence the terms of this debate. Much of the controversy revolved around the Federation's perception that the Bill in its original state 'contained so much state control over

72 See: D Mullins, 'From regulatory capture to regulated competition: an interest group analysis of the regulation of housing associations in England' (1997) 12 *Housing Studies* 301–19.

73 Hancher and Moran, *Capitalism, Culture and Economic Regulation*, above n 14.

74 *Every Tenant Matters: A Review of Social Housing Regulation*, above n 3.

75 See English Partnerships website: www.englishpartnerships.co.uk/about.htm.

76 Interview with David Orr (18 February 2008).

associations that it risked their being reclassified as public bodies'.[77] This was portrayed as a fundamental concern about associations' independence, an issue taken up in chapter eight. Of interest here are three matters that relate to the 'regulatory community' argument of this chapter. First, the nature of the Federation's involvement with this Bill is fundamentally different from its engagement with the Bill that led to the 1974 Act. Here, the Federation's role was lobbying for change to a Bill devised by government, which contains powers that were seen as a threat to the sector. Secondly, David Orr may perceive the changes to be 'more profound' for the Corporation but others see the Bill, and the other associated changes in regulation/funding, as being as fundamental for associations as the 1974 Act.[78] One thing is clear: that whilst the new funding body, the Homes and Communities Agency, has taken on some of the Corporation's staff, its origin in English Partnerships will initiate a culture change. English Partnerships is seen as the dominant partner, its mentality arising from 'doing deals' in the private sector, not managing a 'public interest' programme. As for the Tenant Services Authority, senior staff of some housing associations may have been cheered when Anthony Mayer, a 'popular former head of the Housing Corporation'[79] was appointed as its first chair, but it remains to be seen to what extent the 'very close relationship' with the Housing Corporation can be replicated by associations. Pertinent to this relationship is an entirely unconnected threat arising from an event in October 2007, when Ujima Housing Association became the first ever association to go into insolvency. This event, according to the housing press, created 'a huge blot on the corporation's [sic] previously unblemished record of presiding over a default-free sector'.[80] It resulted in changes in the Housing and Regeneration Bill[81] and casts a shadow over the new regulator's ability to maintain the confidence of private lenders in the housing association sector.

The third issue that arises out of the 2008 Act is how the rules of the game will be formulated in the future. Despite the Housing Act 2004, few developers have so far sought to access Social Housing Grant. For, whilst the Act made it possible, the detailed accountability terms required, which were similar to those for housing associations, made the grant generally unattractive to the private sector. The 2008 Act seeks to remedy this, but has the effect of allowing private house builders to operate within a weaker regulatory framework than associations, for low cost home ownership at least.[82]

[77] NHF, 'Housing and Regeneration Bill: Second Reading—28 April 2008' briefing for peers: see www.housing.org.uk.

[78] Conversation with James Tickell, formerly deputy chief executive NHF, now a freelance housing consultant (12 June 2008).

[79] K Cooper, '"Sharp-minded" Mayer to oversee birth of regulator' (16 May 2008) *Inside Housing* 4.

[80] K Cooper, 'Ujima: why didn't anyone step in?' (6 June 2008) *Inside Housing* 26–30, 27.

[81] *Ibid.*

[82] Above n 77 at 6.

No doubt there are those in the housing association world who can see the potential threat to freedoms gained within the confines of regulatory territory. Others, no doubt, have begun to eye up new territories to be conquered. What this exploration of regulatory territory has shown is that the emergence of any new regulatory regime is not only contingent on the nature of the state's regulators; just as critical are the characteristics of those others who will inhabit the territory. In the twenty-first century, the profile of social housing providers in England is significantly different from the 1960s and 1970s. A number of very large housing associations dwarf the municipal providers and any regulatory body. Private lenders are now crucial to the funding of the sector. Norms have changed significantly; both government and many associations are pushing private sector values. The boundaries have moved: private house developers, also large organisations which profess levels of 'expertise', have entered the 'social housing' system; diversity among the existing housing association sector is much reduced as smaller, community-based associations are swallowed up by the largest in the name of 'efficiency'.

What arises from the current re-drawing of boundaries is very hard to predict. Martin Cave, in his report on the review of social housing regulation, used the term 'social housing domain' to encompass the not-for profit and *for* profit providers of social housing in the future. 'Domain' like 'territory', contains the idea of an area controlled or ruled by a common ruler.[83] Does the introduction of profit making businesses into the social housing domain/territory stretch commonality too far? Housing associations long ago threw off the 'voluntary' mantle; what else must they discard if they are to stay in this new domain? As a prominent housing academic has put it: 'the very fabric that has held the system of affordable housing together is being unpicked'.[84]

[83] *Concise Oxford English Dictionary* (10th edn).

[84] P Marsh, 'New landscapes in affordable housing' in D Chevin (ed), *Moving up a Gear: New Challenges for Housing Associations* (London, Smith Institute, 2008) 20.

6

Money

Introduction

GAINING ACCESS TO financial resources has arguably been the *most* critical factor in moulding and shaping housing associations. The mission of associations to provide housing for those unable to afford the alternatives, has led to a continual search for resources to bridge the gap between costs of housing provision and what tenants could afford. Indeed, one reading of the history of the housing association sector would be as a series of attempts to resolve the problematic of 'affordability'.

The relationship between money and the housing association sector can thus be seen to lie at the heart of this book. Finance dominated the beginning of the Federation's story when associations failed to get a central financing corporation; and for the last year, the fallout from the 'credit crunch' has led to weekly news stories of the impact of a heavy reliance on private loans. Financial concerns have also been at the heart of housing associations' concern about their identity as private or public bodies. And financial issues have arisen in each of the preceding chapters, where the shaping and structuring aspect of money has often been central to the power relations at work in the delivery and performance of 'social housing'.

And so it is that accessing financial resources has required the housing association sector to create allies, aligning its interests with those of potential funders who might invest in this project of affordable housing. Through the process of creating allies, money has become one of the most ubiquitous mechanisms of governing.[1] In accessing funding from a range of sources—philanthropists, the local and central state, private companies and lending institutions—associations have not only had to persuade others that their interests lie in funding affordable housing; they have had to acknowledge and internalise at least some of the priorities of their funders. Money therefore creates

[1] The same can be said for local government, where changes to subsidy regimes have been a particularly shaping powerful tool used by central government: see above, ch 4 and, eg, P Malpass and H Aughton, *Housing Finance: A Basic Guide* 5th edn (London, Shelter, 1999).

two-way processes of governing, through mechanisms of 'direct governing'[2]—clear and visible relationships between donor and receiver, governor and governed—and 'governing at a distance'[3]—where both sides come to internalise and normalise the priorities of the other. Money has a way of making both the funder and receiver responsible to each other. The receiver becomes responsible for delivering the demands of the funder, whether a particular rate of return, or a specified number of new homes each year. Funders become responsible for maintaining a flow of funds, ensuring the financial survival of the other. The problem for the social housing providers, however, is that whilst they must remain located in the 'local', private investors in a globalised world have the possibility of taking flight when risk becomes too great.[4]

The chapter begins by considering the language of financial expertise, and the ways that language itself constructs the field through terminology and attempts at scientism. Then follows an exploration of the ways in which the Federation has sought to *translate* the norms of the housing association sector onto those of funders, whilst at the same time translating the priorities of funders back again to members in reminders of the *responsibilities* of housing associations. The first of these is the campaign to lift post-Second World War rent restrictions, the success of which was seen to tie associations closer to the priorities of the State. Then, with the Housing Act 1974 came the means for dramatic expansion, alongside the creation of an asset base which was to become the basis for the future transformation of the sector as an option attractive to private investment. When public funds became threatened by the changing government's neo-conservative ideology, sections of the housing association sector pushed hard at the door of private finance. This became an actuality in the Housing Act 1988 with the deregulation of rents, and once again rents became a battleground, this time with the Federation attempting to govern members' urge to continue expansion through raising rents. The final section considers how private finance has transformed the sector. Attracting private funders required *appearing* to be like private organisations, and so the 1990s saw accountants transforming housing association accounts—the public face of association finance—to make them *look* and *act* like businesses. Now, with private developers entering the social housing domain, the face of social housing looks set to change again.

[2] D Cooper, *Governing Out of Order: Space, Law and the Politics of Belonging* (London, Rivers Oram Press, 1998).

[3] See, eg, P Miller and N Rose, 'Governing Economic Life' (1990) 19 *Economy & Society* 1–31 and above, ch 1.

[4] Z Bauman, *The Individualized Society* (Cambridge, Polity, 2001).

Structuring Relations through the Language of Finance

Whether from the inside or the outside, housing finance appears highly complex. A 'dog's breakfast',[5] and 'whimsical in the extreme'[6] was how Anthony Crosland described it when, in 1975 as Secretary of State for the Environment, he set up a housing finance review. No review, however, has achieved simplification and so a system (or rather, several systems) continues that layers new schemes on top of old, the possibilities of disentanglement becoming ever more distant. The governing relationships that these systems put in place are often obscure, but this obscurity gives scope for both 'governors' and 'governed' to redefine terms to meet varying objectives.

Take the seemingly simple issue of how much housing costs to provide, the answer to which will determine how much funding is required, raising issues of *affordability* and *subsidy*. The answer is by no means simple and raises questions of what is meant by 'housing'. From a development perspective, housing costs are the sums required to build properties and make them ready for occupation. These would include: purchasing land or property; materials and labour costs; fees to consultants; and costs incurred in loan finance (since organisations can seldom fund development from cash). However, if housing is seen as a long-term investment, other costs come into view: paying back the loan, including interest to the lender; keeping the property in an acceptable condition and modernising it to accommodate changing needs and life-styles. Furthermore, since housing 'the poor' has always been seen as a process of *managing* the occupants and their lifestyles,[7] management costs become a significant, if contested factor. These would include staff costs to find tenants, collect rent, taking action on unpaid rent and time spent governing occupants and their relations with neighbours. Viewed from this long-term perspective, the funding of housing becomes a complex and contested affair. Defining 'housing costs' involves judgements about standards: how much space does each person require and what amenities should be provided (central heating is now considered a 'norm', central wiring for computers may become a new 'norm'). It involves judgements about responsibilities towards improving the surrounding environment: shops, leisure facilities, transportation to work—and so the list goes on. Where 'housing' responsibilities end and the responsibilities of others begin is another contested arena. However, I would argue that, in deciding what is 'affordable' housing, decisions on *social*

[5] B Kilroy, *Housing Finance—Organic Reform?* (London, Labour Economic Finance and Taxation Association, 1984).

[6] M Harloe, 'The Green Paper on Housing Policy' in M Brown and S Baldwin (eds), *The Year Book of Social Policy in Britain 1977* (London, Routledge & Kegan Paul, 1978) 4.

[7] See, eg, M Brion and A Tinker, *Women in Housing: Access and Influence* (London, Housing Centre Trust, 1990); D Cowan '"Social" housing and security: some observations' paper to Law and Society Conference (Chicago, May 2004).

needs are frequently made by *financial* experts, accountants whose training contextualises all decisions in terms of *financial* demands and knowledge.[8]

These experts in housing finance create their own division and boundaries for their own convenience. Look at any standard text on housing finance,[9] and expenditure is divided into *capital spending*, incurred in acquiring long-term assets that will have a life beyond the current financial year; and *revenue*, referring to expenditure that occurs in the current financial year and will recur in subsequent years. Buying land is clearly capital expenditure, but annual interest payments on loans is sometimes capital, sometimes revenue. There is rarely debate that salaries of housing managers are revenue, but paying in-house architects, surveyors and development officers might be counted as capital. Repair costs are incurred year on year, but as such work is necessary as an insurance against the diminution of the capital value of the asset, it too could be *capitalised*. These distinctions are not simply a matter of semantics, but have significant impacts on the fortunes of organisations. For example, to avoid politically and socially damaging rent increases, local authorities have allocated the cost of repairs to capital budgets.[10]

All the above considerations are, of course, connected to the problem of *affordability*[11] thereby to the (often contentious) need for *subsidy*. The need to make housing 'affordable' for those on low incomes has given rise to the need for *subsidy*. How much subsidy is required depends on your definition of *affordability*, but attempts at definition create need for further definition. Consider the following:

> Affordability is concerned with securing some given standard of housing (or different standards) at a price or rent which does not impose, in the eyes of some third party (usually government), an unreasonable burden on household incomes. A number of judgements and assumptions are made in putting the concept into practice, and, in broad terms, affordability is assessed by the ratio of a chosen definition of household income to a selected measure of household income in some given period.[12]

In the UK, high land and property values have been principal factors driving housing policy.[13] Nineteenth century philanthropic organisations tried to bridge the gap with charity, offering 5 per cent return on investment; their failure to

[8] M Power, 'Education Accountants: Towards a Critical Ethnography' (1991) 16 *Accounting, Organizations and Society* 333–53.

[9] Eg, K Gibb, M Munro and M Satsangi, *Housing Finance in the UK: An Introduction* 2nd edn (London, Macmillan, 1999); D Garnett and J Perry, *Housng Finance* 3rd edn (Coventry, Chartered Institute of Housing, 2005).

[10] For more detailed discussion, see: D Cowan and M McDermont, *Regulating Social Housing: Governing Decline* (London, Glasshouse, 2006) ch 4.

[11] Affordability can be achieved in two ways: by lowering standards to levels that people can afford from income (the Word Bank approach in the developing world); or by setting a standard and subsidising the homes of those who cannot afford to meet it.

[12] D Maclennan and R Williams, *Affordable Housing in Britain and America* (York, Joseph Rowntree Foundation, 1990) 9.

[13] Malpass and Aughton, above n 1 at 10–11.

provide sufficient working class housing at 'acceptable' standards arguably led to the necessity for state *subsidies*.[14] Here again, the boundaries are blurred: what *counts* as subsidy is highly contestable. Housing economists have defined it as 'action initiated by government which, by means of an implicit or explicit flow of funds, reduces the relative cost of producing or consuming housing'.[15] Grants, housing allowances, sub-market interest rates and reduced total loan costs are all examples of explicit flows of funds. Subsidies are either directed at the housing producer ('bricks-and-mortar' subsidy), or at the housing occupier (personal subsidies). The term 'subsidy' becomes political: for many years the Treasury refused to call tax relief on owner-occupier mortgages subsidy, preferring 'income foregone'.[16] Similarly, tax relief claimed by charitable organisations can also be seen as state subsidy.[17] It is political because it can be used to obscure the impact of political programmes: housing benefit, a social security payment, has become an integral element in the housing finance system. When the Conservative Government in the 1980s wanted to reduce public expenditure, it cut grant levels for housing association schemes; to cope with this, associations increased rents which resulted in soaring housing benefit costs.

Finally, the *public–private distinction* plays itself out in a highly complex way in housing finance. Chapter two demonstrated how this distinction has been critical to housing associations' finances at various points since the 1940s. Current Treasury rules that limit the amount of public borrowing have been crucial in recent transformations of social housing in England. For an organisation to borrow outside the Public Sector Net Cash Requirement (PSNCR) it must be in private ownership and control.[18] This rule meant that central government set strict limits on borrowing by local authorities, which has resulted in them being unable to fund the necessary improvements to their housing stock. Freedom from this constraint, and the many other financial restrictions on local authority spending and borrowing, has provided impetus for local housing authorities to transfer their housing stock to housing associations; associations as *private* bodies are not subject to PSNCR limits and other constraints.[19]

However, under European Union (EU) competition law, state subsidies to housing associations themselves may not be legal if they 'upset the level playing field'.[20] EU competition law makes no allowances for hybrid organisations, drawing a sharp line between public and private.[21] The reidentification of

[14] S Merrett, *State Housing in Britain* (London, Routledge & Kegan Paul, 1979) 19.

[15] MEA Haffner and MJ Oxley, 'Housing Subsidies: Definitions and Comparisons' (1999) 14 *Housing Studies* 145–62, 148.

[16] P Malpass, 'Policy making in interesting times: the Housing Finance and Policy Review, 1975–77' (2008) 2(1) *People, Place and Policy Online.*

[17] See above, ch 3.

[18] Garnett and Perry, above n 9 at 81.

[19] *Ibid*, 94–95.

[20] H Priemus, 'Real Estate Investors and Housing Associations: A Level Playing Field? The Dutch Case' (2008) 8(1) *European Journal of Housing Policy* 81–96, 82.

[21] *Ibid.*

housing associations in England as *private* organisations in the context of the Housing Act 1988 and private finance has other contentious spin-offs, not least the question as to whether housing associations must comply with the Human Rights Act 1998 (discussed below in chapter eight).[22]

Finance, and financial distinctions, are then both rigid (in that they are tied by rules and regulations) and malleable (in that the obscurity of rules can be put to work). A central point in this rigidity/malleability has been the setting of rents: the extent of housing associations' freedom to determine their income from rents has not just signified their commitment to their mission of affordable housing, but has been a symbol of their independence. Judgements about 'affordability' become intertwined with judgements about housing standards, tenants' lifestyles and the organisation's viability and potential for expansion, a story which occurs in several forms in the next section.

The Federation Intervenes

Rent Restrictions and Responsibilisation

For the housing association sector, the Second World War meant limited activity: new building and maintenance work were subject to tight statutory control and income was restricted by the rent freeze under the Rent and Mortgage Interest (War Restrictions) Act 1939.[23] Nevertheless, the Federation's *Bulletins* were full of hope that the end of the war would mean an important new role for associations in post-war reconstruction. However, the continuing existence of the 1939 Act after 1945 meant that the Federation's principal preoccupation became a campaign to lift rent restrictions.[24]

'Campaign' is very much what it appeared. It began in 1947 with the submission of a 'substantial memorandum' to the Ministry and an all-party meeting attended by eighty MPs.[25] The Federation wanted the issue to be seen as 'wholly non-political', merely one of basic arithmetic: 'a rent of 1s. 6d. will not cover the

[22] See *Donaghue v Poplar HARCA* (2001) 33 HLR 823–46; for discussion, see: M McDermont, 'The elusive nature of the "public function": *Poplar Housing and Regeneration Community Association Ltd v* Donoghue' (2003) 66 *Modern Law Review* 113–23; most recently, *London and Quadrant Housing Trust v Weaver* [2009] EWCA Civ 587.

[23] The Act froze all rents, except those of local authorities, at September 1939 levels: P Malpass, *Housing Associations and Housing Policy: A Historical Perspective* (Basingstoke, Macmillan, 2000) 114–15.

[24] The 1945 Labour Government's emphasis was on facilitating local government to deal with the housing crisis by introducing more a generous subsidy regime for local authorities whilst retaining stringent wartime restrictions on the private sector: see *Malpass, ibid* at 117–23. As noted above in ch 2, the Federation did succeed in persuading the Labour Government to approve appropriate housing association schemes that local authorities considered met local housing demands.

[25] *QB* 58, July 1951, 3–5.

cost of repairs'.[26] However, the a-political approach of the campaign failed to create allies since the matter was, indeed, *highly* political. The Labour Government 'would rather deprive the local authorities of their exemption from the Rent Acts than give it to voluntary housing associations'; and the Conservative Party said that 'if housing associations were exempted, then all other landlords must be exempted from the Acts'.[27] Attempts to persuade the Minister of Health by taking him to see estates 'where the ceilings were falling down' and the association's accounts showed them to be 'practically bankrupt', produced no shift in government policy.[28]

However, the Federation gathered other allies. *The Times*, concerned about the effect of the continuing restrictions on private renting, published a letter from the Federation's chairman and continued a campaign on the issue for several years. In November 1953 its leader column spoke out stridently against the policy, now continued by the Conservative Government:

> The greatest cost of all is the widespread, inexorable, cumulative decay to which millions of useable dwellings are being condemned by their owner's want of means to keep them in good repair [. . .] Britain will not have a rational housing policy until she begins by taking proper care of the dwellings she has, rather than sacrificing them for those she might have.[29]

The restrictions were eventually lifted by the Housing Rents and Repairs Act 1954. The Federation's chairman claimed this as a great success for the organisation, a demonstration of its power to influence government:

> It is true that we have been pressing for changes for some years past and I was even able last year to suggest that some changes might come about, but I cannot remember any case where the demands of an organisation have been met in such full measure as we have received.[30]

The Federation, as a representative body rather than a 'productive' body, relied on the actions of others to effect change. It had to call into question existing modes of governing and then align its members' interests with the interests of others. It then needed to ensure that its solutions were seen as 'obligatory passage points' for the resolution of the problems of others.[31] However, this process was not uni-directional. It had an important role in translating its members' needs into the programmes of others; and in aligning with the interests of others, it needed to recognise and take on board the interests of allies. The process of persuasion

[26] *Ibid*, 3.
[27] *Ibid.*
[28] *Ibid.*
[29] *The Times* leader column (November 1953): quoted in *QB* 64, January 1953, 18.
[30] National Federation of Housing Societies (NFHS), *Report of the Seventeenth Annual Meeting* (28 May 1954) (London, NFHS, 1954) 3.
[31] M Callon, 'Some elements of a sociology of translation: domestication of the scallops and the fisherman of St Brieuc Bay' in J Law, *Power, Action and Belief: A New Sociology of Knowledge?* (London, Routledge & Kegan Paul, 1986).

and aligning of interests became one of acting on *both* the interests of external actor-allies, *and* of members, for both must come to recognise and accommodate the interests of the other.

The Federation portrayed its 'success' in campaigning against rent restrictions as to an alignment of central government policies with housing association needs. It now sought to align associations' interests with those of the Conservative Government that had brought about their new financial freedom. Federation officers argued that, with the freedoms and powers associations had gained under the 1954 Act, came 'new responsibilities'. The financial freedom to raise rents to cover the costs of repairs to existing properties should free up associations' resources. Ministers expected these resources to be used to support its programme to improve the condition of the older housing stock through reconditioning. The Minister 'hopes [that] the Housing Rents and Repairs Bill will enable Housing Associations to play an important part in the reconditioning and he .. await[s] developments with great interest'.[32]

Lord Gage, president of the Federation's council, also argued that the 1954 Act implied another, 'more subtle, responsibility': to act responsibly and not to impair the 'high reputation of associations in Parliament'. It was the new power of eviction which was the subject of his warnings:

> [E]viction always gets publicity and a few injudicious cases of eviction might cause harmful publicity out of all proportion to the hardship which this eviction actually causes.[33]

Any amendments to the Act which might become necessary to deal with 'what, in the opinion of Parliament, might be thought abuses . . . would undoubtedly affect the whole of the Housing Association Movement'.[34] These new powers were particularly symbolic. In order to achieve financial freedom to set their own rent levels, associations' responsibilities had became aligned to another agenda—increasing the housing supply through buying up and improving existing property. 'Reconditioning' as this work was termed, had been promoted by the Federation as a housing association expertise from the outset (see above,chapter two) and so the aligning of the Federation's and governmental interests appeared 'natural'. 'Our object' said the Federation chairman, 'is to serve the cause of housing through the channels appropriately available to us, and also in the manner required of us by Parliament'.[35]

The 1954 Act created a new area of expertise for the Federation, guiding associations through circulars and standard forms of letters to tenants, advising on how to deal with these new responsibilities.[36] However, it could not assume

32 (NFHS), *Report of the Seventeenth Annual Meeting*, above n 30 at 4.
33 *Ibid.*
34 *Ibid.*
35 *Ibid* at 7.
36 *QB* 73, April 1955, 15.

that its members would be enrolled as allies to central government priorities: associations perceived a number of competing priorities on their financial resources. At the 1956 AGM, the president berated associations for still not playing a key role in housing,[37] but delegates raised the need to alleviate hardship caused to tenants by the 1954 Act rent increases. Seeing a conflict between affordability and obligations towards a government that had enabled their financial freedom, they argued for the establishment of rent rebate schemes to help particularly their older tenants. Some associations had already set up their own informal schemes and in 1956 the Ministry of Housing and Local Government issued a circular on Differential Rent Schemes.[38]

Private Funders and Responsibilities

Whilst relations with government created its own set of responsibilities, so too did attempts to seek funding from private sources. It had been the practice of associations to raise funding through the sale of shares. In 1938, the Federation set up the Housing Societies Investment Trust (HSIT), its objectives being to help 'new Societies with finance in the early days' and to address the issue of the lack of marketability of shares in housing associations.[39] The first objective, however, got lost as the Trust became embroiled in the conflict of *responsibilities* of the second. The motive behind this second objective appears as a strange combination of responsibilities: towards member societies, who needed public confidence in their share value in order to attract new subscribers; and towards the executors of estates of deceased shareholders. This conflict is exemplified in a dispute between Hugh's Settlement[40] and the Registrar of Friendly Societies.[41] The society wanted to pay off shares of an 'elderly shareholder', 'deprived . . . of her chief means of livelihood by bomb damage'. 'Every right-minded Society aims at making its shares worth their par value' claimed the Society's secretary (though acknowledging the difficulty of ascertaining the value of shares at any particular point in time). The Registrar appears not to have agreed.

The HSIT suffered from lack of investment which made its activities of buying shares in societies difficult. Its freedom of operation was further limited by a rule made by the Minister of Health, which allowed that anyone could invest in Trust loan stock, but only societies which were members of the Federation were allowed to take up shares.[42] By 1951, the capital of the Trust amounted to £12,000, £2000 from Housing Societies and £10,000 invested by individuals in

[37] *QB* 78, July 1956, 8.
[38] *Ibid* at 34.
[39] Reginald Brown, Secretary of NHFS, *OB* 35, September 1945, 10–11.
[40] A society registered with the Registrar of Friendly Societies (RFS) as an Industrial and Provident Society.
[41] BH Nixon (honorary secretary, Hugh's Settlement) 'The Right to Pay off Shares' in *OB* 35, September 1945, 11.
[42] *QB* 58, July 1951 6.

loan stock. Only 31 of the Federation's 400 societies had any money invested in the Trust, despite its alleged position as 'an integral part of the Housing Society Movement'.

The longer-term significance of the failure of HSIT was its inability to construct allies among building societies or other lending institutions. There is little evidence that the Federation had much impact in persuading institutional investors to invest either in HSIT or directly in associations. The Federation reported various negotiations with the Co-operative Building Society 'with a view to enabling housing associations to borrow money on improved terms',[43] but no significant successes.

The Housing Act 1974: Asset Building

Failure in raising significant support from the private finance sector continued, even the Conservative Government's 1960s experiment in cost-rent housing societies producing little.[44] However, rising public concern about poor housing conditions produced increases in support from charitable donations (see below, chapter seven) and some local authorities. This contributed to mobilising central government support (both politicians and civil servants), resulting in the Housing Act 1974. This Act was a momentous piece of legislation, both for the registration and monitoring system it established for the sector[45] and the new funding system that it put in place, based on 100 per cent funding from the Exchequer, in the form of a mix of loans and grants—Housing Association Grant (HAG). Particularly important was that HAG was not a *revenue* subsidy to meet part of the running costs, as nearly all housing subsidies for both local authorities and housing associations had been up until then,[46] but a *capital* grant paid in tranches throughout the project. The grant was paid by the Housing Corporation (or local authority if sponsor) and rents were set by the Rent Officer (a state official). HAG was not a flat-rate grant per unit, but calculated at the end of the project on the basis of what the scheme could afford, given the allowed rent. Out of rental income received, associations could deduct standard amounts for managing and maintaining the property. What was left would be used to fund a *public* loan. The new grant system was, therefore, virtually risk-free for associations whilst at the same time not tying government into long-term subsidies. Its principal architect was John Baker, a civil servant with little previous background in housing. It was, he believed, his career history that had been responsible for the capital grant system:

43 *OB* 31, January – March 1944, 2.
44 This episode is discussed above in chs 2 and 5.
45 See above, ch 5.
46 Above n 1 at 49.

> The Nat[ional] Fed[eration]'s lobbying stance with the politicians was revenue subsidies. The policy of the Heath government of the day, and certainly the policy of the Treasury, was that open-ended revenue subsidies should be avoided like the plague, a view to which I happen to subscribe . [. . .] I'd been in the Ministry of Transport where I'd worked on the finances of the nationalised transport industries. [I had seen] the way revenue deficit grant doesn't work, because it gives no incentive to management to be efficient and it gives no certainty to the tax-payer that you ever get value for money. When I was transferred [. . .] into the housing policy [division], I brought with me what I had learned in the Department of Transport, and I was also by then Business School trained. So I had two very different features to the people who had worked in housing finance all their lives, who had always been in the business of handing out subsidies to local authorities. So, I think if I hadn't had that background, I doubt the legislation would have come out the way it did.

The HAG system signalled distinction from the old because it arose out of a different type of expertise. Baker's designs were an act of 'translation': he was translating current political anxieties and imperatives into systems that could encompass the demands of this external environment—the housing association sector.

Defending Boundaries, Becoming Private: The Housing Act 1988

The capital grant system allowed housing associations to develop and grow very rapidly. Instead of developing tens of new properties each year, associations like Notting Hill HT began to develop hundreds. There was no shortage of money—quite the opposite according to Richard Best, who recalls chairman of the Corporation Lou Sherman

> exhorting the associations to 'spend the money. If you do not spend the money it won't be there next year!' Then it was 'you didn't spend it, I've had to struggle to keep the money up, you've got to work harder'. They really were pressed to achieve.

Associations grew rapidly, from small voluntary organisations to large bureaucracies employing many paid, professional staff. Indeed a Federation publication in 1976, advocated rapid growth rather than incremental change.[47] Such a rate of development produced its own momentum. Many associations established large teams of architects, surveyors and development managers to run their development programmes—development became their driving force. The Conservative election victory in 1979, with its ideological commitment to cutting public spending, threatened this growth leading some to look for opportunities that would reduce reliance on public funding, 'innovations' and new tenures to take them outside the restrictions of public funding. The development of shared ownership homes (in which an occupier owns a proportion of the property and

[47] NFHA, *Growing Pains: Coping with the Problems of Growth in Housing Associations* (London, NFHA, 1977) discussed below in ch 8.

pays rent to the association for the other share) required associations to bring in an element of private finance. Such innovations were very much in line with the Thatcher Government's ideology of promoting home ownership, but nevertheless only came about through battles with public and private bodies. The Department of the Environment (DoE) had to be persuaded that this was an appropriate direction for associations to take and the Building Societies Association, which had little understanding of housing associations, was 'very difficult'.[48] It was partly through the support of the Nationwide Building Society, the renamed Co-operative Building Society, that such schemes were enabled to work.

The importance of this move was in the normative shift it induced: some, of the new regulatory community that the 1974 Act had produced, could see a future of less reliance on public grant, a spurning of the 'public' status that associations had been glad to accept under the 1974 Act terms. There were, however, hurdles to be overcome and as in previous legislative changes, alliances to be made and battles to be won. In 1983, the board of the Housing Corporation had to be persuaded to set up a working group to consider private finance for housing associations, 'very much against the Board's political judgement about what was feasible. They considered that in terms of financial policy, private borrowing by associations was most unlikely to be acceptable'.[49] The Federation set up a Private Finance Working Party in 1986 and through joint working between the Federation and the Corporation, persuaded first the DoE and then the Treasury that private financing of housing associations was possible and necessary.[50]

The critical actor, as ever, was the Treasury.[51] For the Treasury, the issue was whether private finance would bring in any *additional* funding. According to Treasury rules, unless there was a transfer of *risk* to associations, any private loans would still be counted as *public* borrowing. It was the cash limits on public borrowing that associations were trying to escape. A number of experimental schemes were set up. North Housing Association, a large, financially strong association based in the North East of England,[52] started a project in 1986 based on 30 per cent grant which relied on developing in areas of high property values (so North Housing moved south, to the affluent Home Counties), land contributed by local authorities at no cost and with a substantial contribution from association reserves. Most critically, properties had to be let on private sector

[48] Interview with John Coward: Notting Hill Housing Trust pioneered shared ownership (30 June 2003).

[49] Interview with Ken Bartlett, who was Policy Director at the Housing Corporation in 1983 (30 June 2003).

[50] Federation interviewees spoke of joint working; however, David Edmonds, Chief Executive of the Corporation at the time, claimed the credit.

[51] See above, ch 5, and the need to find a way forward acceptable to the Treasury for the 1974 Act to be possible.

[52] See P Malpass and C Jones, *Home Housing Association: A History* (Newcastle, Home Housing Association, 1995).

assured tenancies so that rents were not constrained by the rent officer's 'fair rent' determination. These 'assured' rents were in effect 25 per cent higher than fair rents.[53] The Federation worked on a pilot scheme with the Nationwide Building Society and 30 per cent HAG from the Corporation. Having convinced the Nationwide to become involved with the shared ownership programme, they had now become important allies in demonstrating that private funding could work. To the government, their support demonstrated that sources of funding could be found, and to other funders they could act as translators of the business of associations.

In technical terms, the most significant hurdle was removed once the Treasury accepted that associations could become risk bearers; now the private finance element of a mixed funded regime would not count as public borrowing, even if the public grant were more than 50 per cent of the project costs. The Housing Act 1988 which de-regulated rents on new schemes, and on all new tenancies, enabled associations return to private finance.

The Impact of the Housing Act 1988: Reshaping Housing Associations

Looking back, we can now see that the 1974 Act capital grant system was highly significant for the long-term financing of housing associations. The system enabled associations to build up an asset base unencumbered by private loans and funded by subsidy that future governments could not withdraw, in the way that they could withdraw revenue subsidy.[54] Inflation further improved their financial situation 'by eroding the burden of debt incurred on new projects'.[55] It was this asset base, built up by the direct application of *public* funds, that could be put to work as security against which they could raise private finance. However, what is frequently overlooked in contemporary narratives is that the translation of the sector from public to private in the late 1980s was highly controversial at the time. A recent article in *Inside Housing*, the magazine for housing professionals, entitled 'Look how far we've come',[56] concentrates on the massive changes created, the professionalisation of the sector and the bright future it brought for associations: 'Without the '88 Act [the legislative change required to enable private finance to happen] we would have withered on the vine' was the verdict of one housing association chief executive. Richard Best, then Director of the Federation, identifies the changes in the housing association

[53] Malpass, *Housing Associations and Housing Policy*, above n 23 at 179.

[54] This is a slight oversimplification, since it would have been open for government to consider directing the use of associations' reserves.

[55] P Malpass, 'The Rise of Housing Associations' in R Rowlands and P Malpass (eds), *Housing Markets and Policy* (London, Routledge, 2009).

[56] D Blackman, (28 March 2008) *Inside Housing* 15–18.

sector in the 1980s with the subsequent fundamental shift in the delivery of public services: 'It was a precursor to all the public private initiatives that have happened in other sectors'. The article makes no reference to the opposition of many in the housing association sector to what was seen as a 'selling out' of principles. However, David Edmonds, Housing Corporation chief executive at the time, described resistance from *within* the housing association sector as obstructive. From this perspective the housing association sector was

> a very well-meaning [sector], not withstanding a few big players, and a very amateur movement. [. . .] there were tensions within the [Federation] and it was very difficult to get coherence. If you went along to a meeting of the Federation Council, you saw that it was dominated by a kind of block vote, and therefore the people you were looking to drive forward the big changes, were often I think constrained by what they could say and do.

In his view, the 1988 Act was brought in 'in the teeth of resistance from the National Federation and much of the housing association movement'.[57]

There were two principal concerns within the sector. The first was the threat to diversity. Smaller associations and co-operatives would be unable to raise private loans (because they did not have a large asset base to act as security), or would be unable to obtain favourable lending rates. The fear was that where the registration system had not succeeded in narrowing down the field of associations, private finance would. Only a limited number would be able to compete in the 'brave new world'.[58]

The second concern arose from the new freedom to set rents at levels that suited private funding. The deregulation of housing association rents (accompanied by simultaneous reforms in the commercial rented sector) was a key aspect of the 1988 Act.[59] The freedom to vary rents to ensure that loans repayments could be met was a necessary condition for private funders to make loans to the housing association sector. However, this freedom, along with the competitive bidding environment set up by the Housing Corporation, brought associations once again into conflict with their 'mission' of providing affordable housing. Once again, the Federation sought to govern its members on the issue of rents.

The Federation's Affordability Campaign

The issue of affordable rents was to dominate the Federation's agenda for some time following the 1988 Act. The fear was that rents would become unaffordable to the poorest households whom associations still considered to be their main clients. The rationale of the new grant funding system was 'value for money': in order to make their bids more 'competitive', that is, require less grant, associations

57 Interview with David Edmonds (30 July 2003).
58 See above ch 2, text associated with fn 89.
59 Malpass, *Housing Associations and Housing Policy*, above n 23, at 202–03.

could either cut costs or increase borrowing. Higher loans meant higher rents. Alongside this, a plethora of 'initiatives' to tackle homelessness were devised by central government, local authorities and housing associations, which involved associations managing private sector properties and letting them at market rents. Higher rents almost became a rationale of housing policy. For the government, affordability was not the issue: cutting capital spend was the goal; personal subsidies in the form of housing benefit would take the strain of higher rents. The Federation, however, argued that this created a poverty trap. Tenants would have to remain on benefit if they were to pay their rent, and new tenancies could only be let to people in receipt of benefit (or in well-paid employment, potentially counter to associations' objectives).

In an attempt to define affordability, the Federation carried out an extensive survey of housing association tenants' income and expenditure. Their initial assumption was that rents should be no more than 20 per cent of net household income, subsequently revised to 22 per cent. The Federation set up a system for recording and monitoring housing association rents called CORE (COntinuous REcording). Associations' CORE returns were compared against the acceptable 'affordable' rents, with reports appearing periodically in the Federation's in-house magazine, showing proportions of associations with rents above target. In December 1993, the Federation's council adopted a new policy:

> Rents are affordable if the majority of working households are not caught in the poverty trap because of dependency on housing benefit or paying more than 25 per cent of their net income on rent.[60]

The Federation was, in effect, attempting to govern its members through a form of performance monitoring, for it was competition between associations, as well as government policy, that was pushing up rents. Many in the sector would not have recognised it as an attempt at regulation, but the shaming of associations setting high rents to win grant competitions was a tactic similar to school league tables and the Audit Commission's publication of inspection results. Tables showing percentages of rents above affordability levels had the effect of differentiating the 'bad', a distinction that had echoes of the labelling of the 'fee-grabbers' in the early 1970s.

Eventually the Treasury realised it could not sustain the massively increased housing benefit bill that high rents had created. It was then that the Housing Corporation began to judge the value for money bids on the basis of 'total public subsidy', a calculation that took account of housing benefit as well as capital subsidies, and associations were forced to limit rent levels to stay competitive. To David Edmonds, the Federation's affordability campaign had been 'unrealistic' as well as a failure, but as a tactic of governing it was facing several ways at once. The

[60] NFHA, *Facing the Future: Annual Report 1993–94*, 13.

Corporation and the Federation may have shared the same regulatory community, common language and frequently the same goals, but each had a different role to play and different history. For the Federation, affordability was of central importance in holding together a diversity of organisations that still saw themselves as part of a 'voluntary housing movement', 'motivated by a desire to contribute to society or help the needy'.[61] It *had* to take a stand. So CORE was a public statement, a symbol of intent, aimed at members and local authorities. And CORE had other targets of governing: the Housing Corporation and central government. By attempting to define affordability and to control rents, the Federation was making a statement about what good, responsible government should be. Nevertheless, it was the financial implications of a more sophisticated understanding of *value for money*, not unaffordable rents, that drove government to take affordability seriously.

Accountants and Lenders Shaping Housing Associations

Despite the Federation's attempts to pull associations back to their 'mission', the focus and identity of the housing association sector had completely changed. Private finance had realigned the sector with the interests of private markets. Accountants, finance managers and ratings agencies became significant shapers of the once 'voluntary' housing sector. In this reshaping, housing association accounts played a significant role.

Accounts can appear as a relatively dull, perhaps impenetrable, aspect of associations. Nevertheless, along with annual reports, they are an integral aspect of their public imagery. As such they became the focus of the Federation's expertise. Since the 1970s, the Federation had worked with the Housing Corporation to formulate a recommended form for the accounts of associations. Initial objectives were limited: to achieve consistency and comparability so that officials in central and local government and the Corporation could understand housing association accounts and make comparisons. This was an accountants' exercise in tidying up the 'mess'[62] of a myriad of hybrid forms that management committees had invented to meet their own requirements. In creating order out of chaos, accountants began the process of inscribing their own normative values on the sector, a set of values that were sourced in their training and in the norms of the corporate business sector.[63] Their specialist knowledge base could translate the affairs of associations into formats that made them readable by those who funded

[61] A Kearns, *Voluntarism Management and Accountability* (Glasgow, Housing Associations Research Unit, University of Glasgow, 1990) 44: findings from a survey of the motivations of voluntary management committee members.

[62] Interview with Stephen Duckworth (13 November 2002).

[63] Power, above n 8.

associations.[64] The exercise was not simply rearranging the pieces on a board; accountants were changing the nature of the game itself. For, as the need to raise private finance became paramount, the 'audience' that associations were speaking to changed significantly. In the lead again was one of the pioneers of private finance, North Housing, which changed its name to Home Housing so as not to deter local authorities and lenders in the south of England. Home's board decided to adopt a more commercial set of accounts, *plc* (public limited company) accounting. Stephen Duckworth, the Federation's Finance Director, recalls the importance of this decision: 'The old formats were largely torn up, and a lot of new concepts came in, which made the accounts come fairly close to a commercial company form'. Legislative changes followed which allowed housing associations to adopt company-style accounts.[65]

Like statistics and maps, accounts can have the appearance of neutrality. They are better understood as part of a range of techniques that are extremely influential in 'making up' organisations.[66] Accountants understand the interrelationship between accounting practices and making individuals and organisations responsible, but outside the accountancy profession this is little recognised.[67] The format of accounts acts as an influence on the actions of others in two ways. First, by presenting information in a particular manner they produce a certain set of (financial) truths, removing others from view and so structure the decisions of decision-makers (for example, housing association boards and their funders); and secondly, by requiring that 'facts' be presented in a particular format, they structure an organisation's possible field of action. Formats and rules of accounts have become the domain of the accountancy profession, with the Accounting Standards Board (ASB). The ASB establishes principles of accountancy through sector-specific Statements of Recommended Practice (SORPs). Just as principles of affordability involve value judgements, these principles 'appeal not only to judgment but to conscience'.[68] The SORP principles are

> not a statutory requirement but something auditors will expect. It's a recommended form, but it incorporates financial reporting standards which any audit firm will require as effectively a mandatory requirement on their clients, but if the clients did not want to do it themselves, there is a bit of argy-bargy. But because a sector like our sector

[64] *Cf* B Latour, 'Visualisation and Cognition: Thinking with Eyes and Hands' (1986) 6 *Knowledge and Society: Studies in the Sociology of Culture, Past and Present* 1–40.

[65] NHF, *Statement of Recommended Practice (SORP): Accounting for Registered Social Landlords* (London, NHF, 1999) para 304.

[66] See, eg, I Hacking, 'Making Up People' in TC Heller (ed), *Reconstructing Individualism* (Stanford, Stanford University Press, 1986) 222–36.

[67] P Miller, 'Accounting and Objectivity: The Invention of Calculating Selves and Calculable Spaces' (1992) 91 *Annals of Scholarship* 61–86.

[68] The chairman of the ASB interview with Mary Keegan, chairman of the Accountancy Standards Board, reported in *The Guardian* (16 February 2002).

> needs tweaks to a purely commercial model, what SORP does is make those tweaks, primarily to get consistency across the sector, for a sector which has a number of oddities.[69]

In 1992, the Federation approached the ASB to develop a housing association SORP. However, the new SORP adopted in 1999[70] was clearly not simply a matter of 'tweaks' or changing appearances. These were new practices that could dramatically alter the fortunes of housing associations: 'William Sutton plunges into the red as new SORP regime takes effect' was the headline in *Social Housing*[71] following the William Sutton Trust's adoption of revised accounting practices.[72] It was not only William Sutton, however, that should be concerned:

> The deterioration in the Trust's financial position comes at a time when the DETR is examining the scope for restructuring council and RSL rents and converging rents in the sector.[73]

The change in accounting format and standards was one vital and visible alteration of housing associations' practices, in which the Federation worked to create sector-wide good practice.

Restructuring Rents

So whilst this chapter began with the ways in which the state's control over financial resources (freedom to set rents and subsidies) shaped housing associations, the story ends with associations being shaped and controlled by *private* funders. There is, however, an interesting twist to the tale, contained in central government's most recent *re-structuring* of social housing rents.

Proposals to change the way in which all social landlords—local authorities and housing associations—set their rents were 'one of the most high-profile and fundamental changes'[74] presented in the New Labour Government's Housing Green Paper published in 2000.[75] The Government claimed that the need to restructure rents arose in part from the disparities between local authority and housing association rents (in 2003, housing association rents were on average £8.00 higher than local authority rents); and also to provide 'a closer link between

[69] Interview with Stephen Duckworth, above n 62.

[70] *Ibid*, n 65.

[71] (July 2000) *Social Housing* 15.

[72] NHF, *Statement of Recommended Practice (SORP)*, above n 66.

[73] See above, n 71.

[74] B Walker and A Marsh, 'Setting the Rents of Social Housing: The Impact and Implications of Rent Restructuring in England' (2003) 40 *Urban Studies* 2023–47, 2027. For a detailed of rent restructuring see: A Marsh, 'Restructuring social housing rents' in D Cowan and A Marsh (eds), *Two Steps Forward: Housing Policy for the New Millennium* (Bristol, The Policy Press, 2001).

[75] Department of the Environment, Transport and the Regions/Department of Social Security, *Quality and Choice: A Decent Home for All*, The Housing Green Paper (London, HMSO, 2000) ch 10.

rents and the qualities tenants value in their properties'.[76] The rent-setting formula for all social landlords was set out in government guidance, taking into account property value, number of bedrooms and local earnings.[77] Now, what is interesting about this episode is that, whilst it was argued in 1988 that deregulation of rents was an absolute requirement for attracting private funders to the housing association sector, the subsequent imposition of rent restructuring on the housing association sector has been achieved with little complaint that it would lead to the demise of private finance.[78] An element of private funders' acceptance of the new regime may lie in the underpinning rationale that there should be a clearer link between 'price signals and hence incentives for tenants to optimise their housing consumption' and in its incentive to invest in areas of appreciated asset values.[79] These are two ways of thinking that private funders understand.

Conclusion: Into the Future?

This chapter has sought to demonstrate the ways in which financial systems, mechanisms and indeed the *language* of finance have been significant in shaping and re-shaping the housing association sector. Associations have sought various levels of freedom in their financial affairs: in particular, the freedom to set rents has been central to their idea of *independence*. However, with freedom comes *responsibilities*. In the 1950s, the Federation used its success in releasing associations from the government restrictions of the war-time rent freeze to argue that associations had responsibilities to government to implement housing policy. Following the removal of rent-setting restrictions under the Housing Act 1988 (necessary for associations to be able to access private finance), the Federation again tried to *govern* associations, emphasising that their commitment to meeting the housing needs of the poorest tenants required them to keep rent levels within certain levels.

Following the Housing Act 1974, the housing association sector was happy to exchange a large degree of independence for 100 per cent public funding; associations lost responsibility for rent setting, which became the domain of the rent officer. However, such acceptance of an essentially *public* status was temporary and contingent. When it became clear that public funds could no longer fund their ambitions for expansion, associations looked to reclassify themselves as *private* organisations, and turned to the private finance markets to fund their

[76] *Ibid*, para 10.1.

[77] Department of the Environment, Transport and the Regions (DETR), *Guide to Social Rent Reforms* (London, DETR, 2000).

[78] Many thanks to Peter Malpass for this interesting observation.

[79] Walker and Marsh, above n 74 at 2043.

programmes. This move has, over the two decades since the 1988 Act, transformed completely the housing association sector. In no sense can twenty-first century housing associations be considered 'voluntary'; they prefer to think of themselves as 'social businesses', a term that, whether deliberately or not, blurs the line between profit-making and not-for-profit. Associations see themselves as adopting a more commercial approach[80] and some associations can be seen benchmarking themselves with commercial organisations such as Marks and Spencer.[81]

Associations have changed in size too. The need to be able to raise finance on the best terms has prompted mergers and group structures. Now the largest associations dwarf local authorities; their financing deals now in billions, not thousands or millions.[82] Associations' need for private finance in effect means that they are running out of options for funding from their traditional sources of banks and building societies, particularly with the 'credit crunch' prompting 'lenders to lose their housing appetites', as the housing press puts it.[83] For some of the largest associations, their need for private finance is making them question their not-for-profit status, as they consider what would have once been the unthinkable—floatation on the stock market.[84]

Unsurprisingly perhaps, the whole world of social housing finance and regulation is being questioned, with previously unthinkable ideas now being thought, even aired in public. The Homes and Communities Agency which will take over the funding of social housing once the Housing Corporation disappears, is considering abandoning the existing grant system, replacing it with an investment-based system that would enable the Agency to 'take a slice of the profits if homes it invests in increase in value'.[85] new regulatory regime proposed by the Cave Review[86] of social housing regulation also sees the world of social housing regulation from an economist's view. Despite the report's title, *Every Tenant Counts,* the economists view prevails. 'Key parts of the review's proposals relate to attracting new providers and increasing efficiency of existing providers'.[87] Expanding supply can be neatly shoe-horned into a strategy that seemingly puts tenants first, because what tenants want (allegedly) is choice. The review is

80 R Chaplin, M Jones, S Martin, M Pryke, C Royce, P Saw, C Whitehead, C Hong Yang and J Hong Yang, *Rents and Risks: Investing in Housing Associations* (York, Joseph Rowntree Foundation, 1995) 11.

81 K Murray, 'Street smart' (20 September 2002) *Inside Housing* 18.

82 C Stothart, 'Billion pound breakthrough' (February 2007) *Inside Finance* 10–13.

83 C Dowler, 'Crunch prompts lenders to lose their housing appetites' (11 April 2008) *Inside Housing* 3.

84 M Hilditch, 'Landlord explores flotation' (5 January 2008) *Inside Housing* 1; 'Flotation considered by many of sector's big hitters' (26 January 2008) *Inside Housing* 3.

85 B Nadeem, 'Investment over grant as agency moots funding shift' (25 April, 2008) *Inside Housing* 3.

86 M Cave, *Every Tenant Matters: A Review of Social Housing Regulation* (Wetherby, Yorks, Communities and Local Government Publications, 2007) and www.communities.gov.uk/index.asp?id=1511391.

87 *Ibid*, para 5.15.

also careful not to upset the private lending community, which requires the protection that a regulated sector provides to their investments. So whilst deregulation is not considered viable, its recommendations are concerned with reducing the regulatory burden and achieving a level playing field for developers to enter the domain (as he insists it should be) of social housing.

The story ends as it began, with the financing of the housing association sector in a state of flux. Perhaps the present 'credit crunch' will force a re-think, as the riskiness and unpredictability of a reliance on private funding is exposed. Or, is it more likely that the sector's appetite for private funding will mean that it finally breaks its links with the, once sacred, not-for-profit motive?

7

Shelter, the Federation and Social Movements

Introduction

ON 1 DECEMBER 1966, Shelter—the National Campaign for the Homeless—was launched. Only two weeks before, the BBC had screened a drama-documentary about a homeless family, *Cathy Come Home*. The drama was watched by a quarter of the population in the UK, and the coincidental proximity of both events ensured that Shelter very rapidly became a 'national campaign'. Within three years, Shelter had raised nearly £2 million and ensured that homelessness and its impact on the lives of 'ordinary people' was very much in the public eye. And crucial for the story of this book, it had also helped to transform the housing association sector.

Previous chapters have told stories of the ways in which housing associations have been shaped by *governmental* strategies: by charitable giving and its regulation; by the sector's relationship with local government; by the establishment of a system of state regulation; and by the funding (public and private) that has established and sustained the sector. The limitation of this approach is that it appears very programmatic; a picture of a sector subject *to* forces external to itself. It is true that, in telling these stories I have tried to show how housing associations (in particular, through their Federation) have interacted with these governmental processes and have themselves shaped modes of governing. However, there is a danger of ignoring the 'extra-governmental'[1]—the inspirations, motivations, indeed emotions that have driven the people who are the actors in these organisations, those who act *out* these governmental strategies. For that reason, this chapter about the role Shelter might have played in shaping the housing association sector has been included—to explore some of the ways in which *ideas* and *ideals* have been a force for transformation.

In the 1960s and early 1970s, that part of the housing association sector that was to come to dominate the Federation was inextricably tied up with Shelter, in

[1] J Clarke, 'Subjects of Doubt: in search of the unsettled and unfinished' paper prepared for CASCA Conference (Ontario, Canada, May 2004).

terms of people, funding and aims. Many events in that period contributed to a transformation of the sector, and the Shelter connection was an important one. It is this period that is therefore the focus of this chapter. The first section considers the formation of Shelter and its early funding of associations, which, from the outset, like other social movements sought to produce alternative forms of knowledge that could question and unsettle common sense. The following section then examines what happened post-Housing Act 1974, when associations no longer required the charitable funds from Shelter. In this period, Shelter was to focus on developing a network of housing advice centres, which were critical not just in the help they provided to homeless people, but in the production of understandings of the impact of housing policies on individual lives. It was also a time when Shelter, along with a group of charities, played an instrumental role in making a piece of legislation now iconic in the housing world, the Housing (Homeless Persons) Act 1977. In the final section, I use this history of Shelter and housing associations to look at the changing identity of housing associations as a social movement.

The Formation of Shelter

Establishing a National Campaign for the Homeless

From the perspective of those Federation actors who were involved in Shelter at the beginning, one key motivation behind Shelter's formation came from the housing association sector itself.[2] A key force in establishing Shelter was Bruce Kenrick who, in 1963, set up Notting Hill Housing Trust in West London along with others from the Methodist Church. John Coward, the Trust's first housing manager, described Notting Hill at the time as a 'sort of sink place of London'.[3] Successive waves of immigration had created an area of such high housing demand that private landlords could easily charge exorbitant rents. There was a great deal of poor quality housing and overcrowding as the poorest families could only afford the very small flats created from the division of large buildings. Following the Rent Act 1957 (which had introduced immediate decontrol of high-valued properties, and for lower valued properties, decontrol at change of tenant) some landlords were using harassment and illegal eviction to remove

[2] This version of Shelter's beginnings arises from my interviews with those housing association actors who, within a few years, were running the Federation. It is also the version told by Chris Holmes in *The Other Notting Hill* (Studley, Warks, Brewin Books, 2001). It is not particularly apparent in the 'official' story of Shelter's launch and first three years published by Shelter itself, *The Shelter Story: A Brief History of the First Three Years of SHELTER's National Campaign for the Homeless and a Handbook on its Current Activities* (London, Shelter, 1970), which made much more of the role of Des Wilson, sidelining Bruce Kenrick's contribution. As will be seen later, Des Wilson was not very sympathetic towards housing associations.

[3] Interview with John Coward (30 June 2003).

existing tenants so that they could raise rents.[4] Their tactics became notorious through the activities of Peter Rachman, and the term *Rachmanism* became synonymous with private landlordism, still used today as a term of abuse.[5] A Labour government was elected in 1964 and acted quickly to remove the worst abuses.[6] Then the Rent Act 1965 brought back protection for tenants,[7] but still left occupants of furnished tenancies unprotected.[8] Housing pressure intensified—local authority slum clearance and the rebuilding of new estates provided housing only for the long-standing white, working class households who were mostly financially better off. Newer occupants, and occupants of furnished tenancies, were seldom re-housed by local authorities. Particularly affected were the new immigrants to Britain from Jamaica and the Caribbean, many of whom sought housing in west London, not anticipating the racial discrimination. Riots in 1959 and the funeral of a Jamaican carpenter became the focus for action against racism. The Methodist Church established a team ministry in Notting Hill, joined in 1962 by Bruce Kenrick.

It was in part Kenrick's reaction to the appalling housing conditions that led to the establishment of a new housing association in Notting Hill. The initial aim of 'Project Notting Hill' was to buy up and convert houses for homeless families in the area. However, Kenrick thought in a grand scale; for him this was a 'pilot'. His paper to the first meeting of the new association stated that the aim should be to 'buy local houses on the largest possible scale' and then to 'launch similar work in other needy cities throughout the UK'.[9] He was also a very successful fund-raising entrepreneur. From street stalls to a donation from Christian Action, an interest free loan to collections in local churches, the Trust raised thousands in its first years. It launched an advertising campaign and Kenrick made appearances on primetime television and radio, at the time highly innovative tactics for a housing association. In 1965, £81,000 was donated[10] and an extensive mailing-list of donors was established which became important in Shelter's launch.[11]

Kenrick's grander plans for the Trust to become a nationwide organisation, however, created tension and opposition among the trustees of Notting Hill

[4] P Malpass, *Housing and the Welfare State: The Development of Housing Policy in Britain* (Basingstoke, Palgrave Macmillan, 2005) 88.

[5] See Holmes, *The Other Notting Hill*, above n 2, ch 1.

[6] Protection from Eviction Act 1964 was a 'holding operation', unlawful eviction a criminal offence.

[7] Harassment also became a criminal offence under this act: see www.lag.org.uk/shared/asp/files?GFSR.asp?NodelD=92091.

[8] Shelter ran a powerful lobbying campaign against this. Amid considerable opposition from the right-wing press and the Conservatives, the Rent Act 1974 rectified this. Thanks to Les Burrows of Shelter for this.

[9] Paper prepared for first meeting of the Project on 18 December 1963, quoted in Holmes, *The Other Notting Hill*, above n 2 at 8.

[10] Holmes, *The Other Notting Hill*, above n 2 at 33.

[11] Interviews with John Coward (above n 3) and Ken Bartlett (30 June 2003).

Trust, who saw their organisation as based in the local community.[12] Nevertheless, they supported the setting up of a national organisation, and relations were established with four other national organisations—the Housing Societies Charitable Trust (HSCT) (set up by the Federation to raise charitable funding which it would channel to associations);[13] the British Churches Housing Trust; Christian Action (which had sponsored the Housing the Homeless Fund); and the Catholic Housing Aid Society (which co-ordinated a number of advisory and other services for Catholics and non-Catholics).[14] One (academic's) interpretation of the motivation for these organisations working together was a concern that the success of Kenrick's fundraising model, and his desire to go nationwide, threatened the income of their own charitable organisations.[15] Interviewees tend to put a more benign interpretation on this alliance, portraying it as a coming together of like-minded individuals.[16] Certainly, one factor behind the launch of Shelter was the success of Kenrick's Notting Hill funding-raising scheme, a mailing list of donors who could be appealed to regularly. The agreement with the Notting Hill Trust to allow this mailing list to be used to launch Shelter was a significant factor in the latter's immediate fundraising success. Indeed, financial agreements between the five founding organisations were key: the five agreed to suspend all fundraising in favour of the new charitable trust[17]— which was to be called 'Shelter— the National Campaign for the Homeless'. Shelter's launch was carefully prepared for many months, led by its first full-time worker Des Wilson, a 'journalist and publicity adviser'.[18] In the months leading up to the launch, research was carried out in what were considered to be the areas worst affected by homelessness: London, Glasgow, Liverpool and Birmingham. The launch was accompanied by full page advertising in the *the Guardian, The Times* and other national newspapers. By the beginning of January 1967, £50,000 had been raised; in Shelter's first fourteen months, £373,041 and by October 1969, £1,750,000.

There was another event, entirely separate from the planning involved in the launch of Shelter, that nevertheless became an important ingredient in Shelter's immediate success. Two weeks before Shelter's planned launch the BBC showed *Cathy Come Home.* a powerful portrayal of the everyday reality of homelessness and its destruction of a family.'A quarter of Britain's population tuned in to see

[12] Holmes, *The Other Notting Hill*, above n 2 at 35.

[13] The remit of the HSCT was to '(i) allocate by way of grant or interest free loan, funds from charitable bodies who prefer to use the Trust as their agent, rather than receive applications from individual Housing Associations, and (ii) operate an interest free loan fund which it has itself built up over a period of time, in support of Associations' in NFHS, *Annual Report* 1969; also see above, ch 3.

[14] Shelter, above n 2 at 11.

[15] P Seyd, 'Shelter: The National Campaign for the Homeless' (1975) 46 *Political Quarterly* 418–31, 419.

[16] In interviews with John Coward, Ken Bartlett, above n 11; Barry Natton and David Bebb (11 August 2003) the formation of Shelter was discussed.

[17] Seyd, above n 15 at 419; Holmes, *The Other Notting Hill*, above n 2 at 36.

[18] Shelter, above n 2 at 11.

the appalling story of Cathy and her family';[19] the timing was pure coincidence.[20] The power of this television portrayal, along with the months of planning and research, meant immediate and phenomenal success for Shelter's initial appeal. But coincidences are seldom quite so random as we think. Many activities had developed awareness in the public domain of the deficiencies of the housing system and the homelessness it created. The oppressive tactics of some private landlords had become exposed through the media, and there was criticism of local authorities in the findings of a government committee, the Milner Holland Report in 1965.[21] It was perhaps then hardly surprising that in 1966 the BBC commissioned Ken Loach (as director) and Jeremy Sandford (as writer) to make a television drama as part of the 'Wednesday Play' series about homelessness,[22] at the same time that those who adopted a pragmatic approach were working to set up a new campaigning organisation.

The 'Rescue Operation'

The terminology of Shelter's campaigning in its early years has biblical connotations: it was 'saving families' through its 'rescue operation'.[23] The majority of the funds it raised were distributed to housing associations for buying up properties and renovating them to house homeless families.[24] From the outset, it was decided that funds should be targeted on four urban areas considered to be high stress areas, those that Des Wilson described as the 'worst-hit cities' of London, Birmingham, Liverpool and Glasgow.[25] Shelter wanted to work with only a small number of associations believing that '"mass production" is more economical'.[26] Associations were asked to put in proposals to Shelter. There would then be a

[19] Shelter, *40 Years On* (London, Shelter, 2006, and www.shelter.org.uk).

[20] Holmes, *The Other Notting Hill*, above n 2 at 37, and also in interview with Ken Bartlett, above n 11.

[21] M Holland, *Report of the Committee on Housing in Greater London* (London, HMSO, 1965).

[22] 'Jeremy Sandford obituary' *Guardian* (15 May 2003); also from the same obituary: 'During the 50s and early 60s, Jeremy made many short documentaries for BBC radio with distinctly socially conscious themes. His first TV commission in 1963 was a portrait of the Savoy Hotel, which had requested coverage to mark an anniversary. Entirely unaware of the consternation his procedure would cause, he focused especially upon the overworked and under-paid staff in the kitchens, laundries and back stairs, rather than celebrating the well-heeled glamour of the lobby, the elegant suites and the famous grill. At a preview of the finished programme, the management of the Savoy were so incensed by this disrespectful approach that they attempted to take out an injunction (which failed)'. An earlier 'Wednesday Play' by Ken Loach, *Up the Junction* (broadcast 3 November 1965), had been considered 'groundbreaking for its ellitical style and inclusion of a controversial abortion sequence' (BFI screenonline, Ken Loach, www.screenonline.org.uk/people/id/458945/).

[23] Shelter, above n 2.

[24] Eg, in 1970, it was intended that 60% of money donated would be used for the rescues operation by housing associations: Shelter, above n 2 at 37.

[25] D Wilson, 'Shelter' (1967) 1(4) *Voluntary Housing* 127–28 (*Voluntary Housing* was the magazine of the National Federation of Housing Societies, started in 1967 and published by the Federation until 1996).

[26] Shelter, above n 2 at 33.

process of assessing the association: the Housing Director would visit the association, looking for 'evidence of a professional and workmanlike approach' and to ensure that 'the kind of families to be helped are, by SHELTER's definition, homeless'.[27] A report would then be prepared for Shelter's 'distributive committee', a joint committee with the Housing Societies Charitable Trust (see below). This was, in many ways, a system of 'registration' with elements of the system set up by the Housing Corporation following the 1974 Act.

The associations supported were a mix of new associations established by Shelter such as Liverpool Housing Trust and a few existing associations. So, for example, in Liverpool, Merseyside Improved Homes was supported.[28] In Birmingham, Shelter funds were used to establish two new associations, Birmingham Housing Trust and Midland Area Improvement HA. They, along with Copec (a housing trust formed in 1925) received funding throughout the 1960s and early 1970s to run what they termed 're-housing agencies', offering financial support services alongside re-housing.[29] On occasions, associations refused Shelter's funding. Mulberry Housing Trust, chaired by Sir Keith Joseph (Minister for Housing in the Macmillan Conservative Government) refused funding to prove the point that housing associations could survive without either state subsidy or charitable funding, in a similar vein to the nineteenth century model dwelling companies. His project failed.[30] Similarly, Kensington Housing Trust, a long-established West London association, refused Shelter's offer; it too believed that the longevity of its existence and experience meant it needed no help from outside.

How the funding was to be used was something of a delicate matter. Publicly, Wilson stated that the funds would go into the direct provision of housing for homeless households through purchase and improvement, and should only 'very exceptionally' be used to enable associations to employ staff, or to go towards their administration.[31] The reality, however, was somewhat different. These charitable organisations ran their operations by employing staff, not purely through voluntary workers as some of the earlier charitable trusts had done. For public relations reasons (donors like to see their money providing a positively identified 'thing'—see, for example, Oxfam's 'buy a teacher') the myth that donations went direct to homeless people was perpetuated.[32] On the ground, Shelter funds had to be used in part for administration and staff if new housing

[27] *Ibid*, 37.

[28] Interestingly, one of my interviewees, Barry Natton, who was to become Director of Merseyside Improved Homes, said Shelter thought it was doing 'a terrible job'! The organisation later became Riverside Housing Association.

[29] K Gulliver, Passionate About Communities: Keynote, *Prime Focus and Midland Heart Housing Associations 1925 to 2006* (Studley, Warks, Brewin Books, 2006) 13.

[30] See Holmes, *The Other Notting Hill*, above n 2 at 36.

[31] Wilson, above n 25.

[32] Interview with Chris Holmes (15th February 2008); *The Shelter Story*, above n 2, also suggests that funds went to pay staff in exceptional cases.

was to be created. Liverpool is a good example. In 1968, half a million pounds was pledged by Shelter to an area in Liverpool 8 in what became known as SNAP—Shelter Neighbourhood Action Project. This was half of all the income from donations for that year and the deal with Liverpool Corporation was that they would declare a General Improvement Area and also put in similar funding. This was a big, high-profile, high-risk project that had to work. Liverpool Improved Homes received a third of a million over three years, with the instructions

> [w]e don't care how you spend the money, so long as you spend it to provide homes. You can spend it as bridging finance, because you're gonna have trouble. You can spend it on staff because you can afford it. You can spend it on *mistakes*, as long as you don't repeat the mistakes. But for god's sake ... house people in housing need.[33]

Shelter's version of philanthropy was a long way from the polite, moralistically-driven housing trusts that had come out of the Victorian era, whose lack of activity had been criticised by both the Cohen and Milner Holland committees.[34] It was an organisation largely run by young people; a great deal of its fundraising came from activities run by school children and teenagers. The tone of those activists engaged in this 'new philanthropy' was very different. On writing about Liverpool SNAP at the end of its three-year life, the project's workers said of themselves:

> We were contentious, arrogant, opinionated and heavily biased in favour of an immediate new deal for the deprived. We wanted jam on it and we wanted it today. The important point is that we were completely unaligned and independent of other actors in the urban crisis.[35]

But they concluded that their project had

> left behind one of the most complex and difficult but one of the most successful General Improvement Areas in Britain. ... If commentators say this does not add up to success, we can only agree.[36]

It is easy to see how these housing activists from Shelter, and the housing associations and projects they spawned, felt that they were part of a social movement. They saw themselves as a force to bring an awareness of the devastating effects of homelessness; their tactics and strategies involved an understanding of *communities* as being central actors in dealing with the housing crisis; and their resources seemed way beyond those previously imagined by housing associations. This might not have been mass action in terms of street protests, but what they had been able to call up could surely be called mass action

[33] Interview with Barry Natton, above n 16.

[34] Cohen Committee, *Housing Associations: A Working Paper of the Central Housing Advisory Committee* (London, HMSO, 1971); Holland report, above n 21.

[35] Liverpool SNAP, *Another Chance for Cities: SNAP 69/72* (Liverpool, Liverpool SNAP, 1972).

[36] 'Preface' by JD McConaghy, Director, Liverpool SNAP, *ibid*, 6.

in terms of 'mass-giving'? I return to the idea of social movements in the conclusion; here I merely want to highlight that the Shelter activists might legitimately have thought themselves as part of a social movement, despite the fact that historian Adam Lent, in his book *British Social Movements since 1945*[37] makes no mention at all of Shelter and the anti-poverty campaigners.

The 1970s and Beyond

In the first few years of Shelter, its relationship with the housing association sector was close. Shelter used the Housing Societies Charitable Trust (HSCT) to allocate funds, making use of 'the Trust's expertise and experience ... to co-ordinate charitable gifts—or interest free loans—throughout the whole movement'.[38] The chair of Shelter was Ken Bartlett, Director of Paddington Churches Housing Association (PCHA), an association set up with the support of Notting Hill Housing Trust (NHHT). Despite his position, PCHA continued to receive financial support from Shelter. John Coward, Director of NHHT, and Anthony Fletcher of Quadrant HA, were also trustees. However, the issue of probity that this would have raised in current ethical regimes did not appear as an issue then, as Chris Holmes, Deputy Director of Shelter 1974–77 explains:

> It would be frowned on now, but that group of people were both on Shelter's grants committee when their own associations were receiving quite a lot of money from Shelter—I think they did it quite honourably, certainly never any hint of corruption, but it would not be seen as good practice now.[39]

David Bebb, Shelter's Housing Director in the early 1970s, explained that the importance of the Shelter-inspired associations was wider than a revival of philanthropy:

> The role that Shelter played was crucial in transforming housing associations. Until the mid '60s, housing associations had operated on a small scale, not really contributing significantly to housing policy. But Shelter's dramatic success in raising money from 1965 onwards enabled it to fund not only Notting Hill Housing Trust and four other London associations. Shelter went on quickly to generate new associations and support the growth of existing ones in Birmingham, Liverpool, Manchester, and in Glasgow and Edinburgh. Their 'rehab' work was an important factor in the shift of national policy from clearance and large-scale redevelopment to neighbourhood improvement. Shelter was the key link in the network of these 'stress area' associations, which went on to become active in what was then the National Federation of Housing Societies.[40]

[37] A Lent, *British Social Movements since 1945: Sex, Colour, Peace and Power* (Basingstoke, Palgrave, 2001).

[38] National Federation of Housing Societies (NFHS), *31st Annual Report* (London, NFHS 1967).

[39] Interview with Chris Holmes, above n 32.

[40] Interview with David Bebb, above n 16.

Des Wilson, unlike Bruce Kenrick, had come to Shelter without a background in the world of voluntary housing and consequently had less sympathy for housing associations. He argued for more tenant control: 'Wherever possible … SHELTER and housing associations should aim to enable tenants to realize their full potential',[41] and criticised them for being 'conservative and undemocratic and failing to meet the needs of the homeless in inner-city areas'.[42] As the amount raised from Shelter's fundraising increased dramatically, Wilson decided that its funds should be controlled directly by Shelter,[43] leaving only small amounts to be channelled through the Federation's Housing Societies Charitable Trust. In 1975, Shelter's trustees took control of the allocation of all funds.[44] However, by then there had been a fundamental change in the funding climate for both Shelter and housing associations. The Housing Act 1974 had brought in a 'new and highly generous subsidy structure for registered housing associations',[45] negotiated by the Federation, mostly by those who worked for the new breed of housing associations supported by Shelter.[46] Associations had no need of funding from charitable sources.

The influence of Shelter on the Federation and the whole housing association sector was significant. The 'new philanthropists' whose organisations Shelter funding had helped to get off the ground, took control of the Federation in 1973. The 1974 Act brought statutory support as well as funding for the urban renewal policies that Shelter and these associations had been pursuing. These were times of political and organisational change, reflected also in a hiatus in the leadership of Shelter. Des Wilson left Shelter in 1971; John Willis (previously Housing Director) took over as Director in 1972 and then the trustees appointed Geoffrey Martin who took over as Director on 1 January 1973. Martin attempted to introduce major changes to Shelter's staffing structure, causing bitter disagreements between him and existing staff and some of Shelter's local groups. Eventually Martin was dismissed by the trustees.[47] The chair of the trustees, Ken Bartlett (by then a leading actor in the Federation) took responsibility for what had become a very public and damaging row, and resigned. The detachment of Shelter's organisational and funding structures from the housing association sector became more apparent, and for Shelter the public disagreement caused disaffection among local Shelter groups and meant that Shelter's income almost halved in 1974.[48]

[41] In a speech to a conference of the National Federation of Housing Societies in 1969, reported in *The Shelter Story*, above n 2 at 26.

[42] Seyd, above n 15 at 419. Patrick Seyd published this article in 1975 as an academic in Sheffield. The article reflects his observations of Shelter's policies and practices at the time.

[43] Interview with David Bebb, above n 16.

[44] National Federation of Housing Associations (NFHA), *1975 Annual Report*.

[45] C Holmes 'The Party's Over: the Government's Retreat from its Housing Strategy' (October 1975) *ROOF* 17.

[46] See above, ch 5.

[47] Seyd, above n 15 at 428.

[48] Interview with Chris Holmes, above n 32.

Challenging Homelessness: Housing Aid and the Homeless Persons Act 1977

Housing Aid: Creating Alternative Knowledge

Like the housing association sector, in the Shelter story, the Housing Act 1974 was a pivotal point:

> That's when Shelter changed its funding from, essentially, from support going to housing associations where most of Shelter's charitable money had gone in the first ten years, and into the development and support of housing aid centres.[49]

A nationwide network of housing advice centres had been recommended by the Seebohm Committee in 1969.[50] The Shelter (Family) Housing Aid Centre (SHAC) had been launched as 'an experiment in housing aid'[51] in 1969, Shelter claiming 'experimentation' as one of its key roles alongside 'rescue'. SHAC had followed on from the success of the Catholic Housing Aid Centres and was part of a partnership to form a London-wide housing advice service which included the National Federation, with a member of the Federation staff serving as a Trustee.[52] Some independent housing aid centres were established and Shelter began setting up centres elsewhere in country. Some of the impetus for establishing housing advice centres came from Shelter's regional officers, who found they were giving housing advice, were not trained to do so but thought that they should be.[53]

With the 1974 Act funding leaving associations no longer in need of Shelter funding, housing advice could became a core activity for Shelter. The value of advice centres was not simply in their advice role: casework also produced knowledge, information and 'facts' that challenged prevailing understandings. Shelter could draw on the experience of thousands of households who turned to the housing aid centres because they had been failed by the housing system. Their research and lobbying was backed up by 'real life' stories. This alternative knowledge became a powerful tool in power relations with central government. It was knowledge that could disturb—like the Christmas 1967 fund-raising poster, a picture of a family on the doorstep of a damp Glasgow tenement with the title 'Christmas? You can stuff it for all we care.' It was knowledge difficult to ignore because it arose from 'real lives'.

[49] *Ibid.*

[50] Seebohm Committee, established in 1965, with a remit to 'review the organisation and responsibilities of Local Authority Personal Social Services in England and Wales' (Seebohm Committee Report, para 1).

[51] Holmes, *The Other Notting Hill*, above n 2 at 34.

[52] NFHS, *1969 Annual Report*, 6.

[53] Interview with Chris Holmes, above n 32.

Shelter, Christmas 1967 poster

In the 1970s, Shelter moved away from the church roots it had shared with many in the housing association sector, arguably becoming more radical.[54] Compared with the stance in its first report—'[t]his report is not a protest … all they [homeless families] need is money'[55]—by 1973 Shelter's tone had become more strident and critical. In *The Kids Don't Notice* the critique was blunt, even critical of their own earlier approach to 'rescue':

> [p]ouring money and energy into the 'rescue' work of the welfare services is but a mopping up operation which is often too late to provide more than superficial help.[56]

This move to the radical, historian Adam Lent argues, was prevalent in social movements in the 1970s, when the 'moderate universe' was overtaken, 'effectively sidelined' by a 'sudden explosion of radicalism'.[57] From the outset, Shelter had backed up campaigns with research. Now, in a series of reports—*the Grief report*,[58] *Blunt Power, Sharp Practices*[59] and *Reprieve for Slums*[60]—they were publicly critical of local authorities and their lack of concern for homeless households: even the limited duty that local authorities had under the National Assistance Act 1948[61] to provide temporary accommodation for households with children, they argued, was used by few.[62] Here the front-line experience of housing advisers interacted with campaigning to create a climate for change:

> As housing advisers, we lived on our wits cajoling local authorities to accept responsibility for homeless people. We had little to use by way of enforcement. Something needed to be done, but what?[63]

For the Federation of the 1970s, transformed in part by its association with Shelter, the priority had been to bring about legislative reform to produce a funding regime that could expand the sector. For Shelter, its priority had to be a major transformation of statutory definitions of homelessness, and the duties of local authorities to prevent and deal with homelessness. Its challenge to status

[54] Seyd, above n 15.

[55] Reported in S Weir, 'The Hypocratic Oath' (November 1979) *ROOF* 200.

[56] *The Kids Don't Notice* (London, Shelter, 1973), reported in Weir, *ibid* at 200.

[57] Lent, above n 37 at 7.

[58] R Bailey and J Ruddock, *The Grief Report: A Shelter Report on Temporary Accommodation* (London, Shelter, 1972) which 'set out to prove that here is widespread default of the National Assistance Act 1948 by local authorities' (at 4).

[59] B Widdowson, *Blunt Powers, Sharp Practices: A Survey of Local Authority Policies on Homelessness* (London, Shelter, 1976).

[60] Shelter, *Reprieve for Slums: A Shelter Report* (London, Shelter, 1972).

[61] Section 21(1)(b), placed a duty on local authority welfare departments (which then became social services) to provide 'temporary accommodation for persons who are in urgent need thereof, being need arising in circumstances which could not reasonably have been foreseen or in such circumstances as the authority in any case may determine'.

[62] 'Foreword' to *Grief Report*, above n 58, which 'set out to prove that there is widespread default of the 1948 National Assistance Act by local authorities'.

[63] B Widdowson, 'Making the Law' (November/December 2007) *ROOF* 32–33, 32. The article describes the making of the Homeless Persons Act 1977 from the perspective of the voluntary sector; *cf* P Somerville, 'Homelessness Policy in Britain' (1994) 22 *Policy and Politics* 163–78, discussed below.

quo understandings of 'homelessness' as 'rooflessness' was a central platform from the outset: '"Shelter" regards any family, or any elderly person, as homeless if, because of the physical conditions under which they are forced to live, they cannot lead a normal family life', Des Wilson wrote in 1967.[64] The Local Government Act 1972 made matters worse, removing the local authority duty to provide for homeless households, reducing it merely to a power. The increased hardship this caused was a catalyst for Shelter, SHAC, the Child Poverty Action Group, the Catholic Housing Aid Society and the Campaign for Homeless and Rootless to establish the Joint Charities Group (JCG).[65] This group lobbied and campaigned for legislative change to the law relating to the homelessness duties of local authorities, the end result of which was the Housing (Homeless Persons) Act 1977.

The 1977 Act was a critical piece of legislation in that it created a clear, decisive break from the Poor Law tradition, which had been the normative background to all previous legislative responses to homelessness.[66] It repealed those sections of the National Assistance Act which had placed limited duties on social services authorities for dealing with homelessness persons, making it the duty of *housing* authorities to provide temporary accommodation. This had been one of Shelter's demands from the beginning. The Act also placed a legal responsibility on local authorities to find *permanent* housing for homeless households, but only provided they passed certain 'tests'.[67]

Shelter saw its role as central to achieving legislative change; most housing literature since then has considered Shelter and the JCG as key agents to change.[68] In this view, it was the JCG's lobbying that was instrumental in bringing about a Department of the Environment (DoE) circular in 1974[69] which 'emphasised prevention, introduced the concept of priority groups including vulnerability and discouraged the punitive practices then current'.[70] The JCG worked with civil

[64] Wilson, above n 25 at 130

[65] Widdowson, 'Making the Law', above n 63; the Women's Aid Federation and the Public Health Action Group later joined the JCG.

[66] Somerville, above n 63, says (at165) that the Act created a 'clearer more decisive break from the Poor Law tradition than the 1948 Act'.

[67] Housing (Homeless Persons) Act 1977, s 2; see Shelter, *Where Homelessness Means Hopelessness: An Appraisal of the First Year of the Housing (Homeless Persons) Act* (London, Shelter, 1978). The three criteria, all of which were subject to extensive litigation, were (1) must be homeless or threatened with homelessness (in terms specified by the Act); (2) must fall into one of the 'priority groups' which included—families with dependent children, pregnant women, and people classified as vulnerable because of old age, mental health or physical disability. The 'Notes' to the 1977 in *Current Law Statutes Annotated* (London, Sweet & Maxwell, 1977) comment that ' the Act in its final form largely reflects the views of … those [MPs] who wanted to create only vague duties and allow local authorities to retain broad discretion in deciding who should be helped'.

[68] Eg, D Donnison and C Unger, *Housing Policy* (Harmondsworth, Penguin, 1982); N Raynsford, 'The 1977 Housing (Homeless Persons) Act' in N Deakin (ed), *Policy Change in Government* (London, Royal Institute of Public Administration, 1986) 33–62; J Richards, 'A new sense of duty' (November/December 1991) *ROOF* 34–37.

[69] DoE circular: 18/74.

[70] Widdowson, 'Making the Law' above n 63 at 32.

servants to draft a homelessness bill; when the Labour Government dropped it from the 1976 Queen's Speech, it then persuaded a backbench MP[71] to put it forward as a Private Member's Bill. This version of history, however, is not universally accepted. In Peter Somerville's analysis it was the civil servants from the DoE who were centre stage.[72] The Bill, which formed the basis of the 1977 Act, he argued, was 'essentially the Department's own work'.[73] It was drafted following a consultation exercise that had come about because the lack of a standard duty on *all* local authorities to deal with homelessness had become a high-profile political problem. Technically, Somerville may be right, but his argument ignores the way alternative forms of knowledge can become prevalent, powerful and understood as 'common sense'. Shelter, in producing research reports and in their often high-profile advertising, was seeking to educate and inform public opinion at the same time as raising money. They were not alone: in 1965, Brian Abel-Smith and Peter Townsend had published their challenging book *The Poor and the Poorest*[74] and the Child Poverty Action Group had also been formed. The work of all these campaigners was, in effect, engaged in constructing what Gramsci would have termed 'counter-hegemonic' knowledge,[75] challenging the prevailing 'common sense' that the welfare state had ended poverty. The fund raising success of Shelter alone suggests that this challenge was understood by many. Hardly surprising, then, that local authorities' lack of any action against homelessness became a 'high-profile political problem'. It was a 'complex, compound, multi-layered terrain of thought and action'[76] that led to these shifts in understanding, shifts that the politicians would understand must have a response. Such complexity is summed up by Les Burrows, who worked for Shelter from 1973 to 2009:

> I think the Joint Charities Group, effectively led by Nick Raynsford, was the driving force—partly because of the unremitting pressure it kept up, and partly because of the weight of evidence it provided, and partly because of the high media profile it maintained. This was a time of economic and political turmoil. The 'Party is over!' as Crosland had said. In a very real sense the Housing (Homeless Persons) Act becoming law ran counter to the economic and political time. A Bill of sorts may have been on a DoE shelf somewhere but I doubt very much it would have seen the light of day without the Joint Charities Group work, Stephen Ross agreeing to table a Private Member's Bill and the influence of the Lib-Lab Pact.[77]

[71] This was Stephen Ross, a Liberal Party MP. On 23 March 1977 the Liberals and Labour had signed the Lib-Lab Pact.

[72] See 'Making the Law', above, n 63.

[73] *Ibid*, 168.

[74] B Abel-Smith and P Townsend, *The Poor and the Poorest: A New Analysis of the Ministry of Labour's 'Family Expenditure Surveys' of 1953–54 and 1960* (London, Bell, 1965).

[75] A Gramsci, *Selections from the Prison Notebooks* (London, Lawrence Wishart, 1971).

[76] Clarke, 'Subjects of Doubt', above n 1 at 4.

[77] Les Burrows wrote this in response to an earlier draft of this chapter. Les has worked for Shelter in many roles, as caseworker, researcher, lobbyist and statistician. He wrote *Shelter's Guide to the*

In Shelter's history, what is clear is that its perception of its role in the making of the 1977 Act was a critical point, just as the Federation perceived its role in the 1974 Act as central. And so, at Shelter's thirty year anniversary, the 1977 Act was held up as a high point of the organisation's campaigning activity.[78]

However, Shelter staff and Federation officers had differing perspectives on how they should conduct their relations with government. Take the account of Bob Widdowson, caseworker at SHAC and author of a number of Shelter's research reports, of the story of the making of the 1977 Act at its fortieth anniversary.[79] He recalled the concern of some members of the JCG that Nick Raynsford, who had become de-facto leader of the group, 'was getting too close to government' because he developed a close working link with a key DoE official.[80] None of the stories told by any actors in the Federation showed any concern for the proximity of their relations with civil servants or ministers. Indeed, I was told a story by Ken Bartlett (Associate Director at the Federation in 1974) about how, following the Housing Act 1974, he effectively wrote the DoE's paper on the allowances associations could claim for administering housing schemes under the Act. He put into this paper everything the associations wanted, took it to Patrick Jackson, a senior DoE official who 'read it, crossed out Nat Fed at the top, and wrote DoE'.[81]

As the discussion of the Federation's role in the making of the 1974 Act in chapter five demonstrated, the Federation never had any qualms about close working relations with government, both civil servants and politicians. Indeed, it has been these connections and networks, which have always been social as well as organisational, that have been a key tool in the Federation's advancement of the cause of housing associations. Such connections have acted as a vital conduit for translating the needs of associations into the needs, and therefore the programmes, of government. However, concern that too close a proximity to governmental actors can lead to co-option has frequently been expressed by actors in social movements. Concerns about co-option have a long history: one sees it, for example, in Marxist debates about reform versus revolution. Social movement activists have often treated such close links with mistrust. Here, perhaps, lies a critical moment that creates a fissure between the housing association sector and other voluntary sector organisations which saw themselves more at the critical edge.

Housing Act 1988 (London, Shelter, 1989). His comments on this chapter have also been incorporated elsewhere and I am extremely grateful for his time, research and insight.

78 D Wilson, 'Backdoor' (January/February 1997) 22(1) *ROOF* 44.

79 See 'Making the Law', above n 63.

80 *Ibid*, 33.

81 Interview with Ken Bartlett, above n 11.

Shelter and Housing Associations: A 'Movement' Moving Apart?

In 1975 Shelter set up *ROOF*, intended to be

> a magazine that was well informed, would focus on the housing issues, which was not directed to Shelter's direct campaigning objectives, so was not about raising money, would not be about promoting process.[82]

In the pages of *ROOF*, the period after the Housing Act 1974 appears as one in which a division opened up between Shelter and the housing association sector. In an article in 1978, Chris Holmes accused associations of taking on the 'conservative mantle' of local authorities.[83] Chris had been Deputy Director of Shelter from 1974–76; his target was none other than Notting Hill Housing Trust, the organisation in part responsible for Shelter:

> . . . [T]he Trusts are viewed with a mixture of scepticism and distrust by a substantial proportion of tenants and community groups in the area. They are seen as alien bodies. Their weakness in organisation seized on avidly; their allocation policies suspected and criticised; their management polices and recruitment procedures dismissed as elitist.[84]

Suggesting that the emergent division was based around diverging conceptions of the rationale for action, Holmes accused the 'housing association movement' of lacking 'a coherent moral, ideological or political base for its activities'.[85] At the same time, *ROOF*'s editorial attacked the sector's lack of accountability to tenants and communities;[86] its focus, attempts by the DoE to ensure that associations would become responsive and accountable. The department's interventions were significantly weakened when the Housing Corporation came under 'substantial pressure from the associations'. The associations' concerns for their freedom and independence led them to oppose a 'uniform principle' that all allocation and management policies should be published. *ROOF*'s attack on associations continued in the editorial in November/December 1980, which reported on the announcement, at the Federation's conference, of a moratorium and severe cuts in housing association public funding:

> [W]hat was most noticeable about the reaction to these cuts was the disturbing tendency of the delegates to over-emphasise the organisational effects of the cuts. … Housing associations would do well to foster once more a closer identification with those in need.[87]

[82] Interview with Chris Holmes, above n 32. Chris said that *ROOF* was an idea he had in discussion with Richard Blake when they were both deputy directors of Shelter. Blake had previously worked for the Advisory Centre for Education which had set up a magazine with similar aims.

[83] C Holmes, 'The Elusive Panacea' (July 1978) *ROOF* 110–111, 110.

[84] *Ibid.*

[85] *Ibid*, 111.

[86] 'The third arm's second thoughts about first principles' (3 July 1978) *ROOF* editorial.

[87] 'Cold comfort conferred' (November/December 1980) *ROOF* editorial, 5.

ROOF reported the findings of a Federation survey of housing association tenants carried out in 1985 which showed that '[h]ousing association tenants are poorer, older and more representative of ethnic communities that those in other forms of tenure'.[88] Unsurprisingly, *ROOF* was critical of Notting Hill Housing Trust and Family Housing Association for increasing rents by 25 and 30 per cent respectively in 1989 as a result of the deregulation of housing association rents in the Housing Act 1988.[89]

One element of this division arose from their differing conceptions of what sort of alternative knowledge they are trying to create. Shelter, as we have seen, based much of its campaigning material on the experiences of people who found themselves at the 'wrong end' of the housing system: those households made homeless, or living in intolerable housing conditions, often as the direct result of a landlord's actions. And it was not just the actions of private landlords which caused people to come to housing aid centres, but of local authorities and housing associations too. The housing association sector's attempts to create alternative knowledge started from a different point, frequently looking to their connections in social and political elites: the Federation's Inquiry into British Housing, chaired by the Duke of Edinburgh, was a prime example. *ROOF's* editors were scathing about the outcome. Under a headline of 'No politics please, we're British', the editorial[90] accused the Inquiry report of being 'politically conservative' in its recommendations:

> Its approach has been to find the magic formula ... which will allow existing institutions—particularly the financial institutions—to play their part without any limits being placed on the pursuit of their own interests. . . . It seems that the chairman of the Midland Bank and the chief general manager of the Nationwide Building Society made the most of their membership of the inquiry.

The editorial was equally critical of the Inquiry for making no recommendations to extend the duty of local authorities to house to single people and childless couples. Accusing the private sector, housing associations and local authorities of a lack of care, the editorial reported that 'the idea was quietly dropped from the inquiry's report', commenting 'That's politics'.

Conclusion: Some Reflections on Being a 'Movement'

This chapter set out to understand some of the ways in which the idea of being a part of a 'movement' has shaped the housing association sector. To suggest that those who worked in the housing association sector saw themselves as part of

88 'Providing for the most vulnerable' (November/December 1985) *ROOF* 7.

89 C Grant, 'Housing association rents—onwards and upwards' (May/June 1989) *ROOF* 8; also see above, ch 6.

90 (September/October 1985) *ROOF* editorial, 10, 2.

that 'movement' is no artificial construct, but a connection that many in the sector have themselves made. From the earliest pages of the Federation's *Bulletin*, we find references to the Voluntary Housing Movement, the Housing Society Movement and the Housing Association Movement. Even in 1985, the Federation's fiftieth year, the annual report still made references to 'the Movement'.[91] In the 1960s and early 1970s, we can see the 'anti-poverty movements' championing housing association activity as a means to 'challenging and improving state provision'.[92]

There are now many literatures studying social movements; it is certainly not the place of this chapter to review those literatures.[93] My point here is, given that many critical theorists acknowledge that social movements (as phenomena) 'signal profound shifts in the social reality and provoke new analytical, theoretical and political questions',[94] the *understanding* of many housing association activists in the 1960s and 1970s that they were part of a social movement is important in itself as a possible shaping factor. That a British historian may not include Shelter or the housing association activists as one of the country's social movements is irrelevant.[95] Social movements are not so easily definable, they have an ephemeral quality, are 'diffuse agglomerations of individuals within civil society who are linked together by ideology, beliefs, or collective identities'.[96] They exist, at least in part, because people believe they exist and that they are part of one: and the 'being part of' is an essential element keeping the movement together and defining its actions. For example, one of those I interviewed for this book described her involvement in the Federation as like growing up together:

> [G]oing back to the Nat Fed annual conferences [in the 1970s], we were all very young, in our twenties ... The conferences were held at universities, we sometimes slept on the floor, ... it was a, kind of, 'socialist' movement...we all felt very strongly...the values of getting people decent housing . . . because it is such a fundamental human need, we were very passionate about it.
>
> ... it has intrigued me that, the older we got as a Movement, and we have sort of aged together . . . the annual conference is now in Birmingham's International Convention

[91] NFHA, *1984 Annual Report*, 9 (published for AGM 12 June 1985).

[92] D Mullins and A Murie, *Housing Policy in the UK* (Basingstoke, Palgrave Macmillan, 2006) 181–85.

[93] One of the most widely-used overview texts is D Della Porta and M Diani, *Social Movements: An Introduction* 2nd edn (Oxford, Blackwell, 2006).

[94] JM Conway, *Identity, Place, Knowledge: Social Movements Contesting Globalization* (Halifax, Nova Scotia, Fernwood Publishing, 2004) 21; also eg, S Hall, 'The Meaning of "New Times"' in D Morley and Kuan-Hsing Chen (eds), *Stuart Hall: Critical Dialogues in Cultural Studies* (London and New York, Routledge, 1996); C West, 'The New Cultural Politics of Difference' in S During (ed), *The Cultural Studies Reader* 2nd edn (London, Routledge, 1993).

[95] Lent, above n 37 and associated text.

[96] EL Rubin, 'Passing through the Door: Social Movement Literature And Legal Scholarship' [2001] *University of Pennsylvania Law Review* 1, 4.

> Centre, we stay in hotels with en suite rooms but we grew out of sleeping on floors. But I hope that that hasn't diminished the passion that we have for the old values.[97]

The tactics of the housing association sector, however, have rarely been radical; from the beginning it has used lobbying and its contacts in elitist structures.[98] It was committed to a role of non-political 'independence'.[99] Shelter and the other charities campaigning in the 1970s for homelessness legislation, were far more likely to see mass action, protest and resistance as appropriate; for them, the solution was grounded in politics. Shelter's caseworkers in housing advice centres were in close proximity to those whose lives were threatened by the housing system of landlords and mortgage companies. Housing associations, on the other hand, have always been concerned with relations with government to secure housing association grant, and now with private lenders to secure loans and private developers and contractors to get 'value for money' developments. The hierarchical structures developed by associations as they rapidly expanded with 1974 Act funding,[100] created distances within associations between frontline housing management workers and their finance and development staff. As competition for grant, and then private funding, became inbuilt into the housing association sector,[101] finance increasingly gained dominance. Housing associations' knowledge and understanding of the housing system became increasingly differentiated from that of Shelter's caseworkers and campaigners. The 'ordinary people'[102] who were failed by the system were sometimes failed by the housing associations, by 25 per cent rent increases in response to grant cuts, or by decisions taken by associations to exclude applicants.[103]

However, looking for linear relations between radical social movement activists of the 1960s and continuing challenges to 'the system' would be false: the creation of subjects/subjectivities is much more complex than that. At the fortieth anniversary of May 1968 much was written about the present-day impact of the student and worker protests. The consensus seems to be that the legacy of 1968 is

[97] Interview with Andrea Titterington (28 October 2003).

[98] Historian Adam Lent in *British Social Movements since 1945*, above n 37, identifies social movements of this period by their tactics, which (he says) involve radical attitudes, mass action, protest and resistance; these he distinguishes from the 'moderate values, polite lobbying and elitist' structures of earlier groups (at 7).

[99] See, eg, the Federation's *Bulletin* in 1946: 'The Federation is not primarily concerned with the political aspect—it IS concerned with seeing that men and women of goodwill all pull the same way for the common objective: ADEQUATE AND BETTER HOUSING FOR THE NATION' *OB* 40, December 1946, 1.

[100] NHFA, *Growing Pains: Coping with the Problems of Growth in Housing Associations* (NHFA, London, 1977) discussed below in ch 8.

[101] R Walker, 'New Public Management and Housing Associations: from comfort to competition' (1998) 26 *Policy & Politics* 71–88; also see D Mullins, 'Redefining "Competition" as "Competitiveness"—the Best Value Activities of Registered Social Landlords' (April–June 2002) *Public Money & Management* 25–30.

[102] Shelter, *Ordinary People: Homelessness in the Housing Crisis* (Shelter, London, 1982).

[103] See D Cowan, M McDermont and K Morgan, *Risk, Trust and Betrayal: A Social Housing Case Study* (2008): www.bris.ac.uk/law/research/centres-themes/nominations/index.html.

anything but radical: the politics of the Right, not of the Left, have come to dominate.[104] Lent argues that by the mid-1980s, 'the social movements which had been born with the scent of revolution in the air were growing into professional organisations with moderate goals integrated more closely with the political establishment'.[105] This could be a description of the housing association sector. The young idealists who went to Federation conferences in the early 1970s, who slept on floors and saw themselves as part of a social movement, all grew up.

So finally I return to the initial puzzle this chapter set out to consider, of the ways in which the idea of a 'movement' has shaped the housing association sector. We can identify institutional transformations, for example in the use of Shelter funding to develop a new breed of associations that came to dominate the sector's agenda. It is less easy to identify the role of the emotional attachment, but then identities are in constant re-formation in a complex way, and it is possible to hold two or more contradictory positions at once.[106] Perhaps what the radicalised Shelter of the 1970s onwards enabled was a division of identity in the housing association sector. Housing professionals, as they became, could be both radical and campaigning, as members of Shelter, and be part of delivery organisations that more and more became the bureaucracies that Shelter was campaigning to change. In this sense, the impact of 'movement' cannot be detected in direct transformation, but in a more dispersed, diverse way through the subject-positions adopted by housing professionals in their everyday roles.

[104] See, eg, G Wheatcroft, 'It was fun, but 1968 left us sybaritic, self-absorbed and ruled by the right' *Guardian* (1 May 2008); on the impact on French politics, see: A Bidou, 'The Communist Hypothesis' (2008) 49 *New Left Review* 29–42.

[105] Lent, above n 37 at 167.

[106] See, eg D Holland and J Lave, 'History in Person: An Introduction' in D Holland and J Lave (eds), *History in Person: Enduring Struggles, Contentious Practice, Intimate Identities* (Sante Fe and Oxford, School of American Research Press and James Currey, 2001) 29.

8

'Independent Spirit'

Introduction

HAVING AN 'INDEPENDENT spirit' was how a senior Federation officer described associations, in an article explaining the Federation's re-branding of the sector through the 'iN business' campaign at the beginning of the new century.[1] He suggested that independence was a property intrinsic to housing associations, one that had been endangered by a reliance on the State produced by the Housing Act 1974. By re-branding associations as 'iN Business for Neighbourhoods' the Federation aimed to restore this 'independent spirit' to the sector.

Independence has been a primary claim of the sector and its representative body for the whole of its history. What is it about 'independence' that is so critical to associations? What do the Federation and housing associations mean by 'independence'? How is, and has, the idea of independence been put to work as a tool of governing? What mechanisms has the Federation used to produce independence in the sector? These are the questions that not only animate this last chapter, but run through the whole book. The search for freedom through independence, as Nikolas Rose said, has come to define 'the problem space within which contemporary rationalities of government compete'.[2] The Federation, in asserting the sector's freedom through independence, attempts to carve out a space in this arena, one in which the sector's own ways of thinking can become tools of governing. And so 'iN Business' seeks to provide tools for associations to become 'champions of communities'.

Independence is a complex concept; nevertheless, of late it has come to mean just one thing for many in the sector; associations as *private bodies*, independent from the State. This binary imaging of the positioning of housing associations, as non-state as opposed to State, private as opposed to public, has been the focus of recent campaigning, not just the Federation's 're-branding' of the sector. The

[1] J Tickell, 'Independent Spirit' (13 September 2002) *Inside Housing* 22–23.

[2] N Rose, *Powers of Freedom: Reframing Political Thought* (Cambridge, Cambridge University Press, 1999).

Federation campaigned against the Housing and Regeneration Bill[3] because, it argued, the powers of the new regulator were so broad that associations might be considered as 'public bodies'. And the largest associations are now lining up to appeal against a recent decision of the Court of Appeal in *London and Quadrant Housing Trust v Weaver*[4] which decided that the Trust's housing management and allocations were *public functions*. The argument throughout this book has been that associations are now so inextricably tied up with their private funders that to understand independence only as the freedom from *state* control misses the point. Therefore, whilst the first part of this chapter considers the mechanisms the Federation has deployed to create independence, the second part seeks to explore the more complex role of associations as being in 'states of dependence', suggesting a more nuanced understanding than the rhetoric of the public–private debate suggests.

The first part of this chapter briefly draws together material from previous chapters to explore the concept of independence, and the different meanings it has held at different times. It will then consider how the Federation sought to prepare associations for meeting the demands of the Housing Act 1974, to set associations free of a dependency on charity and of their image as well-meaning but amateur voluntary organisations. It will then examine the Federation's response to what has been particularly important in making claims of independence—the governance of housing associations by their voluntary committees, or boards of management. The second part of the chapter looks at the 'iN Business' campaign, which, despite its focus on independence, in fact brings into focus associations in their hybrid form; in being not simply housing providers, but community builders, with the desire to develop health, education and employment resources alongside housing, deploying state-like powers such as anti-social behaviour orders (ASBOs) and parenting orders. Therefore, it is argued, the Court of Appeal's conclusion that London and Quadrant Housing Trust is a *hybrid* public authority is a far more useful descriptor of the sector, one that acknowledges the complex nature of associations, in between the public and the private.

[3] Introduced in the parliamentary session 2007–08, the Bill received Royal Assent on 22 July 2008.

[4] *London and Quadrant Housing Trust v Weaver* [2009] EWCA Civ 587.

Securing Independence

Independence through Expertise

Housing associations and the Federation have always had concerns about their status, but threats to independence have not always been from the same direction. In the Federation's early history it did not have the same anxieties about the public–private distinction as it does today, as was seen in chapter two. Indeed, the Federation campaigned in the post-Second World period for associations to be considered as public authorities so that they too, like local authorities, would have access to both subsidies and scarce building materials for new building and repairing war damaged properties. To have been considered as private developers would have been contrary to their interests. In chapter five, too, we saw that the Federation campaigned for associations to be treated like local authorities to enable war-time restrictions on rent increases to be removed.

In the 1960s, what mattered to associations was to be independent from the restrictions of charity, as shown in chapter three. For the confines of charity law (in particular within the regulatory regime of the Inland Revenue) meant that associations could only ever house those who met a very narrow definition of being in poverty, and that they would have to evict any households which stepped over this basic threshold. At this point, associations were unconcerned that freedom from charity meant state regulation; indeed, (as shown in chapter five) the Federation actively worked with civil servants in developing a new regulatory regime that came into force through the Housing Act 1974. The Federation recognised that financial resources from central and local government that would provide freedom to develop (new associations and new housing) required state regulation to signal the trustworthiness of associations. Indeed, the regulatory regime that came out of the Housing Act 1974 was much more controlling than present-day systems, with intensive oversight not just of associations, but of each housing scheme they developed; and in the initial stages of the new regime this oversight occurred twice, from the Housing Corporation *and* the Department of the Environment!

In this period what mattered for securing independence was that housing associations could be trusted for their *expertise*. Producing expertise in member organisations was an aim of the Federation from the beginning and continued as an important role. In the first four decades, besides promoting expertise in housing management, it was expertise in urban renewal that was used to position associations. This positioning became inscribed in statute in the Housing Act 1974, primarily an Act to promote the renewal of inner cities, but which included a funding and regulatory regime for housing associations that would enable them to be key partners in this programme. The 1974 Act was, however, a dramatic step-change in government's expectation of associations' role. The new system of Housing Association Grant delivered by the Act was designed to provide the 'rocket fuel' and the Housing Corporation demanded growth in order to meet spending targets. The pressure to achieve growth placed many strains on associations, both in the production of housing and in managing significantly more tenants and properties. Addressing these concerns, in 1975, the Federation published a code of conduct for the management associations' operations[5]. Following this, a working party was set up to consider how associations would cope with the problems of growth that the new funding implied. The working party included housing association staff, alongside representatives from the Housing Corporation, the Department of the Environment (DoE) and the Institute of Housing. Its secretary was Richard Best, Director of the Federation. The housing association representatives came mainly from the new, Shelter-sponsored associations. However, older ways were seen as an asset, as Richard Best commented: 'the big old trusts were quite a help—they were not growing so fast so they were a nice ballast' and so the Guinness Trust[6] was also represented on the working party. In 1977, the working party's report, *Growing Pains: Coping with the Problems of Growth in Housing Associations* was published.[7]

Growing Pains established growth as the norm. Indeed it argued for rapid, *large-scale* growth, commenting that 'it might be preferable not to expand at all' than to grow slowly, because a slow rate of growth makes 'sensible' staff appointments difficult.[8] It was silent on the arguments against growth. Rather, the assumption was that 'each association has already thought this through and concluded that growth is necessary in its case'.[9] Such unquestioned assumptions arose (in part) from the selection of members of the committee; the new philanthropic associations set out to tackle what Shelter had described as a 'national crisis' of homelessness[10] and saw expansion as the only way to meet perceived levels of need; others already operated in large bureaucracies and so knew no other form.

The publication of *Growing Pains* was described in a recent interview with Richard Best as 'seminal'.[11] Whilst its seminality may be contested, the direction of rapid growth that it prescribed has been consistently pursued by some in the

[5] National Federation of Housing Associations (NHFA), *Housing Management Practice in Housing Associations* (NFHA, London, 1975).

[6] The Guinness Housing Trust was one of a number of housing trusts established in the late nineteenth century to provide housing for poor households. Its large charitable income meant that it was able to ignore many of the dictates of the State, while also enabling it to develop into a large, nationwide organisation. See P Malpass, *Housing Philanthropy and the State: A History of the Guinness Trust* (Bristol, Faculty of the Built Environment, University of the West of England, 1998).

[7] NHFA, London, 1977.

[8] *Ibid.*

[9] *Ibid*, 4.

[10] Shelter, *The Shelter Story: A Brief History of the First Three Years of SHELTER'S National Campaign for the Homeless and a Handbook on its Current Activities* (London, Shelter, 1970); see above, ch 7 of this book.

[11] Interview with Richard Best for this book (12 August 2003).

sector since its publication. But its significance was also in the changing management and governance systems it proposed: it recommended that associations should take on paid staff, and that the voluntary committee should move away from day to day control of associations' affairs into a role of monitoring, oversight and the strategic management. This shift, along with recommendations to adopt formal, written procedures, policies and practices, sought to discard the image of amateur voluntarism, proposing a bureaucratisation of the housing association sector.

Having set out to challenge local authorities' narrow interpretation of housing need,[12] *Growing Pains* was setting associations on a path to becoming the new welfare bureaucracies. In seeking to set associations free of a dependency on charity and of their image as well-meaning but amateur voluntary organisations, there was silence on the possible impact that this transformation might have on their status as independent organisations; both their financial dependence, and newly acquired professionalism and expertise, made them appear as 'public bodies'. Questions were not asked as to whether unchecked growth would distance associations from the communities whose housing needs they had set out to solve. Nor were questions asked about the benefits of members of a community being involved in running their own association. The sector saw the transformation not as a compromise to its objectives, but rather that *growth* would alter power relations leading to influence:

> It must not be thought, however, that the relations between associations and central government (and the Housing Corporation) and local authorities must inevitably lead the association to compromise its own objectives: as the Movement grows, associations can increasingly influence at these two levels and make their contribution of much wider importance.[13]

Independence through Governance

It was the fact of housing associations having management committees of volunteers that was frequently cited as a principal claim to independence. Unlike local authority councillors, housing association committee members claimed that they did not owe their positions to affiliation to a political party, nor were they meant to represent any other interest or make any financial gain from the association. Nevertheless, as we saw in chapter seven, the rapid expansion of housing associations in places like Notting Hill led to an amount of disenchantment from local communities, and there were continuing concerns about the sector. Some saw associations as 'unaccountable self-perpetuating oligarchies'.[14] Some Conservative politicians blamed associations for their party's loss of

[12] See above, ch 4.
[13] *Growing Pains*, above n 7 at 8.
[14] P Malpass, *Housing Associations and Housing Policy: A Historical Perspective* (Basingstoke, Macmillan, 2000) 257.

constituencies in the 1992 general election, believing that associations' development policies had altered 'the social and political balance'.[15] Elsewhere, the governance and accountability of business organisations was called into question, in the failures of Robert Maxwell's empire and the Bank of Credit and Commerce International (which wiped out the savings of many), followed by the Cadbury report (the Report of the Committee on the Financial Aspects of Governance).[16] There was a growing awareness that failings in the governance of private organisations could have a much wider impact. The housing association sector came to understand that trust in the sector could not simply be ensured through a system of state regulation; internal governance mechanisms, too, must provide assurance. In 1994, an 'independent inquiry comprising respected professionals from a range of disciplines' to 'overhaul the governance of the [housing association] sector' was established by the Federation.[17]

Internal pressures on associations also provided impetus for the Inquiry. Board members now had to contend with levels of financial risk following the Housing Act 1988 and the introduction of private finance in the funding of associations.[18] The increased financial risk faced by associations meant boards were under pressure to take on members with specific professional expertise; but at the same time they were accused of being unrepresentative and encouraged to take on members from the communities in which they operated.[19] Also significant was the Page report,[20] which had set out a scenario of an impending crisis for associations, building ever larger estates to house the ever-increasing number of homeless households. Part of the solution advocated by Page was that associations should assert their independence from local authorities, and in particular from being too tied in to their needs-based allocations systems. There was considerable focus in the Inquiry on the 'independence' of associations and establishing the Inquiry appears in part to be the Federation's response to the Page report.

Funding for the Inquiry came from the Joseph Rowntree Foundation, which had a reputation for producing high quality research independent of government

15 *Ibid.*

16 The Cadbury Report, *Committee on the Financial Aspects of Corporate Governance, Draft Report* (London, Financial Reporting Council, 1992).

17 NFHA, *1995–96 Annual Report.* The Inquiry and the background to it have been extensively discussed in other publications: see J Ashby, 'The Inquiry into Housing Association Governance' in P Malpass (ed), *Ownership, Control and Accountability: The New Governance of Social Housing* (London, Chartered Institute of Housing, 1997); A Kearns, *Going by the Board: The Unknown Facts about Housing Association Membership and Management Committees in England* (Glasgow, Centre for Housing Research and Urban Studies, University of Glasgow, 1994).

18 See above, ch 6.

19 Ashby, above n 17 at 68.

20 D Page, *Building for Communities: A Study of New Housing Association Estates* (York, Joseph Rowntree Foundation, 1993) discussed above in ch 4. Despite its widespread influence in the housing associations sector, this report was commissioned and published not by the Federation but by the Joseph Rowntree Foundation whose Director was Richard Best, who had been Federation Director from 1973 until 1988.

and other organisations, funded by income from the Trust's charitable legacy. The composition of the Inquiry Panel was also critical in conferring legitimacy on the Inquiry's recommendations with external constituencies. It 'would need to be independent if it was to have the necessary credibility'[21] according to its Secretary, Julian Ashby.[22] The panel included representatives of the Housing Corporation, the Charity Commission, the Registrar of Friendly Societies and the Department of the Environment (DoE), with only three housing association representatives. An executive director of Hambros Bank and previous permanent secretary in the Department for Education and Science, was chosen as chairman. I would suggest that, as with *Growing Pains*, the panel's composition not only accorded legitimacy, but influenced possible outcomes, for the organisational cultures of panel members would be brought to bear in their deliberations. Choosing a prominent figure from the banking sector as chairman indicated a desire that the practices in the private finance sector should be taken on board, as well as making outcomes acceptable to that sector. There was no tenant representative on the panel.

The panel's recommendations were by no means radical. In leading the sector, the Federation rarely attempted radical change. The Federation had its own long-term interests to consider, which relied on the support of a spectrum of views within a diverse sector. In any case, in the prevailing political climate of 1995, with a Housing Bill going through that was intended to allow developers to access social housing grant, and an almost universal assumption that New Labour would win the next general election,[23] radical outcomes would not find acceptance. The message from the Inquiry chairman conveyed to the internal and external environment was that 'housing associations should be competent, accountable, independent and diverse'.[24] In explaining that competence meant 'building homes that work for a competitive price . . . enjoying the confidence of tenants ... staying solvent . . . discharging financial, statutory and regulatory obligations'[25] it was clear that the Inquiry meant its recommendations to be understood by business and markets. Independence meant being independent of party politics, pressure groups and ministers.

The panel proposed a 'Code of Governance', borrowing a mechanism of self-regulation from the financial services industry, no doubt hoping that like the financial services industry's adoption of the Cadbury Code, it would avoid statutory controls. Indeed, the Federation claimed the Inquiry as a success in

[21] Ashby, above n 17 at 69.

[22] Ashby was Managing Director of HACAS, an advisory service for associations formed by the Federation and the Corporation in the 1980s.

[23] A Rawnsley, *Servants of the People: The Inside Story of New Labour* (London, Hamish Hamilton, 2000) vii.

[24] NFHA, *Competence and Accountability: Report of the Inquiry into Housing Association Governance* (London, NFHA, 1995) 5.

[25] *Ibid.*

fending off a review of housing associations by the Nolan Committee on Standards in Public Life.[26] Nolan 'overwhelmingly endorsed the code's principles'.[27]

This shift in the ways in which the Federation has sought to establish independence was contested at the time, as is shown by some of the evidence submitted to the Inquiry panel. These submissions demonstrate a range of perspectives on independence often missing from the present-day hegemony of the image of associations as private business organisations focused on expansion. In particular, it was the suggestion in the Inquiry's terms of reference that a change in the legal structure of associations might be necessary to accommodate a more business-style mode of operations, that focused submissions on the nature of housing associations. Evidence submitted by the Voluntary Committee Members groups was particularly strident in its opposition to any changes in the statutory basis of associations, which, they feared would move them out of the voluntary 'not for profit' sector into either the statutory or the private 'for-profit' sector. 'There is virtually no pressure from within the housing association movement for such radical change',[28] they stated. Equally, the London Voluntary Committee Members Working Group considered comparisons with the Cadbury report were 'not . . . appropriate' as associations were not commercial organisations.[29] The Scottish Federation of Housing Associations challenged the assumption of the need for continued growth as a driving factor behind the search for new legal structures, and warned that:

> There is a real danger that this success [in difficult urban regeneration work, supported housing, etc] could be undermined by a short-term stampede for growth [..] SFHA believes that changes to the legal basis to plc forms, or which changed the voluntary control of housing associations, would mean that new organisations would no longer be housing associations as they are currently understood.[30]

It is these nuances and contestations in understandings of independence that we turn to in the next section.

[26] The Nolan Committee on Standards in Public Life, *Standards in Public Life: Local Public Spending Bodies: Further and Higher Education Bodies (including universities), Grant-maintained Schools, Training and Enterprise Councils and Local Enterprise Companies, Registered Housing Associations* vol 1 (Cm 3270-I, London, HMSO, 1996).

[27] NFHA, *A Step Ahead: National Federation of Housing Associations' Annual Report 1995–96* (London, NFHA, 1995–96) 9.

[28] Evidence from National VCM Forum cited in NFHA, *Much in Evidence: Selected Submissions to the Governance Inquiry* (London, NFHA, 1995) 5.

[29] *Ibid.*

[30] *Ibid*, 10.

States of Dependence

What I want to explore here is a concept of independence as relational; the idea that independence is not a property intrinsic to a particular body or type, but that independence can only exist in relation to independence *from* some other state or being. Following the sociologist, Zygmunt Bauman, I would argue that independence, like freedom

> exists only as a social relation; that instead of being a property, a possession of the individual himself, it is a quality pertaining to a certain difference between individuals; . . . it makes sense only as an opposition to some other condition, past or present.[31]

Liberal democracies in Europe, particularly since the Second World War, have understood freedom in terms of the 'maximization of individual liberty and, in particular, with the defence of that liberty against the State'.[32] In Bauman's analysis, freedom as an 'ability to master one's own fate' is a very modern understanding of the condition, associated with an 'artificiality of social order'.[33] Within the context of the discussion about housing associations in this chapter, their 'social order' concerns perceptions of where they stand in relation to organisations of the State. For those very large associations like London & Quadrant (the subject of the most recent court case to consider the public nature of associations, discussed further below), who own and manage far more properties than any single local authority, their understanding of their position is of autonomous organisations able to order their own affairs. Their identity is that of a *private*, not *public*, body. But if we go beneath the rhetoric, we begin to see a far more complex situation: we see organisations that have been given powers of the State in, for example, their ability to apply for Anti-Social Behaviour Orders and Parenting Orders as tools for managing anti-social behaviour on their estates. We see a sector that remains 'financially underpinned by government expenditure through grants and particularly Housing Benefit',[34] whilst at the same time, an individual association is able to raise £265 million in a bond in its own name.[35] But should we be surprised that claiming independence from the State is a false claim? According to English seventeenth-century philosopher, John Locke, a state of freedom must be secured by laws, for freedom is but 'a Liberty to dispose and order, as he lists, his person, Actions, Possessions and his whole Property, *within the Allowance of those laws under which he is*'.[36] Economist and

[31] Z Bauman, *Freedom* (Milton Keynes, Open University Press, 1988) 7.

[32] B Hindness, *Discourses of Power: From Hobbes to Foucault* (Oxford, Blackwell, 1996) 65.

[33] See above, n 31.

[34] K Gibb and C Ngaard, 'Transfers, Contracts and Regulation: A New Institutional Economics Perspective on the Changing Provision of Social Housing in Britain' 21(6) *Housing Studies* 825–50, 830.

[35] 'New bond issue busts records' (14 November 2008) *Inside Housing* 4.

[36] J Locke, *Second Treatise on Government* 2nd edn (London, Cambridge University Press, 1970) para 57 (emphasis added).

philosopher Friedrich Hayek also saw freedom as contained by mechanisms of control: 'the discipline of civilization ... is at the same time the discipline of freedom'.[37] And so, in post-Second World War Europe, the European Convention on Human Rights was formulated by nation-states as a means to ensure freedom, in an attempt to avoid the atrocities that had occurred. This Convention has been incorporated into the legal structures of most of its signatory states.[38]

The binary divide, state–non-state, public–private, is no longer (if it ever was) useful in describing our present states of being. Just as, in the 1960s, the boundaries of charity law produced sterile debates, unable to acknowledge modern understandings of poverty (see chapter three), so now arguments about public versus private have become sterile. This can be illustrated by looking at what associations do, and aspire to do, at the present time.

Housing Associations as Hybrid Bodies: 'iN Business for Neighbourhoods'

Perceptions of a *lack of independence*, led to a major initiative by the Federation to 're-brand' the association sector under the slogan 'iN Business for Neighbourhoods', launched at its 2003 annual conference. The intention was that 'iN Business' would create a 'national alliance of housing associations working to create good neighbourhoods in cities, towns and villages across England'.[39] The campaign aimed to 'identify housing associations collectively'[40] and included a new logo for the sector, the letters 'iN' inside an orange circle. 'iN' represents a person standing next to a house, the circle, an orange sun, meant to signify hope! The terminology of the campaign, as well as many of the tools, were deliberately reflective of the consumer paradigm that associations considered they were located within. The exercise was called a 're-branding' and the brand was to be stamped on the imagination of tenants, government and funders through the common logo displayed on stationery, signboards and other publicity material.

To understand this desire to re-brand the sector, we need to go back to 1993 and the Page report, *Building for Communities*.[41] This was associations' rediscovery of community but, critically, in the context of maintaining financial security and minimising risky tenancies through strategies for exclusion. Creating *sustainable communities* became the 'holy grail of housing policy': housing allocations policies should ensure a mix of poor with not-so-poor households, requiring

[37] FA Hayek, *The Constitution of Liberty* (London, Routledge & Kegan Paul, 1960) 163.

[38] In the UK, now in part incorporated through the Human Rights Act 1998.

[39] National Housing Federation (NHF), *In Business for Neighbourhoods: who we are, what we do* (London, NHF, 2003) 1.

[40] J Coulter, NHF chief executive quoted in C Griffin, 'Interview: Jim Coulter' (2003) 57(9) *Axis: Housing, Planning and Regeneration* 6.

[41] Above n 20.

abandoning (or at least suspending) 'the universalist notion of need'[42] The Page report urged associations to reassert control over where and what they built and who they housed, in effect to reassert their independence. In this new role envisioned by 'iN Business', housing associations were to become 'the independent champions of neighbourhoods and communities, and [..] the vital intermediaries between the state and the people'.[43]

As with the need for a governance inquiry, much of the driving force behind re-branding was a self-perception of a sector vulnerable to criticism and requiring a new image. The Federation's chief executive knew that the Government perceived social housing to be 'a problem' prior to its 2000 spending review and 'did not want to be investing in failure'.[44] The Federation's chair, Richard McCarthy,[45] saw a growing frustration among members that they were 'modernising' their organisations and activities but receiving no recognition. Associations directed their frustration ('unfairly', he said) at the Federation. In particular, some of the bigger players were beginning to question whether they were getting enough from being part of the Federation. For McCarthy, 'iN Business' was born out of the Federation's search for a 'Big Idea'. At the same time, the Federation was receiving other, more mixed messages, from its members and central government. The 2000 Housing Green Paper[46] proposed much tighter controls over associations by moving towards a system of unified rents across the whole social housing sector in one section[47] at the same time as proposing to allow them much broader discretion in social housing allocations.[48] 'iN Business' can be seen as the Federation's attempt to take control of this growing problematisation of the future of social housing.

In adopting the slogan 'iN Business for Neighbourhoods' the Federation located associations within two dominant languages of current political discourse, consumerism and communities. Government urban policy, particularly since 1997, had 'attempted to restructure the terrain of governance by seeking to change the ways in which communities govern themselves'.[49] The Government's

[42] D Cowan and A Marsh, 'Analysing New Labour Policy' in D Cowan and A. Marsh (eds), *Two Steps Forward: Housing Policy for the New Millennium* (Bristol, The Policy Press, 2001) 274.

[43] Tickell, above n 2 at 22–23.

[44] Jim Coulter quoted in *Inside Housing*, Griffin, above n 40.

[45] Interview with Richard McCarthy (17 September 2003).

[46] Department of the Environment, Transport and the Regions/Department of Social Security, *Quality and Choice: A Decent Home for All*, The Housing Green Paper (London, HMSO, 2000).

[47] A Marsh, 'Restructuring Social Housing Rents' in Cowan and Marsh (eds), *Two Steps Forward*, above n 42; B Mauthe, in same volume.

[48] Cowan and Marsh, *ibid* at 272.

[49] R Atkinson, 'Addressing Urban Social Exclusion through Community Involvement in Urban Regeneration' in R Imrie and M Raco (eds), *Urban Policy, Community, Citizenship and Rights* (Bristol, Polity Press, 2003) 102.

policy focus became 'sustainable communities'[50] and strategies for neighbourhood renewal.[51] However, the Federation's interpretation of the 'community' discourse was framed by their claims to independence. The Page report's focus on communities can be seen as little more than a device to save associations from having to house a lot more people in extreme poverty. As the discussion in chapter four showed, an association's business interests can frame their allocations policies, leading them to exclude households who might 'trash' the properties they have invested in, or cause management problems.[52] Although associations try to square the circle of communities and consumerism, they are fundamentally incompatible.

However, such an alignment with the dominant political ways of thinking and speaking provided the sector with a self-confidence that its role was *governmental.* Legislation already recognised its role of *policing* communities, providing associations with powers similar to local authorities, enabling them to apply for ASBOs[53] and parenting orders[54] where behaviour impacted on their housing management functions. 'iN Business' proposed that associations should be approaching their forward planning and decision-making in much the same manner as the State would: they should become knowledgeable about the needs of the whole population (of the neighbourhood), asking questions about *population* need, not simply *housing* need. The launch of 'iN Business' was accompanied by the publication of Federation research, which aimed to provide much of this background population information.[55] Similarly, associations should act to tackle community needs, not just housing needs:

> If health or education are what matter, then we build health centres and schools and if necessary manage them. The same goes for leisure facilities, libraries and public transport.[56]

The idea that housing associations should be providing more than housing is not new. Right up until at least 1945, associations such as the Octavia Hill Housing

[50] Office of the Deputy Prime Minister (ODPM), *Sustainable Communities: Building for a Better Future* (London, ODPM, 2003).

[51] ODPM, *Changing Neighbourhoods, Changing Lives: The Vision for Neighbourhood Renewal* (London, ODPM, 2003).

[52] D Cowan and K Morgan, 'Trust, Distrust and Betrayal: A Social Housing Case Study' (2009) 72(2) *Modern Law Review* 157–181; D Cowan, K Morgan and M McDermont 'Nominatons: An Actor–Network Approach' (2009) *Housing Studies* 24(3), 281–300.

[53] Anti-Social Behaviour Act 2003, Part 2, ss 153A–D.

[54] Police and Justice Act 2006 s 23, amending Anti-Social Behaviour Act 2003, s 25: an association can apply for a parenting order 'where that child's behaviour affects housing management functions' (www.respect.giv.co.uk/members/article.aspx?id=11518).

[55] R Scase and J Scales, *Regional Futures and Neighbourhood Realities* (London, NHF, 2003).

[56] NHF, *In Business for Neighbourhoods: Who We Are, What We Do* (London, NHF, 2003) 5. There seems to be a shift in policy from the 1980s and 1990s 'partnering' approach (see above, ch 4) to an approach of doing it alone.

Trust were providing crèches and other social facilities;[57] and since the mid-1990s the Housing Corporation has been encouraging (perhaps 'pushing' might be more accurate) associations to do 'Housing Plus'. This might encompass providing education and training opportunities as part of a construction contract, constructing offices to be shared with health workers, or employing neighbourhood workers.[58] Maybe what is different, however, is a sense that associations should now be the leaders in such partnerships, whereas in the past this would have been considered the role of local government.[59]

Critically, however, 'iN Business' envisioned a hybrid role for associations, as in this slide explaining the campaign to a Federation national conference shows:

> What it could mean—role
> not a substitute, but an intermediary between ...
> - *people and government*
> - *public and private*
> - *private and private*
> - *public and public*
>
> no political affiliation
>
> *Don't try to emulate councils*

Similarly, the final slide of this presentation asked members to remember that 'the idea of neighbourhood has far-reaching implications [for] culture and mindset, economic model, local focus/sector structure, public policy, standards, buy-in'.[60]

Clearly, the re-branding of associations is complex. The messages also seem contradictory, since suggesting associations should be providing health facilities, or addressing transport needs, looks very like 'emulating councils'. Unlike councils, of course, associations' income stream is almost totally reliant on rents and so these other functions could only be carried out in partnership with others; and their claims to represent 'hope' and act as intermediaries between 'the people and the State' can seem unreal when many are large bureaucracies without even the check of elected councillors. Nevertheless, the idea of being *between* the identities of public and private seems a refreshing message after the rhetoric of associations

57 See, eg, P Malpass, *The Work of the Century: The Origins and Growth of the Octavia Hill Housing Trust in Notting Hill* (London, Octavia Hill Housing Trust, 1999).

58 Eg, see case studies in NHF, *In Business for Neighbourhoods: Action for Change* (London, NHF, 2003) 6.

59 See above, ch 4 on partnering.

60 NHF, 'Housing's Better Future' plenary presentation to NHF conference (Birmingham,19 September 2002).

as *private businesses*. I argue in the final section that the Court of Appeal's decision that the London and Quadrant Housing Trust was a hybrid public authority should be understood as an acknowledgement of this complex, in-between role.

A Housing Association as a Functional Public Authority

The question of identity has arisen in the courts on various occasions. In the 1950s, the issue was whether the Guinness Trust was charitable, as we saw in chapter six. However, as chapter six also showed, by the late 1980s the funding sources for associations had changed; associations wanted to access *private* loans and so be seen as *private* risk-bearing bodies. They were, however, increasingly drawn upon to take over from local authorities the function of housing poor and vulnerable households. It was hardly surprising then when the question as to whether they could be held to the same legal standards as local authorities came before the courts. Being *public* bodies, local authorities were expected to conform to certain standards of fairness and rationality and not contravene legitimate expectations in decision making; and their actions could be subject to judicial review. In *R v Servite Houses*,[61] the Court concluded that Servite Houses, a housing association, was not a public body. However, the judge concluded that the increasing contractualisation and privatisation of the State was 'one of the most important questions in public law today'.[62] More recently, the Human Rights Act 1998 has required that organisations that are *public authorities* should not act in a manner that contravenes certain categories of human rights set out in the Act. The seemingly broad definition of public authority contained in the Act, which includes bodies carrying out *public functions* has led to a series of cases in the courts as to what constitutes 'public functions'. The courts have taken a somewhat restricted view of public function, which left associations in all but a very limited range of cases as private bodies.

The most recent decision of the Court of Appeal appears to change this. In *Weaver v London & Quadrant Housing Trust* the Court was asked to decide whether the London and Quadrant Housing Trust was subject to judicial review proceedings for contravening the legitimate expectations of a tenant, and whether it was subject to the Human Rights Act. This decision is highly significant, for it confirms the hybrid, in-between nature of housing associations. There are a number of strands to this decision. When the case was first heard before the Divisional Court,[63] LQHT conceded that certain of its functions—its ability to request an ASBO or a parenting order—were public acts and therefore that when carrying out these functions it was a hybrid public authority. However,

[61] *R v Servite Houses and another ex p Goldsmith and another* [2001] LGR 55.
[62] Moses J at para 67b.
[63] *Weaver v London & Quadrant Housing Trust* [2008] EWHC 1377 Admin.

the Court of Appeal also confirmed the Divisional Court's decision that the association's housing management and allocation functions were functions that could be considered as *governmental*:

> [A]lthough not directly taking the place of local government, the Trust in its allocation of social housing operate in very close harmony with … the provision of subsidised housing, as opposed to the provision of housing itself, is, in my opinion a function which can properly be described as governmental.[64]

The implication is that a potentially wide range of the association's functions are open to judicial review and human rights claims. It also opens up the possibility of other claims as a public body, for example, to question whether use of CCTV evidence gathering is challengeable under the Human Rights Act.[65] In the previous section, an examination of the functions and powers that associations deemed necessary to be 'iN business for neighbourhoods', suggested an identity in between public and private; the term 'hybrid public authority' seems to capture this identity well.

But this is an identity that LQHT and other large London associations are not prepared to accept. They have set up a 'war chest'[66] to support LQHT in an appeal to the House of Lords (now Supreme Court). Interestingly, there is no talk of the Federation being involved in this challenge to the sector's legal identity. It is not mentioned in press reports; it's role seems to be simply that of briefing members.[67]

What are the concerns about this ruling? One is the associations' fear of the costs of defending claims in the courts, but this is something local authorities have always faced. Organisations that can call on the sorts of powers, and have the impact over people's lives that associations have, surely should be accountable for their actions, including through the courts? Another concern is that they will be classified as public bodies for funding purposes, leaving their private borrowing to be counted against public sector spending limits—but the Federation has sought advice about this and has concluded that it seems unlikely that the *Weaver* decision will lead to reclassification as public bodies.[68] In reality, of course, the concern is about protecting a narrative of independence, one that eschews state control whilst failing to acknowledge that limitations of freedom come from a whole variety of directions—in particular, the controls of being situated in increasingly globalised financial markets.

[64] *London and Quadrant Housing Trust v Weaver* [2009] EWCA Civ 58, LJ Elias at paras 69, 70.

[65] PJ Whitehead, the Managing Director of specialist housing law solicitors Whiteheads, writing in 24dash.com, 10 July 2009: www.24dash.com/news/Housing/2009–07–10-London-and-Quadrant-v-Weaver-what-does-it-mean-in-practice.

[66] C Story, 'War chest to fight L&Q ruling' (26 June 2009) *Inside Housing* 1.

[67] NHF briefing note, '*Weaver v London & Quadrant Housing Trust*' ref NS.GN.2009.BR.12.

[68] NHF briefing note, *ibid* 4.

Conclusion

This chapter has looked at some of the ways in which the Federation has sought to establish an image of housing associations as independent organisations, with the skills and expertise to exercise power over their sphere of operation. The 1977 report, *Growing Pains*, was part of setting associations on the path to becoming large, bureaucratic, hierarchical organisations. It consolidated the expansionist ideas of much of the sector. This was followed, in the 1990s, by a need to demonstrate that these ever-expanding organisations could be trusted to manage themselves. So the sector set up an 'independent' inquiry which created a 'code of governance' for the housing association board. In doing so, they drew upon models and understandings from private corporate governance, in the knowledge that it was private sector bodies as much as government that needed to understand how housing associations worked. The private sector needed to trust associations to be in control of large sums of private funding.

However, despite assertions by the Federation and associations that the key aspect of independence is freedom from state control, the discussion in the second part of the chapter shows that the nature of associations is, by necessity (and desire), hybrid. 'iN Business' sought to position associations between public and private, public and public, private and private. It sought to cement the role of associations as community builders, providers of much more than housing, moving into health, education and transport where necessary. Associations need the powers as well as the resources of the State if they are to be able to fulfil this role. The chapter, therefore, concluded that the Court of Appeal's most recent decision on the legal identity of associations, as *hybrid public authorities*, may be the most helpful descriptor. For Bauman's understanding of freedom as a social relation shows that 'independence' is a miasma: we all exist in conditions of dependency. Better surely to acknowledge that our need for social relations and resources creates and sustains conditions of *inter*-dependency, and to work openly and honestly within these dependent sets of relations? To continually argue for independence is to obscure those relations that, at some future time, will assert themselves, demanding an acknowledgement of responsibility and asserting control.

The fundamental question is, why should housing associations not be considered as exercising public functions and therefore subject to the Human Rights Act? They seem to want to be hybrid bodies at a technical level, but in terms of identity and accountability, to be resolutely private. But associations are deeply embedded in the social: they provide public services, using public funds; they have the ability to exercise coercive power over tenants and possibilities for excluding would-be tenants they consider anti-social. It must be possible to call them to account, and being subject to a regulatory authority is not enough. The 'market-failure' rationale for regulation that Martin Cave proposed, that has become the dominant rationale for regulatory bodies, means minimalist regulation. In calling to account these organisations that have both massive potential for public good, whilst at the same time the ability to exercise powers that can create significant harm, the exercise of rights in the *public* domain becomes a critical tool.

Appendix: Biographies of Interviewees

UNLESS OTHERWISE SHOWN, these biographies have been primarily compiled in August 2008 from information in the Jubilee Album[1] and interview transcripts. (Interview dates are given in brackets.)

Charlie Adams (17 September 2003)

Charlie studied architecture at Liverpool University and became involved with Shelter Neighbourhood Action Project in Liverpool 8. On leaving university, he went to work for Birmingham City Council in urban renewal, working in Small Heath where the council set up a number of housing co-ops. He then worked as development officer for the Co-operative Housing Agency (CHA), set up in 1976 by government on the recommendation of the Campbell Committee to promote housing co-operatives nationwide. CHA subsequently became a satellite of the Housing Corporation. He moved on to work in regulation in the Housing Corporation South London region and then became Regional Director. He was chief executive of Hyde Housing Association when interviewed for this book. Charlie died on 5 May 2006.

Eric Armitage (22 September 2003)

Eric joined North British Housing Association in 1973, and became chief executive in 1983. He was a founder member of the Northern Housing Associations' Group (NORHAG). Eric became a member of the Federation's Press & Organisation Committee, then a member of the executive committee, before being elected as chair of the National Council in 1988, a post that he held for a period of four years. In 1997 he retired as chief executive of North British HA and became a member of the Housing Corporation board. He retired from the Housing Corporation board in 2003.

[1] P Jones *The Jubilee Album: A Celebration of the Housing Association Movement* (London, National Federation of Housing Associations, 1985)

John Baker (11 September 2003)

John was a career civil servant, working in the Ministry of Transport, transferred to the Housing section of the new Department of the Environment (DoE) in 1972. He was put in charge of some aspects of housing policy, in particular, rental policy, and the private rental sector. He participated in the Housing Finance Act 1972, was one of the primary authors of what became the Housing Act 1974. He left the DoE in 1974 to become deputy chief executive of the Housing Corporation, responsible for policy and finance. He left the Housing Corporation in 1978 to become commercial Managing Director of the Central Electricity Generating Board, becoming chief executive and then chairman of National Power plc following the reconstruction and privatisation of the electricity industry. He was chairman of Circle 33 Housing Trust for several years. At the time of interview he was semi-retired and Director of a number of diverse industries, chairman of the Senior Salaries Review Body and of the governors of Holland Park School.

Ken Bartlett (30 June 2003)

Ken became a curate in Paddington, West London, in 1963. In 1967 he set up Paddington Churches Housing Association (PCHA). He was a trustee of Shelter, and then became its chairman. He was a member of the Federation's Improvement Action Committee, and after Richard Best became Director of the Federation, became an Associate Director and improvement advisor to the Federation. He left PCHA in 1979 to work for the Housing Corporation. In 1991–92 he left the Corporation to become an adviser to the Joseph Rowntree Foundation, writing the brief for what became known as the Page report.

David Bebb (11 August 2003)

After an early career in industry and the commercial sector, David joined Shelter in 1971 as Housing Director. In 1973 he became a Founder Director of UK Family Housing Association, a specialist housing association set up to buy in property companies and portfolios of housing for selling on to local housing associations. He joined Liverpool Housing Trust (LHT) as Director in 1976. When interviewed he was group chief executive of LHT Group Limited.

Richard Best (12 August 2003)

Lord Best has been Director of both the Joseph Rowntree Foundation and Joseph Rowntree Housing Trust since 1988. He was a member of the Minister of Local Government's Sounding Board and a member of the Housing Minister's Sounding Board from 1999 to 2001. He has been a member of the Commission on the

Future of Birmingham's Council Housing (2002) and currently chairs the Hull Partnership Liaison Board. He is on the advisory panel of the Home Office Active Community Unit. Among his previous posts have been: commissioner, Rural Development Commission (1989–1998); chair, Inquiry into Social Inclusion in Glasgow (1998–2000). Between 1973 and 1988 he was Director of the National Federation of Housing Associations. Richard Best was created a life peer in 2001.

Source: Joseph Rowntree Foundation website www.jrf.org.uk/about/lordbest.htm

Jim Coulter (13 November 2002)

Jim was head of research for NALGO until he became interested in housing in the early 1970s. He became involved with local authority housing and subsequently became leader of a local authority in Hertfordshire. In 1975 he answered an advert for a Housing Corporation funded scheme which was known popularly as the 'Flower Pot Scheme', whereby the corporation sought to plant, literally, people from other sectors into the new housing association world created by the 1974 Housing Act. Accepted onto the scheme, he spent six months as a trainee. He was then appointed as Director of Leeds Federated Housing Association in 1976, was chair of the Federation's Council from 1985 to 1988. He was chief executive of the National Housing Federation when interviewed for this book, appointed in 1988, retiring in 2005. He is now chair of the board of Bridging Newcastle Gateshead: www.bridgingng.org.uk/.

John Coward (30 June 2003)

John worked for a number of London local authorities as housing manager, finishing up in Richmond as a deputy housing manager, before becoming the first full-time executive of Notting Hill Housing Trust (NHHT), later becoming chief executive. He was a member of Shelter's board of trustees from 1967 to 1969, and a founder member of the London Housing Associations Committee. A committee member of a number of housing associations and voluntary organisations, including Sutton Housing Trust, he served as a member of the Federation's Council from 1969 to 1975, and again from 1980 to 1983. In 1974 he was awarded an OBE and was a member of the Housing Corporation's board from 1975 to 1980. From 1986 to 1989 he chaired the Federation's private finance working party. After retiring from NHHT he continued as trustee of Sutton HT until 2003.

Tony Crook (10 April 2003)

Tony spent two years as a research officer in the planning department of the Greater London Council, working as part of the team that wrote the first draft of the Greater London Development Plan. He was appointed lecturer in Town & Regional Planning at the University of Sheffield in 1968, became a chartered town planner in 1977. He has been chair of South Yorkshire HA, and of the Yorkshire and Humber Regional Council of the Federation. He was elected to the Federation's National Council in the voluntary committee members' constituency in 1982, re-elected in 1985 and served until 1988. He is an adviser to the Institute of Housing. He has been Pro-Vice-Chancellor of the University of Sheffield since 1999.

Source: University of Sheffield website www.shef.ac.uk/trp/staff/crook/index.html

Stephen Duckworth (13 November 2002)

Stephen trained as a chartered accountant. He became involved with community politics in Notting Hill in the 1960s and is a friend of Ken Bartlett. He became a member of the management committee of Paddington Churches HA in 1971. He was appointed Finance Director of Paddington Chuches in 1973 and worked on financial subsidy issues for the NFHA, post 1974 Act, seconded part-time to NFHA from 1980. He was appointed as NFHA Finance Director in 1982. At time of interview, Stephen was projects director of the NFHA.

David Edmonds (30 July 2003)

David Edmonds worked as a career civil servant from 1966 until 1984. From 1984 to 1991 he was chief executive of the Housing Corporation. On leaving the Corporation he became a Managing Director of NatWest Bank, and then Director-General of Oftel, the UK telecommunications regulatory agency, from 1998 to December 2003. He was chair of the board of NHS Direct from 2003 to 2008. In May 2008 he was appointed as the inaugural chairman of the Legal Services Board.

Sources: PublicTechnology.net www.publictechnology.net; Ofcom website; www.legalservicesboard.org.uk

Anthony Fletcher (25 February 2003)

Anthony trained as a barrister. He was Conservative parliamentary candidate for Romford in 1964 and a member of the London County Council from 1961 to 1964. He helped to establish Quadrant Housing Trust (which later merged to become London and Quadrant HT), and was Director from 1968 to 1979. He served as a member of the board of the Housing Corporation from 1979 to 1982, and has been a member of the Federation Council. He has also been a board member of Shelter and of the Empty Homes Agency, set up by Sir George Young to bring empty properties into use as housing accommodation.

Chris Holmes (15 February 2008)

Chris Holmes is self-employed as a researcher and writer; he was a member of the Youth Justice Board, and on the Board of the Housing Corporation until it closed in 2008. He was Director of Shelter from 1995 to 2002, and before that was Director of Housing for the London Borough of Camden. He was Chair of the Mayor's Housing Commission for London, and has also held director positions at CHAR (the Housing Campaign for Single People), East London Housing Association, Society for Co-operative Dwellings and North Islington Housing Rights Project. Chris was awarded the CBE in 1998 for his services to homelessness and Shelter.

Richard McCarthy (17 September 2003)

Richard was secretary of a short-life student housing co-operative while studying geography at university. On leaving university he went to work for Hyde Housing Association in 1979. He became a member of the Federation's National Council in 1998, and was elected chair in 2000. When interviewed for this book he was chair of the NHF and chief executive of Peabody Housing Trust. He left Peabody in October 2003 to become Director-General of Housing and Planning in the Department of Communities and Local Government.

Source: Dept of Communities and Local Government

Barry Natton (11 August 2003)

Barry began his working life in the construction industry. He was appointed chief executive of Liverpool Improved Houses in 1969 (which became Merseyside Improved Homes, and then Riverside Housing Association). He was a member of the Federation's Improvement Action Committee and a founder member of Merseyside Voluntary Housing Group 1971. He became a member of the Federation's Council in 1972, and was chair of NFHA from 1982 to1985. He was also a trustee of the Housing Associations Charitable Trust.

David Orr (18 February 2008)

David Orr is Chief Executive of the National Housing Federation and President of CECODHAS, the European Liaison Committee for Social Housing. He also sits on the board of The Housing Finance Corporation (THFC). He is a member of the Social Investment Task Force which supports the development of social investment in the UK.

John Perry (23 July 2002)

John joined the Chartered Institute of Housing (CioH) in 1991. Prior to that he was Assistant Director of housing with Leicester City Council, responsible for inner city renewal, housing associations and voluntary organisations. As Director of Policy at the Institute until February 2003 he took the lead on a range of issues including housing investment, housing strategies and welfare reform. In 2000 he was a member of the Institute for Public Policy Research Inquiry into the Future of Social Housing. Since March 2003 he has been based in Nicaragua, where he is co-ordinating projects with low income farming families, including a housing project funded by the CIH Presidential Appeal 1998/99. He is now a part-time policy adviser to the CIoH, and his recent work has been on housing finance, BME housing associations and projects for the Audit Commission and National Audit Office.

Source: Chartered Institute of Housing

Andrea Titterington (28 October 2003)

After graduating, Andrea worked as a programme assistant for the Foundation for Co-operative Housing, Washington DC. She joined East Midlands Housing Association (Coalville, Leicestershire) in 1972, working on housing management and development. While at East Midlands HA she was seconded to the Berlin Federation of Housing Associations and Housing Co-operatives from 1975 to 1976. In 1983, she set up the East Midlands Group HA training scheme and worked part-time as the training officer and part-time as regional officer for the NFHA from 1983 to 1986. In 1986, she was appointed as development manager for North British HA, and in 1990 area manager for Housing Corporation, North West Region. She became chief executive of Maritime Housing Association (based in Liverpool) in 1992, retiring in 2003. She was chair of the Housing Federation North until 2003. Andrea is now Regeneration Director for Liverpool Football Club.

Bibliography

ABEL-SMITH, B and TOWNSEND, P, *The Poor and the Poorest: A New Analysis of the Ministry of Labour's 'family expenditure surveys' of 1953–54 and 1960* (London, Bell, 1965).

ALDER, J, and HANDY, C, *Housing Association Law* 2nd edn (London, Sweet & Maxwell, 1991) 355–57.

ALLEN, C, 'The policy and implementation of the housing role in community care—a constructionist theoretical perspective' (1997) 12 *Housing Studies* 85–110, 97.

ARDEN, M, 'The Challenge of Corporate Governance' (2003) 3(1) *Journal of Corporate Law Studies* 1.

ASHBY, J, 'The Inquiry into Housing Association Governance' in P Malpass (ed), *Ownership, Control and Accountability: The New Governance of Social Housing* (London, Chartered Institute of Housing, 1997).

——*In control: The Board Members' Handbook* (London, NHF, 2005).

ATKINSON, R, 'Addressing Urban Social Exclusion through Community Involvement in Urban Regeneration' in R Imrie and M Raco (eds), *Urban Policy, Community, Citizenship and Rights* (Bristol, Polity Press, 2003).

BAKER, CV, *Housing Associations* (London, The Estates Gazette Ltd, 1976) 419–22.

BAILEY, B, *Almshouses* (London, Robert Hale, 1988) 15.

BAILEY, R and RUDDOCK, J, *The Grief Report: A Shelter Report on Temporary Accommodation* (London, Shelter, 1972).

BALDWIN, R and CAVE, M, *Understanding Regulation* (Oxford, Oxford University Press, 1999).

BARKER, K, *Delivering Stability: Securing Our Future Housing Needs* (2004) www.barkerreview.org.uk.

BAUMAN, Z, *Freedom* (Milton Keynes, Open University Press, 1988).

——*The Individualized Society* (Cambridge, Polity, 2001).

BIDOU, A, 'The Communist Hypothesis' (2008) 49 *New Left Review* 29–42.

BILLIS, D, and HARRIS, M, 'Taking the strain of change: UK local voluntary organisations enter the post-Thatcher period' (1992) 21 *Nonprofit and Voluntary Sector Quarterly* 211–25.

BLACK, J, 'Enrolling Actors in Regulatory Systems: Examples from UK Financial Services Regulation' [2003] *Public Law* 63–91 at 65, 70–71.

BLOMLEY, N, Delaney, D and Ford, RT (eds), *The Legal Geographies Reader: Law, Power and Space* (Oxford, Blackwell, 2001).

BLOMLEY, N and SOMMERS, J, 'Mapping Urban Space: Governmentality and Cartographic Struggles in Inner City Vancouver' in R Stamdych (ed), *Governable Places: Readings on Governmentality and Crime Control* (Aldershot, Dartmouth, 1999).

BOURDIEU, P, 'What Makes a Social Class? On The Theoretical and Practical Existence of Groups' (1987) 32(1) *Berkeley Journal of Sociology* 1–17, 5.

BOURDIEU, P, 'Social Space and Symbolic Power' (1989) 7 *Sociological Theory.*

BRAITHWAITE, J, *Restorative Justice and Responsive Regulation* (Oxford, Oxford University Press, 2001) 113–16.

BRAITHWAITE, J and DRAHOS, P, *Global Business Regulation* (Cambridge, Cambridge University Press, 2000) 618–19.

BRION, M and TINKER, A, *Women in Housing: Access and Influence* (London, Housing Centre Trust, 1980).

BURCHELL, G, GORDON C and MILLER, P (eds), *The Foucault Effect: Studies in Governmentality* (London, Harvester Wheatsheaf, 1991).

CALLON, M, 'Some elements of a sociology of translation: domestication of the scallops and the fisherman of St Brieuc Bay' in J Law, *Power, Action and Belief: A New Sociology of Knowledge?* (London, Routledge & Kegan Paul, 1986).

CALLON, M, and LATOUR, B, 'Unscrewing the Big Leviathan: How Actors Macro-Structure Reality and How Sociologists Help Them to Do So' in K Knorr-Cetina and A Cicourel (eds), *Advances in Social Theory* (London, Routledge and Kegan Paul 1981).

CAMERON, A, HARRISON, L, BURTON, P, and MARSH, A, *Crossing the Housing and Care Divide* (Bristol, Policy Press/JRF, 2001).

CAVE, M, *Every Tenant Matters: A Review of Social Housing Regulation* (Communities and Local Government Publications, Wetherby, Yorks, 2007) and www.communities.gov.uk/index.asp?id=1511391.

CHAPLIN, R, JONES, M, MARTIN, S, PRYKE, M, ROYCE, C, SAW, P, WHITEHEAD, C, HONG YANG, C and HONG YANG, J, *Rents and Risks: Investing in Housing Associations* (York, Joseph Rowntree Foundation, 1995) 11.

CLARKE, J 'Subjects of Doubt: in search of the unsettled and unfinished' paper prepared for CASCA Conference (Ontario, Canada, May 2004).

CLARKE, J and NEWMAN, J, *The Managerial State* (London, Sage, 1997).

CLARKE, J, COCHRANE, A, and SMART, C, *Ideologies of Welfare: From Dreams to Disillusion* (Routledge, London, 1987).

CLARKE, J, GEWIRTZ, S and MCLAUGHLIN, E, *New Managerisialism, New Welfare?* (Sage/Open University, London, 2000).

COLE, I, and GOODCHILD, B, 'Local Housing Strategies in England: an assessment of their changing role and context' (1995) 23 *Policy & Politics* 40–60.

COMMUNITIES and LOCAL GOVERNMENT, *Homes for the Future: More Affordable, More Sustainable* (2007, Cm 7191 at http:///www.communities.gov.uk/index.asp?id=1511890).

——*Delivering Housing and Regeneration: Communities England and the Future of Social Housing Regulation* (2007 www.communities.gov.uk/index.asp?id=1511392).

CONWAY, JM, *Identity, Place, Knowledge: Social Movements Contesting Globalization* (Halifax, Nova Scotia, Fernwood Publishing, 2004) 21

COOPER, D, 'Local Government Legal Consciousness in the Shadow of Juridification' (1995) 22 *Journal of Law & Society* 506–26, 508.

——*Governing Out of Order: Space, Law and the Politics of Belonging* (London, Rivers Oram Press, 1998).

COOPER, K, '"Sharp-minded" Mayer to oversee birth of regulator'(16 May 2008) *Inside Housing* 4.

——'Ujima: why didn't anyone step in?' (6 June 2008) *Inside Housing* 26–30, 27.

COWAN, D, *Housing Law and Policy* (Basingstoke, Macmillan, 1999).

COWAN, D and MARSH, A (eds), *Two Steps Forward: Housing Policy for the New Millennium* (Bristol, The Policy Press, 2001).

COWAN, D and MCDERMONT, M, *Regulating Social Housing: Governing Decline* (London, Routledge, 2006) ch 3.

COWAN, D, MCDERMONT, M, and MORGAN, K, *Risk, Trust and Betrayal: A Social Housing Case Study* (2008): www.bris.ac.uk/law/research/centres-themes/nominations/index.html.

COWAN, D, MORGAN, K and MCDERMONT, M, (2009) 'Nominations: An Actor-Network Approach' (2009) *Housing Studies* 24, 281–300.

COWAN, D and MORGAN, K, 'Trust, Distrust and Betrayal: A Social Housing Case Study' (2009) 72 *Modern Law Review* 157–181.

COWAN, D, PANTAZIS, C, and GILROY, R, 'Social housing as crime control: an examination of the role of housing management in policing sex offenders' (2001) 10 *Social & Legal Studies* 435–57, 41.

CRAIG, G, TAYLOR, M, and PARKES, T, 'Protest or Partnership? The Voluntary and Community Sectors in the Policy Process' (2004) 38(3) *Social Policy and Administration* 221–39, at 238.

CROOK, ADH and MORONEY, M, 'Housing associations, private finance and risk avoidance: the impact on urban renewal and inner cities' (1995) 27 *Environment and Planning A*, 1695–1712.

CUNNINGHAM, H and INNES, J (eds), *Charity, Philanthropy and Reform* (Basingstoke, Macmillan, 1998).

DAY, P, HENDERSON, D and KLEIN, R, *Home Rules: Regulation and Accountability in Social Housing* (York, Joseph Rowntree Foundation, 1993).

DEAN, M, *Critical and Effective Histories: Foucault's Methods and Historical Sociology* (London, Routledge, 1994).

——, *Governmentality: Power and Rule in Modern Society* (London, Sage, 1999).

DELLA PORTA, D and DIANI, M, *Social Movements: An Introduction* 2nd edn (Oxford, Blackwell, 2006).

DEPARTMENT OF THE ENVIRONMENT, TRANSPORT and THE REGIONS/DEPARTMENT OF SOCIAL SECURITY (DETR/DSS), *Quality and Choice: A Decent Home for All*, The Housing Green Paper (London, HMSO, 2000).

DEZALAY, Y, 'Territorial Battles and Tribal Disputes' (1991) 54 *Modern Law Review* 792–809.

DOWLER, C, 'Crunch prompts lenders to lose their housing appetites' (11 April 2008) *Inside Housing* 3.

DUNN, A, 'Demanding Service or Servicing Demand? Charities, Regulation and the Policy Process' (2008) 71 *Modern Law Review* 247.

DUROSE, C, and RUMMERY, K, 'Governance and Collaboration: Review Article' (2006) 5(2) *Social Policy & Society* 315–21 at 315.

EDGE, PW, and LOUGHREY, JM, 'Religious Charities and the Juridification of the Charity Commission' (2001) 21 *Legal Studies* 36–64, 36–37

ELCOCK, H, *Local Government: Politicians, Professionals and the Public in Local Authorities* 2nd edn (London, Methuen, 1982) 1.

FERLIE, E, ASHBURNER, L, FITZGERALD, I , and PETTIGREW, A, *The New Public Management in Action* (Oxford, Oxford University Press, 1995).

FINLAYSON, G (1990) 'A Moving Frontier: Voluntarism and the State in British Social Welfare 1911–1949' (1990) 1(2) *Twentieth Century British History* 183–206.

FORREST, R, and MURIE, A, *Selling the Welfare State: The Privatisation of Public Housing* (London, Routledge, 1988).
FOUCAULT, M, *Discipline and Punish* (trans AM Sheridan) (London, Penguin Books, 1977).
——'One ought to read everything, study everything [..] have at one's disposal the general archive of a period at a given moment' in *The History of Sexuality: Part 1 The Will to Knowledge* (trans R Hurley) (London, Penguin Books, 1998) 263.
——*Society Must Be Defended* (London, Allen Lane, 2003).
——Afterword: The Subject and Power' in H Dreyfus and P Rabinow (eds), *Michel Foucault: Beyond Structuralism and Hermeneutics* 2nd edn (Chicago, University of Chicago Press, 1983).
GARLAND, D, *The Culture of Control: Crime and Social Order in Contemporary Society* (Oxford, Oxford University Press, 2001).
GARNETT, D and PERRY, J, *Housing Finance* (Coventry, Chartered Institute of Housing, 2005).
GARSIDE, PL, 'Central Government, Local Authorities and the Voluntary Housing Sector' in A O'Day, (ed), *Government and Institutions in the Post 1832 UK* (Lampeter, Mellon Press, 1995).
——*The Conduct of Philanthropy: The William Sutton Trust 1900–2000* (London, Athlone Press, 2000)
——'Reassessing Voluntary Action in English Housing Provision Post 1900' (2001) 30 *Journal of Social Policy* 613–36.
GEERTZ, C, *Local Knowledge: Further Essays in Interpretive Anthropology* 3rd edn (New York, Basic Books, 2000).
GIBB, K, MUNRO, M and SATSANGI, M, *Housing Finance in the UK: An Introduction* 2nd edn (London, Macmillan, 1999).
GIBSON MS and LANGSTAFF, MJ, *An Introduction to Urban Renewal* (London, Hutchinson, 1982).
GIDDENS, A, *The Third Way: The Renewal of Social Democracy* (London, Polity Press, 1998).
GOODLAD, R, *The Housing Authority as Enabler* (London, Chartered Institute of Housing and Longman, 1993).
GRAMSCI, A, *Prison Notebooks* (London, Lawrence Wishart, 1971).
GRANT, C, 'Housing association rents—onwards and upwards' (May/June 1989) *ROOF* 8.
GREER, A, and HOGGETT, P, 'Patterns of governance in local public spending bodies' (1997) 10(3) *International Journal of Public Sector Management* 214–27.
GRIFFIN, C, 'Interview: Jim Coulter' (2003) 57(9) *Axis: Housing, Planning and Regeneration* 6.
GRIFFITH, JAG, *Central Departments and Local Authorities* (London, Allen & Unwin, 1966) 506.
GULLIVER, K, *Passionate About Communities: Keynote, Prime Focus and Midland Heart Housing Associations 1925 to 2006* (Studley, Warks, Brewin Books, 2006) 13.
GUNNINGHAM, N, and Grabosky, P, *Smart Regulation* (Oxford, Clarendon Press, 1998) 408–13.
GUTCH, R, *Contracting: Lessons from the United States* (London, NCVO, 1992).
HACKING, I, 'Making Up People' in TC Heller (ed), *Reconstructing Individualism* (Stanford, Stanford University Press, 1986) 222–36.

HAFFNER, MEA, and OXLEY, MJ, 'Housing Subsidies: Definitions and Comparisons' (1999) 14 *Housing Studies* 145–62, 148.
HALL, PA, 'Policy Paradigms, Social Learning, and the State: the Case of Economic Policymaking in Britain' (1983) 25 *Comparative Politics* 275–96.
HANCHER, L and MORAN, M, 'Organizing Regulatory Space' in L Hancher and M Moran (eds), *Capitalism, Culture and Economic Regulation* (Oxford, Clarendon Press, 1989).
HARDY, D, *From Garden Cities to New Towns: Campaigning for Town and Country Planning 1899–1946* (London, E & FN Spon, 1991) 204.
HARLOE, M, 'The Green Paper on Housing Policy' in M Brown and S Baldwin (eds), *The Year Book of Social Policy in Britain 1977* (London, Routledge and Kegan Paul, 1978) 4.
HAWKINS, K, *Law as Last Resort: Prosecution Decision-Making in a Regulatory Agency* (Oxford, Oxford University Press, 2002).
HEMS, L, and PASSEY, A, *The Voluntary Sector Almanac* (London, NCVO Publications, 1998).
HILDITCH, M, 'Landlord explores flotation' (5 January 2008) *Inside Housing* 1; 'Flotation considered by many of sector's big hitters' (26 January 2008) *Inside Housing* 3.
HILLS, J, *Ends and Means: The Future Roles of Social Housing in England* (ESRC Research Centre for Analysis of Social Exclusion, CASE report 34, 2007).
——, 'The Voluntary Sector in Housing: The Role of British Housing Associations' in E James (ed), *The Non-Profit Sector in Internationals Perspective* (New York, Oxford University Press, 1989).
HINDNESS, B, *Discourses of Power: From Hobbes to Foucault* (Oxford, Blackwell, 1996) 65.
HOLDSWORTH, W, *History of English Law* vol 1 (London, Methuen & Co, 1922).
HOLLAND, D and LAVE, J 'History in Person: An Introduction' in D Holland and J Lave (eds), *History in Person: Enduring Struggles, Contentious Practice, Intimate Identities* (Sante Fe and Oxford, School of American Research Press and James Currey, 2001) 29.
HOLMES, C, 'The Party's Over: the Government's Retreat from its Housing Strategy' (October 1975) *ROOF* 17.
——'The Elusive Panacea' (July 1978) *ROOF* 110–111, 110.
——*The Other Notting Hill* (Studley, Warks, Brewin Books, 2001).
HOOD, CC, 'The British Tax Structure Development as Administrative Adaptation' (1985) 18 *Policy Sciences* 3–31, 29.
——'A Public Management for All Seasons' (1991) 69(1) *Public Administration* 3–19.
HUGHES, D and LOWE, S, *Social Housing Law and Policy* (London, Butterworths, 1995).
HUNT, A, *Governing Morals: A Social History of Moral Regulation* (Cambridge, Cambridge University Press, 1999).
JENKINS, K, 'A Postmodern Reply to Perez Zagorin' (2000) 39(2) *History and Theory* 181–200.
JOHNSTON, A, *The Inland Revenue* The New Whitehall Series, No 13 (London, George Allen & Unwin Ltd, 1965). 12
JONES, GH, *History of the Law of Charity 1532–1827* (Cambridge, Cambridge University Press, 1969).
JONES, G and STEWART, J, *The Case for Local Government* 2nd edn (London, George Allen & Unwin, 1985).
KEARNS, A, *Going by the Board: The Unknown Facts about Housing Association Membership and Management Committees in England* (Glasgow, Centre for Housing Research and Urban Studies, University of Glasgow, 1994).
KENDALL, J, *The Voluntary Sector* (London, Routledge, 2003).

KENDALL, P, and KENDALL, J, (eds), *The Contract Culture in Public Services: Studies from Britain, Europe and the USA* (Aldershot, Arena, 1997).
KILROY, B, *Housing Finance—Organic Reform?* (London, Labour Economic Finance and Taxation Association, 1984)*ousing Finance – organis reform?* . . ..
KRAAKMAN, R, 'Gatekeepers: the Anatomy of Third Party Enforcement Strategy' (1986) 2 *Journal of Law, Economics and Organization* 53–104.
LANGSTAFF, M, 'Housing Associations: A Move to Centre Stage' in J Birchall (ed), *Housing Policy in the 1990s* (London, Routledge, 1992).
LATOUR, B, 'The Powers of Association' in J Law (ed), *Power, Action and Belief* (London, Routledge & Kegan and Paul, 1986).
—— 'Visualisation and Cognition: Thinking with Eyes and Hands' (1986b) 6 *Knowledge and Society: Studies in the Sociology of Culture, Past and Present* 1–40
LE GRAND, J, and BARTLETT, W (eds), *Quasi-markets and Social Policy* (Basingstoke, Macmillan, 1993).
LENT, A, *British Social Movements since 1945: Sex, Colour, Peace and Power* (Basingstoke, UK, Palgrave, 2001).
LEFEBVRE, H, *The Production of Space* (trans D Nicholson-Smith) (Oxford, Blackwell, 1991).
LEVISON, D and ROBERTSON, I, *Partners in Meeting Housing Need: Local Authority Nominations to Housing Associations in London: Good Practice Guide* (London, NFHA, 1989).
LEWIS, J (1999) 'Reviewing the Relationship Between the Voluntary Sector and the State in Britain in the 1990s' (1999) 10 *Voluntas* 255–70.
——'What does contracting do to voluntary agencies?' in D Billis and M Harris (eds), *Voluntary Agencies: Challenges of Organisation and Management* (London, Macmillan, 1996).
LEWIS, N, and HARDEN, I, 'The Housing Corporation and "voluntary housing"' in A Barker (ed), *Quangos in Britain* (Basingstoke, Macmillan, 1982).
LOCKE, J, *Second Treatise on Government* 2nd edn (London, Cambridge University Press, 1970) para 57.).
LOUGHLIN, M, 'Law, Ideologies and the Political–Administrative System' (1989) 16(1) *Journal of Law & Society* 21–41, 27.
LOUGHLIN, M, *Legality and Locality: The Role of Law in Central-Local Government Relations* (Oxford, Clarendon Press, 1996).
——'Restructuring of Central-Local Relations' in J Jowell and D Oliver, *The Changing Constitution* 4th edn (Oxford, Oxford University Press, 2000).
LUXTON, P, *The Law of Charities* (Oxford, Oxford University Press, 2001).
LYONS, M, *Lyons Inquiry into Local Government, Place-shaping: A Shared Ambition for the Future of Local Government* (London, TSO, 2007) and www.lyonsinquiry.org.uk).
MACLENNAN, D, and WILLIAMS, R, *Affordable Housing in Britain and America* (York, Joseph Rowntree Foundation, 1990) 9.
MALPASS, P, 'Policy Making and Local Governance: how Bristol failed to secure City Challenge funding (twice)' (1994) 22 *Policy and Politics* 301–12.
——*Housing Philanthropy and the State: A History of the Guinness Trust* (Bristol, Faculty of the Built Environment, University of the West of England, 1998).
——*The Work of the Century: The Origins and Growth of the Octavia Hill Housing Trust in Notting Hill* (London, Octavia Hill Housing Trust, 1999) 11.

——*Housing Associations and Housing Policy: A Historical Perspective* (Basingstoke, Macmillan, 2000).

——'The Uneven Development of 'Social Rented Housing': Explaining the Historically Marginal Position of Housing Associations in Britain' (2001) 16 *Housing Studies* 225–42.

——'Wartime planning for post-war housing in Britain: the Whitehall debate, 1941–5' (2003) 18 *Planning Perspectives* 177–96, 177.

——*Housing and the Welfare State: The Development of Housing Policy in Britain* (London, Palgrave, 2005).

——'Policy making in interesting times: the Housing Finance and Policy Review, 1975–77' (2008) 2(1) *People, Place and Policy Online.*

——(ed), *Ownership, Control and Accountability: The New Governance of Social Housing* (London, Chartered Institute of Housing, 1997).

——'The Rise of Housing Associations' in R Rowlands and P Malpass (eds), *Housing Markets and Policy* (London, Routledge, 2009).

MALPASS, P and AUGHTON, H, *Housing Finance: A Basic Guide* 5th edn (London, Shelter, 1999).

MALPASS, P and JONES, C, *Home Housing Association: A History* (Newcastle, Home Housing Association, 1995).

MALPASS, P and MURIE, M, *Housing Policy and Practice* 5th edn (Basingstoke, Macmillan, 1999).

MANDERSON, D, *Proximity, Levinas and the Soul of Law* (Montreal & Kingston, McGill-Queen's University Press, 2006).

MARSH, P, 'New landscapes in affordable housing' in D Chevin (ed), *Moving up a Gear: New Challenges for Housing Associations* (London, Smith Institute, 2008) 20.

MASON, J, 'Qualitative Interviewing: Asking, listening and interpreting' in T May (ed), *Qualitative Research in Action* (London, Sage, 2002).

MCDERMONT, M, 'The elusive nature of the "public function": *Poplar Housing and Regeneration Community Association Ltd v Donoghue*' (2003) 66 *Modern Law Review* 113–23.

——'Territorializing Regulation: A Case Study of "Social Housing" in England' (2007) 32(2) *Law & Social Inquiry* 373–98.

MCDERMONT, M, COWAN, D and PRENDERGAST, J, 'Structuring Governance: A Case Study of the New Organisational Provision of Public Service Delivery' (2009) 29(1) *Critical Social Policy* 677–702.

MCVICAR, M and ATKINSON, R, 'Rate Capping and Local Government' (1985) 19 *Social Policy & Administration*, 121–33.

MERRETT, S, *State Housing in Britain* (London, Routledge & Kegan Paul, 1979) 19.

MILLER, P, 'Accounting and Objectivity: The Invention of Calculating Selves and Calculable Spaces' (1992) 91 *Annals of Scholarship* 61–86.

MILLER, P and ROSE, N, 'Governing Economic Life' (1990) 19 *Economy & Society* 1–31.

MOBERLEY BELL, E, *Octavia Hill: A Biography* (London, Constable, 1942).

MOLE, R, *Cottage Improvement to Sheltered Housing: Oxford Citizens Housing Association—the first 120 years* (Oxford, Oxford Citizens Housing Association, 1987).

MOODY, SR, 'Self Giving in "Charity": The Role of Law' in C Mitchell and SR Moody (eds), *Foundations of Charity* (Oxford, Hart Publishing, 2000) 80.

MORRIS, D, 'Charities in the contract culture: survival of the largest?' (2000) 20 *Legal Studies* 409–27.

MULLINS, D, 'From regulatory capture to regulated competition: an interest group analysis of the regulation of housing associations in England' (1997) 12 *Housing Studies* 301–19.
——'Redefining "Competition" as "Competitiveness"—the Best Value Activities of Registered Social Landlords' (April–June 2002) *Public Money & Management* 25–30.
MULLINS, D and MURIE, M, *Housing Policy in the UK* (Basingstoke, Palgrave Macmillan, 2006).
MURRAY, K, 'Street smart' (20 September 2002) *Inside Housing* 18.
MYDDLETON, DR, *The Power to Destroy: AStudy of the British System* (London, Johnson, 1969).
NADEEM, B, 'Investment over grant as agency moots funding shift' (25 April, 2008) *Inside Housing* 3.
NEWMAN, J, 'Beyond the New Public Management: Modernising Public Services' in J Clarke, S Gewirtz and E McLaughlin (eds), *New Managerialism, New Welfare* (London, Open University/Sage, 2000).
NFHA, *Competence and Accountability: Report of the Inquiry into Housing Association Governance* (London, NFHA, 1995).
——*Much in Evidence: Selected Submissions to the Governance Inquiry* (London, NFHA, 1995).
——*Growing Pains: Coping with the Problems of Growth in Housing Associations* (NHFA, London, 1977).
——*Statement of Recommended Practice (SORP): Accounting for Registered Social Landlords* (London, NHF, 1999).
——*In Business for Neighbourhoods: Who We Are, What We Do* (London, NHF, 2003).
NOBLE, D, 'Policing Voluntary Housing' (July 1979) *ROOF* 122–23, 122.
NOBLE, M, 'From rules to discretion: the Housing Corporation' in M Adler and S Asquith (eds), *Discretion and Welfare* (London, Heinemann, 1981) 175.
OFFICE OF THE DEPUTY PRIME MINISTER, *Sustainable Communities: Building for a Better Future* (London, ODPM, 2003).
——Changing Neighbourhoods, *Changing Lives: The Vision for Neighbourhood Renewal* (London, ODPM, 2003).
OWEN, D, *English Philanthropy 1660–1960* (London, Oxford University Press, 1965).
PAGE, D, *Building for Communities: A Study of New Housing Association Estates* (York, Joseph Rowntree Foundation, 1993).
PAWSON, H and MULLINS, D, *Changing Places: Housing Association Policy and Practice on Nominations and Lettings* (London,The Housing Corporation, 2003).
POWER, M, 'Education Accountants: Towards a Critical Ethnography' *Accounting* (1991) 16(4) *Organizations and Society* 333–53.
——*The Audit Society: Rituals of Verification* (Oxford, Oxford University Press, 1997).
PRIEMUS, H, 'Real Estate Investors and Housing Associations: A Level Playing Field? The Dutch Case' (2008) 8(1) *European Journal of Housing Policy* 81–96, 82.
PROCACCI, G, 'Social Economy and the Government of Poverty' in G Burchell, C Gordon and P Miller (eds), *The Foucault Effect: Studies in Governmentality* (London, Harvester Wheatsheaf, 1991).
RAWNSLEY, A, *Servants of the People: The Inside Story of New Labour* (London, Hamish Hamilton, 2000) vii.
RHODES, R, *The National World of Local Government* (London, Allen and Unwin, 1986).
——*Beyond Whitehall and Westminster* (London, Allen and Unwin, 1988).

——*Understanding Governance: Policy Networks, Governance, Reflexivity and Accountability* (1997).

ROSE, N, 'Government, authority and expertise in advanced liberalism' (1993) 22 *Economy & Society* 283–99.

——*Powers of Freedom:Reframing Political Thought* (Cambridge, Cambridge University Press, 1999).

——'Government and Control' (2000) 40 *British Journal of Criminology* 321–39, 329.

ROSE, N and MILLER, P, 'Political Power Beyond the State: problematics of government' (1992) 43 *British Journal of Sociology* 173–205.

ROSE, N and VALVERDE, M, 'Governed by Law?' (1998) 7(4) *Economy & Society* 541–51.

ROYLE, N, *After Derrida* (Manchester, Manchester University Press, 1995).

RUBIN, EL, 'Passing Through the Door: Social Movement Literature and Legal Scholarship' (2001) 1 *University of Pennsylvania Law Review* 1.

SCASE, R and SCALES, J, *Regional Futures and Neighbourhood Realities* (London, National Housing Federation, 2003).

SCOTT, C, 'Analysing Regulatory Space: Fragmented Resources and Institutional Design", [2001] *Public Law* 329–53.

SEYD, P, 'Shelter: The National Campaign for the Homeless' (1975) 46 *Political Quarterly* 418–31.

SHELTER, *The Shelter Story: A Brief History of the First Three Years of SHELTER's National Campaign for the Homeless and a Handbook on its Current Activities* (London, Shelter, 1970).

——*Reprieve for Slums: A Shelter Report* (London, Shelter, 1972).

——*Where Homelessness Means Hopelessness: An Appraisal of the First Year of the Housing* (Homeless Persons) Act (London, Shelter, 1978).

——*Ordinary People: Homelessness in the Housing Crisis* (Shelter, London, 1982).

SOMERVILLE, P, 'Homelessness Policy in Britain' (1994) 22 *Policy and Politics* 163–78.

DE SOUZA SANTOS, B, 'Law: a map of misreading. Toward a postmodern conception of law' (1987) 14(3) *Journal of Law and Society* 279–302.

STOKER, G, 'Governance as theory: five propositions' (1998) 50(1) *International Journal of Social Sciences* 17–28.

STORY, C, 'War chest to fight L&Q ruling' (26 June 2009) *Inside Housing* 1.

STOTHART, C, 'Billion pound breakthrough' (February 2007) Inside Finance 10–13.

TAYLOR, M, 'Voluntary Action and the State' in D Gladstone, *British Social Welfare, Past, Present and Future* (London, University College Press, 1995) 219.

TAYLOR, M, and HOGGETT, P, 'Quasi-markets and the transformation of the independent sector'in W Bartlett, C Propper, D Wilson and J Le Grand, *Quasi-markets in Public Services: The Emerging Findings* (Bristol, School for Advanced Urban Studies, 1993).

TEUBNER, G, 'Substantive and Reflexive Elements of Modern Law' (1983) 17 *Law and Society Review* 239–85.

TICKELL, C, Governance…the small print: A Range of Model Documents Covering Key Policy Areas 2nd edn (London, NHF, 2008).

TICKELL, J, 'Independent spirit' (2002) (13 September) *Inside Housing* 22–23.

TITMUSS, R, *The Gift Relationship: From Human Blood to Social Policy* (London, Allen & Unwin, 1970).

VALVERDE, M 'Seeing like a city: legal tools of municipal order' paper to the Law and Society Association Conference (Pittsburgh, June 2003)

WADDILOVE, L, (1967) 'Developing a third arm' (26 December 1967) 219 *The Spectator* 7279.
WALKER, R, 'New Public Management and Housing Associations: from comfort to competition' (1998) 26 *Policy & Politics* 71–88.
WALKER, B and MARSH, A, 'Setting the Rents of Social Housing: The Impact and Implications of Rent Restructuring in England' (2003) 40 *Urban Studies* 2023–47, 2027.
WEIR, S, 'The Hypocratic Oath' (November 1979) *ROOF* 200.
WEST, C, 'The New Cultural Politics of Difference' in S During (ed), *The Cultural Studies Reader* 2nd edn (London, Routledge, 1993).
WIDDOWSON, B, *Blunt Powers, Sharp Practices: A Survey of Local Authority Policies on Homelessness* (London, Shelter, 1976).
——'Making the Law' (November/December 2007) *ROOF* 32–33.
WILSON, D, 'Shelter' (1967) 1(4) *Voluntary Housing* 127–28.
——'Backdoor' (January/February 1997) 22(1) *ROOF* 44.
WOLMAR, C, 'Corporation Critics' (September/October 1982) *ROOF* 12–13.
WOODROOFE, K, *From Charity to Social Work* (London, Routledge and Kegan Paul, 1962) 41.
WOOLF, S, *The Poor in Western Europe in the Eighteenth and Nineteenth Centuries* (London and New York, Methuen 1986) 18.

Index

Index

Index